Fitzgerald and
Hemingway on Film

Fitzgerald and Hemingway on Film
A Critical Study of the Adaptations, 1924–2013

CANDACE URSULA GRISSOM

McFarland & Company, Inc., Publishers
Jefferson, North Carolina

LIBRARY OF CONGRESS CATALOGUING-IN-PUBLICATION DATA

Grissom, Candace Ursula, 1979–
    Fitzgerald and Hemingway on film : a critical study of the adaptations, 1924–2013 / Candace Ursula Grissom.
        p.   cm.
    Includes bibliographical references and index.

    ISBN 978-0-7864-7831-6 (softcover : acid free paper) ∞
    ISBN 978-1-4766-1454-0 (ebook)

    1. Fitzgerald, F. Scott (Francis Scott), 1896–1940—Film adaptations. 2. Hemingway, Ernest, 1899–1961—Film adaptations. 3. American fiction—Film adaptations. 4. Film adaptations—History and criticism. I. Title.
PS3511.I9Z6475 2014
813'.52—dc23   2014003646

BRITISH LIBRARY CATALOGUING DATA ARE AVAILABLE

© 2014 Candace Ursula Grissom. All rights reserved

No part of this book may be reproduced or transmitted in any form or by any means, electronic or mechanical, including photocopying or recording, or by any information storage and retrieval system, without permission in writing from the publisher.

On the cover: *The Great Gatsby*, 2013, poster art (Warner Bros./Photofest)

Manufactured in the United States of America

McFarland & Company, Inc., Publishers
Box 611, Jefferson, North Carolina 28640
www.mcfarlandpub.com

Table of Contents

Preface: The Ouroboros of Celebrity Authorship and a Six-Question Approach to Film Adaptation Theory ... 1

ONE • Screening the American Icarus, Part One: Film Adaptations of Fitzgerald, 1924–1962 ... 9

TWO • Screening the American Icarus, Part Two: Film Adaptations of Fitzgerald, 1974–2013 ... 43

THREE • Papa's Grace Under Genre Pressure, Part One: Hollywood Adaptations of Hemingway, 1932–1952 ... 101

FOUR • Papa's Grace Under Genre Pressure, Part Two: Hollywood Adaptations of Hemingway, 1957–2013 ... 163

Bibliography ... 235

Index ... 241

Preface
The Ouroboros of Celebrity Authorship and a Six-Question Approach to Film Adaptation Theory

The cult of literary celebrity is best understood in the context of an ouroboric cycle. In order to cultivate the reputation of an author, a publicity campaign must be built around him. Unfortunately, the extra attention that heavy publicity foists upon authors often stifles their creativity, since a public reputation forces them to produce works that conform to that image. The ultimate result of this cycle is that the later works produced within this artificial environment are often inferior to the earlier works, leaving critics no choice but to declare a celebrity writer's career over, even as his status continues to grow. Thus, the ouroboric cycle of literary celebrity might best be described by the motto on Christopher Marlowe's portrait: *"qvod me nvtrit me destrivt,"* which translates from the Latin as "that which nourishes me destroys me" (Marlowe-Society.org). This motto encapsulates the histories of F. Scott Fitzgerald and Ernest Hemingway as public writers. The public images of Fitzgerald and Hemingway greatly influenced both the critical receptions and film adaptations of their works. Scholars and filmmakers continually seek out the motivations of these men, whose private lives were at times even more interesting and complex than their fiction. Like the ouroboros, both Fitzgerald and Hemingway's careers moved in an endless circle, nourished by the cult of celebrity during their early years, but destroyed by it once the authors actually became famous and were forced to work within the confines of personas that live on today as self-perpetuating legends.

This ouroboros often continues to circle when a celebrity author's works are adapted for film. In his article "Adaptation, the Genre," Thomas Leitch recognizes a trend among film scholars: "Whenever students of adaptation gather, a call invariably arises for an alternative to a remarkably persistent model of adaptation studies: the one-on-one case study that takes a single novel or play or story as a privileged context for its film adaptation" (106). The problem that Leitch notes is genuine. Anyone searching for a persistent theory of film adaptation must wade through endless case studies of films that he or she most likely has not viewed in order to separate the wheat of theory from the chaff of close reading.

Adapted cinema tends to film the author's public image in connection with the original work. Because of this tendency, I have developed a new, systematic method of film adaptation criticism. This theory delineates the parameters of quality film adaptation through a series of six questions in an attempt to define a new term: "cohesive cinema." Cohesive cinema is a term that represents a chorus of collaborative creative voices used to express a consistent artistic vision throughout a film, which the audience accepts as a harmonious visual and aural adaptation of the original printed work and its author in a social context. By working through the six-question cohesive cinema analysis method, critics may determine whether a film adaptation represents a responsible and aesthetically acceptable work derived from its original source.

Question One: Does the work represent a consistent artistic vision of collaborators?

This question represents the central inquiry of the six-question approach, by asking whether the creative interests of all parties involved in creating the film adaptation are represented in a way that creates cohesive cinema. Thematic consistency between the original author and the source text as well as the filmmaker and the adaptation should be the primary concern. If this thematic consistency is maintained in the transference from page to screen, then the adaptation can be considered a work of cohesive cinema, and critics can begin to describe how that consistency is achieved using the remaining five questions. However, if the opposite result is found, critics may use the following five questions to determine when and how during the creative process the film adaptation developed thematic inconsistencies from the original work.

Question Two: Is the filmed work incorporated or unincorporated?

A film adaptation may be considered an "incorporated" work if it includes information about the original author's biographical life and times and/or contains references to other works in the author's canon besides the text claimed as the central focus. In contrast, a film adaptation is considered "unincorporated" if it contains no references to the author or his other works outside the main text. Incorporation of biographical, historical, or canonical detail can be used effectively to fill in the narrative gaps left in the transference from printed work to film.

With short stories and novellas, screenwriters and directors must often add new details of plot and character in order to create a filmable story. If the new details are added from circumstances completely foreign to the original author's life and time period, then the resulting film might be considered anachronistic or overly editorial. However, if such details are carefully selected from sources relevant to the original work's creative circumstances, then narrative and thematic consistency can be maintained to create cohesive cinema.

Question Three: In which of the three styles is the filmed adaptation performed?

According to this analysis instrument, there are three styles of film adaptation: conversion, interpretation, and revision. Conversion occurs when transference from page to screen is made with as little alteration to the original text as possible. This style of adaptation is commonly referred to in critical circles as a "faithful" adaptation. The potential drawback of slavishly faithful adaptation is twofold. First, overly faithful adaptation sets severe artistic limits on the screenwriter, director, cast, and crew of the adaptation. However, perhaps even more detrimental, faithful adaptations sometimes threaten to collapse under the weight of audience over-awareness. This danger is most prevalent with well-known literary classic texts, which audiences attend in hopes of seeing a new angle on an already too-familiar story.

In order to combat an audience's potential for time-worn narrative fatigue, film adapters often choose a second style, interpretation. An interpretation is created when the screenwriter or director keeps the main characters and plot of the original, but sets the film in a more current time period in hopes of making the work culturally relevant for audiences. The six-question approach term, interpretation, assumes that departure is a necessity of form and concentrates instead on the motivations behind the changes made in the transition from page to screen, rather than faithfulness.

In contrast, revision is a style of film adaptation that makes significant, large-scale changes to the plot, characters, and themes of the original work, in order to make the work more appealing to its intended audience and to pursue some new and different artistic vision that the filmmaker draws from the source text. The potential drawback of creating a revisionist adaptation is that filmmakers may range too far into editorialization about underlying social issues of the original work, alienating the target audience.

Despite the potential risks of their styles of adaptation, all three of these sample films were commercially successful when first released, suggesting that it is possible for any of the three styles to find a sizable audience in the marketplace. However, the films which tend to be the most critically acclaimed and enduring are the ones which blend one or more of these styles to balance cultural relevance with thematic purpose to create commercial success.

Question Four: In which of the four contextual manners is the filmed adaptation made?

After filmmakers and critics examine and classify a text according to the three styles described above, it is next helpful to determine the contextual manner in which the work might be approached. The fourth question asks scholars to consider four manners of academic approach concerning both the creation of the source text and its film adaptation: historical, socio-cultural, political, and psychological. If adequate supporting information is available, these four approaches should be combined for maximum critical effectiveness. Also, when producing new films, filmmakers should allow the manner of approach to determine what details to emphasize or downplay from the original work, the author's incorporated life and canon, or from other relevant sources in relation to the themes and plot of the original. With this approach, scholarship and the creative process should be able to develop a mutually beneficial relationship.

The first, and perhaps most common, manner of approach to film adaptation is historical. Although historical adaptations naturally consider the biography of the author and the time setting of the book, they should also include historical discussion of the original text. History of the film should also be pursued by critics, since the circumstances of a film's production, release, and reception in comparison to the source text often yields important scholarly insights.

The second manner of adaption, socio-cultural, focuses on societal trends and cultural attitudes relevant to the setting and creation of the original work, in relation to similar concerns surrounding production of its film adaptation. Also, it is important to take into account that the social-cultural message conveyed in a source text might be altered by the political economics of the filmmaking industry, in an effort to target the widest possible audience while simultaneously avoiding censorship.

The third manner of adaptation, political, is difficult because it forces both filmmakers and critics to consider not only their own political beliefs, but also those political attitudes held by large portions of the adaptation's target audience. If their primary motivation is to create commercially successful films, filmmakers must consider the current tide of political opinion when creating new adaptations and select works that hold timely viewpoints relevant to public concerns. Filmmakers and critics must be careful not to push their own agendas if they have no relevance to the source text. Otherwise, they risk alienating audiences in agreement with the tone of the original work. Still, neutralization of political issues, while it may produce box office success, is not an easy way to please all parties concerned in the adaptation process.

The final manner of adaptation, psychological, is perhaps the most difficult to film, because it involves delving into the minds of characters and the author who created them. Texts with prevalent psychological themes usually contain significant periods of flashback, which disrupt the linear flow of narrative and have the potential to disorient film audiences, who do not have the ability to flip back a few pages to catch important details that they may have missed. Audiences watching their own copies on digital video can revisit scenes, but the flow of visual narrative is still interrupted. The central problem for filmmakers producing a psychological adaptation is how to maintain narrative flow when most of the action takes place inside the mind of a character. The simplest way to accomplish this maneuver is through liberal, though careful, use of flashback sequences. Still, as with any filmmaking technique, flashbacks are not foolproof tools for capturing the psychological spirit of an original text.

In sum, the level of consistency and adherence to one of these four suggested manners of adaptation can determine the success or failure in the process of transferring print fiction to film. The most successful adaptations balance these four contextual manners of adaptation and reflect an understanding of the major themes, plot, and characters contained in the original work.

Question Five: Into which of the five media categories does the original work or filmed adaptation fall?

The five categories into which an original work or adaptation might fall are creative fiction, plays, poetry, and songs; creative non-fiction prose, plays, poetry and songs; moving visual media; static visual media; or multi-modal expression. These categories are named in an effort to simplify meaning and should be understood according to the expected definitions of their words. Each of these five categories of original texts carries with it the cultural expectations for that medium of expression. These intrinsic differences affect the film adaptation process.

One concern that filmmakers seeking to adapt any work of creative fiction often face is the problem of narrative point of view. Most often, films are made from an omniscient perspective, allowing viewers not only to see the activities of the characters, but also to hear their internal thoughts. In contrast, films adapted from creative non-fiction sources present the opposite problem. Directors must often work against the actual facts, which may even be contained in the original work, in order to create an illusion of plausibility that audiences will accept as the truth. The most solid guide for potential films of creative non-fiction works is that they should give the appearance of realism, rather than the fantasticism that fiction allows, because "true story" audiences are less willing to engage their suspension of disbelief.

Although most writers never produce films, paintings, or multimodal pieces on their own, all of these media are used in adaptations of their work. Each of these media categories carries with it a different set of expectations. Films, television programs, and other moving visual media normally seek to entertain audiences, whereas static visual media, such as painting and sculpture, create higher expectations of artistic merit. However, these media can collide in interesting ways to create multimodal pieces, particularly in works of animation that are carefully planned and executed. Today's filmmakers, freed from the technical constraints of older modes of visual media, are now able to create adaptations that continue to break down the boundaries between serious art and entertainment.

Question Six: Is there a balance in levels of creative command among the six types of collaborators for each of the factors controlling the consistency, level of incorporation, style, manner, and category of the final film adaptation product and what might the motivations be for these decisions?

Six types of collaborators work together to produce, distribute, and interpret film adaptations: the original author, producer, screenwriter, director, cast and crew, and audience. Each of these collaborators significantly impact adaptations, and their journey from page to screen can often provide important insights into how to interpret the quality of a final product in relation to the original. As a result, in order to analyze any film adaptation, critics must examine the contributions that each collaborator makes to the process.

In the beginning of the adaptation process, the collaborative team must realize that each original author is a genre unto himself. Thus, adapting a film from a textual work by an author necessarily creates a genre conflict between the general genre of adaptation and the specific genre of an individual writer.

However, this assertion does not mean that the author created his original work in a vacuum. The number of collaborators involved in the creative process for writers is small compared to film. Editors, agents, and publicists, as well as the literary, financial, and cultural interests that they represent, play a large role in a writer's process. Due to the similar collaborative processes of the publishing and film industries, it is no wonder that filmmakers often attempt to collaborate with authors, as well as their production team, in the construction of film adaptations. Full, balanced cooperation among all creative forces is the most consistently successful means of adapting a literary text into a work of cohesive cinema.

As Thomas Leitch notes, filmgoers watch adaptations of novels "to test their assumptions, not only about familiar texts but about new ideas of themselves, others, and the world those texts project against new ideas fostered by the adaptation and the new reading strategy it encourages" ("Genre" 116). Perhaps this is why both filmmakers and audiences continue to gravitate toward making and watching adaptations that include additional information about the author's life and historical times. In his seminal text on film adaptation, George Bluestone quotes Sartre as saying, "One cannot write without a public and without a myth—without a *certain* public which historical circumstances have made, without a *certain* myth of literature which depends to a very great extent upon the demand of this public" (31). Film adaptations that are based upon a source text while also incorporating material from the original authors' biographies and canons allow filmmakers and filmgoers to preserve, expand, and in a way, relive the mythology surrounding their favorite authors.

• One •

Screening the American Icarus, Part One
Film Adaptations of Fitzgerald, 1924–1962

While he was an undergraduate at Princeton, F. Scott Fitzgerald made two remarks to his friend Edmund Wilson that, in hindsight, sum up his existence: "If I couldn't be perfect, I wouldn't be anything," and "I want to be one of the greatest writers in the world, don't you?" (Wilson 484). Although it is possible for a writer acting alone to aspire to create a work that is a perfect distillation of his artistic vision, it is virtually impossible for a writer to insure that same level of perfection in the adaption of his work for the screen. By necessity, filmmaking is a collaborative process among the original writer, screenwriter, director, cast, producer, and audience. In the best adaptations, a balance of power amongst these creative forces aligns to create a product of cohesive cinema that is consistent with the major themes, if not always the exact content, of the original work.

In the novels and short stories of F. Scott Fitzgerald, two themes predominate to such a degree that they must be addressed by any filmmaker seeking to adapt one of his works. First, Fitzgerald relied heavily on his own autobiography as a source of inspiration for his writing. As Robert Wilson describes, "His life and work were so interwoven that the distinction between them blurs; in a sense, he imagined and created his life and lived in his fictional protagonists" (482). Fitzgerald's approach to writing might best be understood as akin to method acting, in which the actor and character become one. In order to achieve the level of genuine emotion and honesty contained in his original writing, filmmakers hoping to successfully adapt Fitzgerald's works for the screen must willingly enter Fitzgerald's ouroboric conception of a life within creative process, while searching their own lives for biographical parallels to Fitzgerald and to lay such insecurities open for public view.

Concurrently, filmmakers must be aware of and prepared to address what has been referred to as the "Icarus complex" in Fitzgerald's life and writing (Wilson 483). Writing in 1955, psychologist Henry A. Murray developed a theory about an individual with the sort of personality that made him or her continually strive for high ideals in order to gain a sense of self-worth, not through actual achievement, but rather the pursuit of it. Robert Wilson, who has applied the Icarus complex to Fitzgerald, identifies all five of the behavioral manifestations indicative of the Icarus complex, including "burning ambition and exhibitionism, desire to ascend to great heights, desire to be the center of all eyes, a precipitous fall, craving for immortality, and depreciation and enthrallment of women" (483). These five traits can be read as a general synopsis of the life of Fitzgerald, and the fictional characters that he modeled after it. Filmmakers who do not address Fitzgerald's Icaric tendencies set themselves up for an epic fall. Over the past century, filmmakers have either ignored or attempted to address these two major themes in adaptations of Fitzgerald's works. Although each possesses some characteristics of other styles, all feature film adaptations can be classified into one of three stylistic categories: revision, conversion, and interpretation.

The revisionist approaches to Fitzgerald's works, including *Conductor 1492* (1924) and *The Great Gatsby* (1949), have historically proven the most difficult to film successfully. Of the pair, *Conductor 1492* might be considered stronger, because of director Johnny Hines's intelligent choice to offer his manner of socio-cultural, historical, and political commentary from the solid foundational platform of Fitzgerald's Irish background. Elliot Nugent's adaptation of *The Great Gatsby* suffers from pressure to conform to both the delicate sensibilities of Hays Code–era filmmaking and the stifling conventions of the film noir genre. Only one conversionist film, *Tender Is the Night* (1962), appeared during the first four decades of Fitzgerald adaptation. Henry King's *Tender Is the Night* is an underappreciated film that delves deeply into the psychological underpinnings of Fitzgerald's novel, which deserve thorough reexamination.

However, Richard Brooks's interpretive adaptation of "Babylon Revisited," called *The Last Time I Saw Paris* (1954), is perhaps the most critically interesting Fitzgerald-based film released from 1924 to 1962. Not only does Brooks's film incorporate large amounts of Fitzgerald lore, but it also includes thought-provoking incidents from Ernest Hemingway's biography. This blending of the two authors' biographies creates what will be referred to here as the "Hemingerald phenomenon" of film adaptation, which means that when filmmakers need to incorporate additional information into a film about the era in which an original work is set, they often rely not only on the life of the work's author, but also on the lives of that author's contemporaries, in order to create the most intriguing plotline possible. Due in part to its incorporation of blended Hemingerald elements, *The Last Time I Saw Paris* can be read as a film with greater philosophical resonance than the short story upon which it is based, proving that interpretation is most often the most effective method of adapting texts to film.

* * *

Conductor 1492 (1924)

Although many of Fitzgerald's early short stories were adapted into silent films, only one, Johnny Hines's *Conductor 1492* (1924), survives today. Hines, the star and sole screenwriter for the film, was a popular comedian of the silent film era. The plot of *Conductor 1492* bears little resemblance to "The Camel's Back," a short story from Fitzgerald's early collection, *Tales of the Jazz Age* (1922); however, both the book and the film are thematically consistent pieces of light, romantic comedy tinged with commentary on race and social class.

Since Fitzgerald himself claimed that his purposes for writing the original story were merely to serve his personal needs for amusement and financial capital, the pressures for a faithful adaptation that is true to the most nuanced details of his original story are virtually nonexistent.

Proof of Fitzgerald's nonchalance in relation to the story's content can be found in his preface to *Tales of the Jazz Age*. As Fitzgerald describes his inspiration for the tale:

> I suppose that of all the stories I have ever written this one cost me the least travail and perhaps gave me the most amusement. As to the labor involved, it was written during one day in the city of New Orleans, with the express purpose of buying a platinum and diamond wrist watch which cost six hundred dollars. I began it at seven in the morning and finished it at two o'clock that same night. It was published in the *Saturday Evening Post* in 1920, and later included in the O. Henry Memorial Collection for that same year. I like it least of all the stories in this volume [799].

Not surprisingly, there is no record of Fitzgerald ever having any involvement with the story's adaptation into film after selling his rights to Warner Bros. Given Fitzgerald's cavalier attitude toward the story's production, it is safe to assume that, so long as the adaptation was a success and he was compensated, any resulting product was acceptable. However, careful screening of *Conductor*

1492 proves that its screenwriter and lead actor Johnny Hines found far more depth in Fitzgerald's material than the original author ever acknowledged to be present.

Fitzgerald's original story, "The Camel's Back," tells the story of Perry Parkhurst, an up-and-coming young attorney from Toledo, Ohio, and the girl he loves, Betty Medill, heir to local tycoon Cyrus Medill's aluminum fortune. When Betty rejects Perry's demand for marriage, Perry goes on a drunken spree, which culminates in his going to a costume party dressed as the front half of a camel. An unnamed cab driver, who seems to be Irish from his working-class accent, stands in as the camel's rear end. After Perry wins the costume contest, he and Betty are facetiously married in a mock ceremony by Jumbo, a black waiter. Later, they learn that the waiter is actually "a sho-nuff minister in the Firs' Cullud Baptis' Church" ("Camel's Back" 845). Also, they discover the marriage certificate that Perry mistakenly handed the waiter/minister in his drunken confusion was the genuine article that he had threatened Betty with earlier in the day. These details render the marriage to both men contained in the camel costume legitimate.

To save her reputation, Betty reluctantly agrees to marry Perry in a real ceremony and move West with him. After all, a society girl like Betty cannot be married to both an Anglo attorney and a working-class Irish cab driver, because, as Perry points out, "that's bigamy" ("Camel's Back" 849). The concluding theme of the story seems to be the same as much of Fitzgerald's early flapper fiction: a young, middle-class Midwestern man can only win the rich girl he loves, not through personal merit, but instead through besting her in the lover's game of flirtation, deception, and intrigue.

In contrast, the plot of Hines's *Conductor 1492* centers on a young immigrant, Terry O'Toole, who leaves his home in Ireland to come to America, hoping to find work as a motorman. During the scene of Terry's going-away party, which depicts Irish men engaging in stereotypical, yet comic, activities, such as drinking and fighting, Terry's father, Mike, gives Terry an Irish doll for good luck. Unbeknownst to Terry, the doll holds his future fortune: the two missing shares of Loteda Traction Company stock which are sought after by both the president of the company, closeted Irishman Denman Connelly, and his rivals who want to take over the company, Vice-President James Stoddard and company attorney Richard Langford.

Upon arriving in America, Terry lands a job at the company. After only a few days on the job, Terry rescues Bobby, a little boy who falls in front of his streetcar. Bobby turns out to be Connelly's son. Edna Connelly, Bobby's lovely sister, sees the rescue and invites Terry to dinner, where a romance blossoms between the pair. The remainder of the film is devoted to the business intrigue among these men, as well as the developing romance between Edna and Terry. Ultimately, it is revealed that Mike, who is visiting from Ireland, bought the two shares years ago and hid them in the Irish doll that he gave to Terry. After saving the day by rescuing the doll and his father from a fire, Terry marries Edna and returns to Ireland, where another party containing many demonstrations of stereotypical Irish drinking and fighting ends the film.

The camel, an instrumental plot device in Fitzgerald's original story, makes only a small appearance in Hines's film, when Terry picks up in his trolley car a well-dressed, drunken young man carrying a camel costume. This young man, presumably an unnamed Perry Parkhurst character, asks Terry to be the rear half of his camel. This question marks the most significant thematic departure from Fitzgerald's original story, in which the unnamed Irish cab driver agrees to be the rear end of the camel. This scene presents a willingness of the working-class Irish immigrant to subordinate his own sense of self-worth in order to please his supposedly superior Anglo employer.

However, in *Conductor 1492*, Johnny Hines chooses not only to name the motorman, Terry O'Toole, but also to give him a sense of cultural pride that causes him to refuse this onerous duty. When the unnamed rich young Anglo man offers to pay Terry twenty dollars for this indignity, Terry considers it, until Mike stops him, saying, "No O'Toole will ever be the South end of a camel!" After seeing how upset his father is at the possible insult to his family name, Terry not only rejects the young man's proposal, but instead makes a counteroffer.

When the rich young Anglo man agrees to this alternative idea, that Terry should be the head of the camel and he the posterior end, an ethnic power shift occurs in the film. Terry goes to the non–Irish, upper-class roller-skating party that the young man was invited to as his equal. During the party, Terry becomes the toast of the event through his skillful skating prowess. Shortly thereafter, Terry saves the day by regaining control of the shares of stock hidden in the Irish doll. After these heroics, Edna is so overcome with love for Terry that she proposes marriage to him, and her father agrees, representing the greatest event of his acceptance into Anglo culture: a marriage to the daughter of a wealthy man, which will presumably make him heir to a fortune.

It comes as no surprise that Edna, who is at least half Irish, falls in love with the working-class Irish immigrant, Terry, nor that Edna's wealthy father, the closeted Irishman Denman/Dinty Connelly, accepts Terry into the family so easily. As historian Thomas Brown suggests, "Irish-American nationalism had its origins in loneliness, poverty, and prejudice" (333). In all likelihood, Dinty Connelly was a self-made man who built the Loteda Traction Company through hiring other Irishmen, as evidenced by the fact that both Terry and

Mike were employed there. According to Matthew Pratt Guterl, many Irishmen deliberately sought each other for personal and business ventures. Guterl claims that "missing their homeland and collectively uncomfortable with the grind of modern industrial America, the Irish in America took comfort in nationalism ... that shared belief ultimately gave grass-roots nationalism in the United States a remarkable strength and longevity" (313). The ultimate result of many American Irishmen's deliberate choice to disregard social divisions between rich and poor members of the Irish community in favor of unifying cultural interests "coincided with the needs of the Irish and Irish immigrant family and imposed strong communal pressures for ethnic solidarity and conformity on ambitious or assimilation-minded individuals" (Miller 107). Based on this information, it is little wonder why Edna rejects her other, wealthier potential suitor in the film, James Stoddard. Not only does Stoddard deviously scheme against her father, but choosing Stoddard over O'Toole would represent Edna's rejection of her own Irish heritage in favor of Anglo assimilation. By selecting O'Toole, Edna legitimates the decision for a wealthy daughter of a secret Irishman to choose a poorer husband who is openly Irish, based not only on his personal virtues, but also a shared willingness to embrace their jointly-held Irish heritage.

Hines's choice to name the Anglo-American villain of the film adaptation Stoddard is most likely deliberate. In 1920, Lothrop Stoddard released his now-seminal text of American scientific racism, *The Rising Tide of the Colored Empires*. F. Scott Fitzgerald was well aware of Stoddard, and subtly criticized him by allowing the villain, Tom Buchanan, of his most famous novel, *The Great Gatsby*, to quote from his works as a demonstration of Tom's blatant and unappealing racism. In what may represent a spoke in the wheel of the ouroboric cycle of literary celebrity culture, it is possible that Fitzgerald saw the villain James Stoddard in Hines's film adaptation of his story "The Camel's Back," in 1924, and then included the reference in his novel in 1925, which was in production at the time of *Conductor 1492*'s release. Regardless, it appears from the connection between these film and printed fiction villains that both Hines and Fitzgerald were in agreement that Lothrop Stoddard's racist politics were worthy of ridicule.

From these inferences, the revisionist message that Hines sends in his film, although thickly veiled in comic farce, is clear for any viewer who chooses to see it. Although it is easy to stereotype the Irish for less desirable behaviors of boisterous drinking and fighting, Irishmen as a race are possibly even more capable of success in business and love than Anglos, due to their propensity for hard work, courage, and resourcefulness, especially when the positive stereotypes of Irish luck, charm, and cunning are added into the mix. The last title card in the film reflects the sentiment that Irishmen should view their cultural heritage as a source of pride, rather than attempt to disguise it so that they can pass into Anglo-American society.

In the card, displayed during the Irish homecoming scene after Terry's marriage to Edna, Mike O'Toole tells the father of his new daughter-in-law, "It's the divil of an Irishman ye are—changing yer name from Dinty to Denman" (*Conductor 1492*). Denman Connelly counters with the accusation to Mike, "Well, at least I didn't change it to Rosenthal!" implying that Mike's choice to pass in America as Jewish was an equal denial of his Irish heritage (*Conductor 1492*). The two fathers almost come to blows in the final scene and must be calmed down by Terry. However, seconds later, all three are dragged into a mass street scene of fighting Irishmen that fades to black at the end of the film. By following this exchange, indicating that Irishmen should retain their names as a source of ethnic pride with a scene of stereotypical Irish temper and confrontational behavior, Hines was able to articulate his subversive message of pro–Irish equality from behind the protective veil of comedy.

Although less obvious than Hines's display, the ending of Fitzgerald's original story seems to indicate that the author also held pro–Irish sentiments that he could express only through the veil of comedy in his work. Fitzgerald was of Irish Catholic descent himself, through his mother Mollie McQuillan's side of the family. According to Matthew Bruccoli:

> Philip F. McQuillan was an exemplar of the American Dream that his grandson, F. Scott Fitzgerald, would respond to complexly in his fiction. Born in County Fermanagh, Ireland, he moved in 1857 from Illinois to St. Paul, Minnesota, where he worked as a bookkeeper. Two years later, at twenty-five, he opened his own small business in the general line. In 1860, he married Louisa Allen, the daughter of an Irish immigrant carpenter. By 1862 he was a grocery wholesaler. Prospering with the post–Civil War expansion of the territory, McQuillan became one of the most substantial businessmen in St. Paul and a benefactor of the Catholic Church [*Grandeur* 11].

Interestingly, the course of Scott Fitzgerald's grandfather's life seems to follow that of Hines's character from *Conductor 1492*, as an Irish immigrant who made good, prompting the inference that Hines may have incorporated elements of Fitzgerald's biographical material into his film adaptation. Certainly, there was enough material circulating in the 1920s for Hines to refer to, since Fitzgerald's life story was heavily circulated in magazines during the height of his fame in the mid–1920s, when Hines was making his film.

However, it makes sense that the non–Irish Hines would pick up on the pro–Irish undertones in Fitzgerald's work that the author himself chose to downplay. Fitzgerald's parents married against custom in Baltimore, the hometown of his father, Edward Fitzgerald, rather than in the bride's hometown of St. Paul. Edward Fitzgerald hailed from a long line of Southern-sympathizing Anglo-American former plantation owners that included Francis Scott Key, for whom the author was named. Although both were Catholic, the bigger problem that prevented their marriage in St. Paul was the fact that the McQuillans, although the richest family in town, were Irish. At that time in St. Paul, "the Irish were regarded as common, a step above the Swedes" (*Grandeur* 12). However, by the time of Fitzgerald's birth, all his father's family money was gone, and the young couple raised their son on Mollie's inheritance from her Irish father. This uncertain social position, in which Fitzgerald was a descendant of pedigreed but poverty-stricken American social elite on one side of his family, and wealthy but culturally ostracized Irish immigrants on the other, is arguably the root of Fitzgerald's obsession with class structure, which permeates all of his writing. By choosing not to name his Irish cab driver in "The Camel's Back," Fitzgerald was effectively disclaiming his own Irish heritage.

Still, Fitzgerald allows his unnamed cab driver to be the *deux ex venit* (God in the camel) in his short story "The Camel's Back." The cab driver, not Perry Parkhurst, is the person who finally moves the story to its climax by pointing out that Betty was married to the whole camel, because she is wearing the ring that Perry borrowed from him for the pseudo-ceremony. The cab driver then gives Betty an ultimatum, claiming that "if you [Perry] don't, I'm a-gonna have the same claim you got to bein' married to her!" Fitzgerald's choice to let the lower-class cab driver rescue the upper-class Perry ends the story with the two men exchanging "a particularly subtle, esoteric sort of wink that only true camels can understand" (849). This wink means that the Irish cab driver and the Anglo-American Parkhurst are both aware of the fact that the greatest fear of a flirtatious upper-class girl like Betty Medill is to be married to a lower-class man. Thus, their choice to play on Betty's social insecurity serves the dual purpose in the story of giving a teasing girl who trades on her looks to manipulate men her comeuppance, while simultaneously proving that sometimes the lower-class members of society, such as the Irish, are the wittiest of all. This wink and nod to flouting social conventions was as far as the still socially insecure Fitzgerald was willing to go in his early story, which was written in 1920 expressly for a decidedly social conservative publication, *The Saturday Evening Post*.

Perhaps because he was more well-known as a comedian, and consequentially less likely to be taken seriously in his social commentary, Johnny Hines was able to bring out more pro-immigrant sentiment in his film adaptation than was Fitzgerald in his original story. The format of silent film allowed Hines to incorporate many sight gags that played on commonly held Irish stereotypes that Fitzgerald, in the print medium, would have been unable to employ. These sight gags allow Hines to draw audiences in, by fulfilling their anti–Irish expectations, and then subversively cause them to root for Terry, Mike, and Denham/Dinty when they defeat the evil Anglo-Americans Stoddard and Langford. In one particularly complex scene near the end of the film, Terry returns to Ireland with the gift of dozens of pairs of boxing gloves that he tosses out to his Irish friends, while the title card reads, "Show your nationality!" (*Conductor 1492*). While on the surface level it is easy to read the rest of the scene, in which all the men spontaneously burst into a massive street-fighting free-for-all with their new boxing gloves, as cheap Irish stereotype exploitation played for laughs, a deeper meaning is present for those who look for it.

By giving them boxing gloves to fight with, Terry effectively tells his countrymen that, if they can learn to control their supposedly fiery temperaments, they can then turn brawling into a sport. In the 1920s, Irish-American boxers, such as Jack Dempsey and Gene Tunney, promoted Irish equality in American society to a generation of young boys who regarded them as heroes. Beyond sports, Terry's gift of boxing gloves could be read metaphorically, suggesting that Irish courage, softened by the temperance of self-restraint, could lead to financial and social success in America. In other words, when Terry's friends ask him, "Terry lad—What did ye bring us from Americky?" the answer is actually that Terry brings back from America a new sense of why they should be proud of their cultural heritage. Just like the Irish doll that Mike gives him, which contains the stock certificates that eventually earn Terry his fortune, the average Irishman holds within himself virtues of determination, ingenuity, and wit that can make his fortune in a new world. Hines's ending message in the film seems to be that with time, grit, and a little Irish luck, any new immigrant can write his own Horatio Alger tale.

Fitzgerald, an author normally given to various re-creations of the Horatio Alger mythos in his fiction, was most likely still too insecure in his own cultural heritage at this point in his career to take up the cause of Irish nationalism that Johnny Hines found lying dormant in his original text. Although in his later career Fitzgerald would often create fictional alter egos of himself with Irish names, such as in his story for *Esquire*, "Financing Finnegan" (1938), the young author was not ready to disclose openly such bold connections to his Irish heritage in 1920, when he wrote "The Camel's Back." Instead, with Hines's revisionist adaptation, *Conductor 1492*, the beginning of a pattern emerges that will exist up to the present day, of filmmakers exploring in greater depth the latent social and ethnic issues in Fitzgerald's fiction that the author could not express explicitly in his original works, due to a hostile cultural climate.

The Great Gatsby (1949)

The second adaptation of Fitzgerald's novel *The Great Gatsby* was made for Paramount in 1949 by Elliot Nugent. Blending elements of 1940s film noir and women's film with his need to conform to the Hays Code, Nugent created a movie in the interpretive style that reflects the historical, social, and cultural sensibilities of his era. However, even though Nugent successfully incorporates some elements of Fitzgerald's biography into the text, it still strays from the author's major themes in an effort to conform with pressures of censorship and genre.

In his introduction to *The Great Gatsby*, Matthew Bruccoli writes:

> *The Great Gatsby* does not proclaim the nobility of the human spirit; it is not politically correct; it does not reveal how to solve the problems of life; it delivers no fashionable or comforting messages. It is just a masterpiece [vii].

Viewers of Elliot Nugent's film adaptation of *The Great Gatsby* must consider Bruccoli's astute observation about Fitzgerald's reluctance to moralize in the novel strange. From its opening scene, during which Nick Carraway reads a Bible verse inscribed on Gatsby's headstone, to its closing sequence, in which Gatsby makes an unequivocal confession of his life's sins, Nugent's adaptation for Paramount screens like a morality play condemning the sins of greed and adultery. Of course, this assessment of a character who sought to acquire the married woman he loved through accumulating an impressive amount of wealth first would have been well accepted in the 1940s, when Hollywood's morality was still heavily regulated by the Hays Code. However, this take on *Gatsby* is almost completely inconsistent with the artistic vision of Fitzgerald's original tale, which sought to present the actions of the characters living in materialistic and promiscuous modern times without passing judgment upon them.

The consistency of Nugent's *Gatsby* with Fitzgerald's original novel suffers from not only an overdose of Hays Code-inspired middle–American morality, but also from the pressures of genre restrictions as well. As a director of numerous films noir, Nugent approached *Gatsby* with the apparent intention of emphasizing the gangster elements of the story, depicting Jay Gatsby as a thinly-veiled, trench-coated mobster, Jordan Baker as the overt femme fatale, and Daisy Buchanan as a damsel in distress. This choice to remain within the confines of genre runs counter to Fitzgerald's original depiction of Gatsby as a complex man who defies typecasting as a man from modest means who turns to crime for an easy livelihood. Whereas Fitzgerald's original Gatsby shuns connections with his shady past, Nugent's Gatsby at first embraces and then confronts his self-perceived moral shortcomings. This depiction is wholly inconsistent with the general attitude of denial and avoidance with which Fitzgerald's original character dealt with his history, and represents a second thematic departure by Nugent's film.

The film also alters Fitzgerald's original depictions of female characters. In the novel, both Daisy and Jordan appear struggling with the confines of their roles as women in the 1920s, a decade which paradoxically allowed women more sexual freedoms, but still left them financially dependent on men for their livelihoods. Fitzgerald's take on the condition of women in the 1920s seems to be one of sympathy. The author presents Gatsby as a potential protector and independence-facilitator for Daisy. By earning enough money to give Daisy the choice to be with the man she would have naturally selected (had financial security not been her primary concern) Gatsby offers Daisy a way out of her life of *de facto* marital prostitution.

After living for several years with his wife, Zelda, a very independent-minded woman, Fitzgerald must have surmised from experience that sexual liberties gained in the 1920s by women did not equate to equal treatment in the job market or social circles. Due to society's slow progress toward occupational equality, the socially independent flapper still remained financially dependent on a benevolent and open-minded man who was fiscally stable in order to survive. However, the Nugent adaptation removes Fitzgerald's realistic approach to women's inequality in the 1920s by making the characters of Daisy Buchanan and Jordan Baker behave like females straight out of a post–World War II women's film.

Although Nugent's intent to show strong, decisive women characters is honorable, it is anachronistic when placed within the 1920s setting of his adaptation. Their strong-shouldered costumes and quick-witted quips are inspired more by Bette Davis's fierce independence than Zelda Sayre Fitzgerald's feisty vulnerability. In sum, Nugent's choice to employ a revisionist strategy by adapting *Gatsby* for the screen as a cautionary moral tale, with flavors of 1940s film noir and women's cinema, creates an entertaining film; however, it is almost completely inconsistent with F. Scott Fitzgerald's original artistic vision.

Nugent's adaptation of Gatsby opens with a scene of a middle-aged Nick Carraway and his wife visiting Gatsby's graveside. Nick notes that the tombstone is oddly simple, given Gatsby's tendency toward making grand gestures, and that it has a Bible verse inscribed upon it. The verse, Proverbs 14:12, reads, "There is a way that seems right to a man, but in the end it leads to death" (*NIV*). The addition of this biblical verse sets the moralistic tone that persists to the end of the film. This choice is a departure from Fitzgerald's natural tendency, as a lapsed Catholic, to shy away from sacred quotation in his works, preferring instead only to have "his secretary read the Bible to him—not for divine inspiration, but because he admired the rhythms of the King James Version" (*Grandeur* 472). The inclusion of this opening biblical reference begs further inquiry as to its possible purpose.

The answer to this question most probably lies in Nugent's effort to make a moral statement condemning the hedonistic culture of the 1920s. In the voiceover immediately following his recitation of the Bible verse inscribed on Gatsby's tomb, Nick Carraway describes the drunken excesses of Prohibition, while a montage of violent gangster images rolls across the screen. This montage ends with Gatsby, attired in a trench coat and fedora, walking toward the camera while looking directly into the lens as Nick concludes, "Out of the twenties and all it entailed came Jay Gatsby, who built a dark empire because he carried a dream in his heart" (Nugent). The overall effect of this opening sequence is to cement in the viewer's mind that Gatsby is, first and foremost, a criminal. Even if he committed his crimes in furtherance of great ideals, those efforts were tarnished by his involvement in illicit activity.

Most likely, Nugent's choice to criticize, rather than glorify, Gatsby's rise to wealth and power came from an effort to tell Fitzgerald's original story in a manner that still conformed to the Hays Code. Initially enacted in 1930 by the Motion Picture Association as a self-regulatory attempt to curb public outcry against alleged immorality in cinema, the Code became the most effective means of imposing middle-class Protestant Christian morality ever introduced into American popular culture. As Michael Brooke states in an article for *BFI Screenonline*:

> The Code was based on three general principles:
> - No picture shall be produced that will lower the moral standards of those who see it. Hence the sympathy of the audience should never be thrown to the side of crime, wrongdoing, evil or sin.
> - Correct standards of life, subject only to the requirements of drama and entertainment, shall be presented.
> - Law, natural or human, shall not be ridiculed, nor shall sympathy be created for its violation ["The Hays Code"].

These three regulatory restrictions made it virtually impossible for a director to adapt Fitzgerald's central theme: that love can cause a man to commit shameful or illegal acts that normally would be regrettable. However, if those acts are committed with honorable intent, they might be considered justifiable and even pitiable if the moral compromise is ultimately made in vain. In order to create a film based on this questionable modern theme, while still conforming to the Hays Code, Nugent had to find another villain in the story besides Jay Gatsby upon whom he could turn the eye of judgment.

As a result, Dan Cody, a minor character in Fitzgerald's novel, becomes the villain of Nugent's film adaptation. Cody's character in the film is quite clearly intended to be a visual interpretation of Satan. The old man has an angular face, sinister laugh, and pointed beard, needing only horns and a pitchfork to complete his devilish depiction. Although in the novel Cody is described by Fitzgerald as a "pioneer debauchee who ... brought back to the eastern seaboard the savage violence of the frontier brothel and saloon," the author does not claim that Gatsby wholly adopted all of Cody's vices without retaining some of his own innate Midwestern virtues (*Gatsby* 106). Instead, Fitzgerald seems to suggest that Gatsby studied the ways in which Cody made money and the ways in which he used it to acquire desirable things, but rejected some of Cody's other bad habits, such as drinking to excess. In short, although Gatsby "filled out to the substantiality of a man" while under Cody's tutelage, this coloring of character was not solely shaded with the dark tint of wholly accepted immorality (*Gatsby* 107).

However, the nuances of this blended sensibility of mentoring by both positive and negative example are dropped in Nugent's film adaption, most likely because only more clear-cut morality would have satisfied the Hays Code censors. Instead, Dan Cody is depicted as a completely evil entity, who seeks to tempt young Gatsby into a depraved lifestyle of lust and money. Ella Kaye, Dan Cody's mistress, who is barely mentioned in Fitzgerald's original novel, appears in Nugent's film as a devious femme fatale who foreshadows Gatsby's later, purer love, Daisy Fay. Cody promotes Gatsby's flirtations with Ella, knowing all the while that Ella will reject Gatsby because of his poverty.

In a manner that recalls Mrs. Havisham's temptation of Philip Pirrip with her niece Stella in *Great Expectations*, Dan Cody appears to revel in the fact that Ella will break the heart of young Jimmy Gatz and harden him into the corrupt adult rum-runner Jay Gatsby. The temptation culminates when Cody addresses Gatsby from his deathbed, saying, "You never could lay a finger on her, could you Jimmy? Old Dan's a devil, but old Dan's always right" (Nugent). From this claim, Cody wants Gatsby to surmise that he will never win the steadfast love of a woman without money. In this film adaptation, Gatsby spends most of the remainder of the film acting in conformity with this belief; however, in Fitzgerald's novel, the author seems to suggest that Gatsby's heart was never so completely hardened, even after Daisy's final betrayal. For Fitzgerald, a man's moral code was never so clearly defined as it is in Nugent's film.

Possibly the most telling influences of the Christian morality inserted into Nugent's film through efforts to comply with the Hays Code occur in the *mea culpa* statements made by each character. Although in Fitzgerald's original, Tom Buchanan makes a half-hearted effort to confess his past wrongs in the confrontation scene at the Waldorf Hotel, his plea for redemption seems repealed by the new sin he commits in the end of the novel, when he fails to prevent Wilson from killing Gatsby. In contrast, the Nugent film shows Tom not only repentant during the Waldorf scene, but also making repeated phone calls in an attempt to warn Gatsby that the murderous Wilson is approaching. Daisy also appears more morally straightforward in Nugent's cinematic version. Whereas in Fitzgerald's original, Daisy is able to say only that she "can't help what's past" and that she "loved [Gatsby] too" throughout her marriage to Tom, in the film version, her choice must be more unequivocal (*Gatsby* 140). According to the Hays Code, a married woman could not carry on an emotional affair with another man; therefore, Daisy must make a decisive choice in favor of Gatsby that is completely out of character with her previous emotional uncertainty about the situation. Last, and perhaps most telling, Gatsby makes a confession of his past sins, saying, "I've beaten a lot of raps in my time, but I'll take this one. I owe it to a kid named Jimmy Gatz," just before being shot in the back by Wilson (Nugent). Gatsby's confessional gives him a moment of redemption just before death, which in turn provides the resolution of justifiable punishment necessary for Gatsby to emerge as a pitiable and tragic figure under the Hays Code.

Taken altogether, these confessional moments added in Nugent's film could be read as an encroachment of Christian morality upon Fitzgerald's theme of reserved judgment. Although Fitzgerald was confirmed as a Catholic, he did not actively practice his religion. Therefore, it is safe to assume that the confessional endings for each character's storyline in the film were additions inconsistent with Fitzgerald's original, which should be read as flaws in the adaptation.

Perhaps compliance with the Hays Code was only part of the reason that led Elliot Nugent to stage his adaptation of *The Great Gatsby* as a film noir. As a veteran of the Paramount studio contract system since 1925, Nugent would have been well aware that the standard film noir formula, of a criminal who strays but wins back audience sympathy through a redemptive final confession, would have been enough to satisfy Hays Office censors. Certainly, Nugent was eager to complete his adaptation as safely as possible, since he confided in a friend that he feared he would not be able to do justice to the book and would instead "betray Fitzgerald as well as my friends at Paramount" with his inadequacy as a director (qtd. in Phillips 116).

The film's star, Alan Ladd, was also personally invested in the film. Ladd, a self-described "Okie kid" whose life had been a sort of Hollywood Horatio Alger tale, impressed the adaptation's co-scriptwriter and producer, Richard Maibaum, as perfect for the role of Gatsby when he "proudly displayed his wardrobe, particularly his collection of fancy shirts" to his future employer upon their first meeting (Phillips 117). Both Nugent and Ladd suffered from alcoholism and persistent depression as adults, stemming from fears of social inadequacy related to their childhoods, which coincided perfectly with parallel themes in Fitzgerald's life and the *Gatsby* novel.

Considering these facts, it comes as no surprise that, in the opening scene of the adaptation, Nugent set the beginning date of Gatsby's life as 1896 (a birth year that Nugent shared with Fitzgerald) and the ending date of Gatsby's life in 1928, the year that Fitzgerald first came to Hollywood. In producing *Gatsby* as a film noir with a redemptive message, Nugent and Ladd ourobor-ically joined their psychological histories within Fitzgerald's circle, creating a composite Hollywood myth of Gatsby. The hope in this film adaptation seems to be that, by making Jay Gatsby socially acceptable, Nugent could save not only his own reputation, but also Ladd's and Fitzgerald's.

The drawback of conforming to film noir conventions as a potential device of character redemption, of course, is that at least one of the female characters must be made into a femme fatale. Jordan Baker is the character who is played to fit this stereotype most closely. In a sharp departure from Fitzgerald's novel, Nugent's film makes Jordan the active agent in setting up the fateful meeting between Gatsby and Daisy at Nick's house, without Nick ever being aware of the situation until their arrival. Unbeknownst to Nick, Jordan has made a deal with Gatsby to arrange the meeting, in exchange for his new Dusenberg automobile. When Nick chides Jordan for assisting in what will inevitably become an adulterous affair, she replies that she will do whatever she pleases, regardless of morality, "when it is worth my while" (Nugent). By making Jordan into a woman who endangers the morality of men, Nugent conforms to the conventions of film noir by transforming her into a typical femme fatale. However, the trade-off is that Jordan has lost the redeemable qualities that would make her a fitting romantic interest for Nick. Thus, this plotline is dropped from Fitzgerald's original novel in the film.

Jordan Baker could also be characterized as a "superwoman" typical of 1940s films. According to Molly Haskell, a superwoman "has a high degree of intelligence or imagination, but instead of exploiting her femininity, adopts male characteristics in order to enjoy male prerogatives, or merely to survive" (505). Although Fitzgerald's original portrayal of Jordan paints her as a coy and cunning professional golf cheater, she does not engage in the same degree of emotional espionage as in Nugent's film. Also, the novel version of Jordan is much more of a reserved romantic than her film counterpart, who makes a suggestive innuendo out of Nick's attempt to correct what he considers to be her lax morality. When he learns that Jordan has arranged the meeting, he scolds her, saying, "I'd like to take you over my knee," to which Jordan replies, "Why darling! Any time, any place!" (Nugent). Jordan's playful naughtiness would have been innocuous enough to slip past Hays Office censors, but still enough to place her firmly in the role of a 1940s superwoman, who took charge of her sexuality, rather than in the position of Fitzgerald's flapper heroines, who remained less secure at the time. Nugent, as a veteran director of romantic comedies such as the Bob Hope vehicles *The Cat and the Canary* (1939) and *My Favorite Brunette* (1947), would have been well aware of exactly how far he could push the envelope of flirtation without censorship. He successfully maneuvers Jordan's character along these lines, safely within film conventions, without ever mentioning her sexual liaison with Nick, which is detailed in Fitzgerald's original novel.

In contrast, Daisy Buchanan, as characterized in Nugent's film, is also a woman very much in sync with the film era of the 1940s; however, she bears little emotional resemblance to the Daisy of Fitzgerald's original novel. Most critics agree that Fitzgerald's original Daisy was modeled after his wife, Zelda Sayre Fitzgerald, a vivacious yet emotionally volatile young woman during the time in Fitzgerald's life in which he wrote *The Great Gatsby*. Although this vulnerability is shown through Daisy's continuous self-doubt and second-guessing in the original novel, Nugent's film adaptation allows no such complex waffling. Instead, Daisy is set to be the damsel in distress in Nugent's film noir version of Gatsby, who must be rescued from society when her decisive resolve proves to be an insufficient weapon in an unfair world.

Molly Haskell describes this character type in 1940s cinema as the "super-female," saying that she is "a woman who, while exceedingly feminine and flirtatious, is too ambitious and intelligent for the docile role society has decreed she play. She is uncomfortable, but not uncomfortable enough to rebel completely; her circumstances are too pleasurable" (505). Evidence of Daisy's conformity to this 1940s character type can be seen by comparing the Waldorf confrontation scene to the post-accident reconciliation scene in Nugent's film. In the Waldorf scene, Daisy demonstrates the nerves of steel that Fitzgerald's original heroine did not possess, when she fires back at Tom after he threatens to take custody of their daughter. "That's all I need, that's the final thing! I'm leaving you, and nothing in the world can force me back" (Nugent). Interestingly, even though Daisy is leaving her husband for another man in this scene, her conduct would still be within the bounds of the Hays Code. She has responded justifiably to protect her child and sever a manipulative relationship, rather than carry on with a secret affair and emotionally desert her daughter.

However, when faced with the setback of her accidental killing of Myrtle in Gatsby's car, Nugent's Daisy retreats just as decisively back to the safety of

Tom's money and power. In her scene with Tom back at their home, Daisy refutes her earlier declaration of love for Gatsby, saying to Tom, "I'll do whatever you say, whatever it takes" because she thinks Tom's plan to pin the killing on Gatsby will make a stronger defense than Gatsby's earlier agreement to take the blame willingly. Oddly, this reversal ends up with Daisy once again in technically safe moral ground under the Hays Code, since she is rejecting a potential lover and returning to her husband and home. After looking through the window and seeing Daisy definitively betray him, it is little wonder that Nugent's Gatsby comes to the cynical conclusion of so many hard-boiled film noir protagonists, when he asks Nick in the final scene, "Look at what I've done to myself and everyone else to get where I am, and for what?" (Nugent). For this Gatsby, there is no moral uncertainty in which he can find comfort. Betrayed by his mentor and the love of his life, he is prepared to make confession and die. The result is that Nugent's film reaches a satisfying resolution that is consistent with the conventions of film noir and the Hays Code.

Still, although Nugent's film is successful as an independent work that provides adequate closure and symmetry with the themes that it chooses to introduce, it fails as an adaptation of Fitzgerald's original work because it strays from his central message. In love, there is no moral right or wrong. Just as in the acquisition and dissipation of a fortune, there is a natural ebb and flow to human emotions, and many more shades of moralistic gray than the black and white of Hays Code–era film noir could delineate. Perhaps this is why Fitzgerald writes that Gatsby's last thoughts were not definitive moral statements, but instead ruminations on lost desires in "a new world, material without being real, where poor ghosts, breathing dreams like air, drifted fortuitously about" (169). For the romantically-minded Fitzgerald, love moved like the breeze through an Aeolian harp, ever-changing and uncontrollable, but consistently self-aware.

The Last Time I Saw Paris (1954)

Richard Brooks's *The Last Time I Saw Paris* (1954) represents an important milestone in cinematic adaptations of F. Scott Fitzgerald's works. Brooks's adaptation of Fitzgerald's "Babylon Revisited" (1931) displays the first appearance of what is referred to in this dissertation as the "Hemingerald phenomenon." The term refers to the tendency of filmmakers, from the 1950s onward, to incorporate portions of the biographical lives of both F. Scott Fitzgerald and Ernest Hemingway into works by either author. Most often, their lives are used to fill in gaps caused by chronological shifts in the time setting between the original print work and its adaptation. When performed well, as in *The Last Time I Saw Paris*, the additional information provided by the Hemingerald phenomenon can both enhance the resonance of the original story by giving studious audience members further literary dimensions to explore and also increase popular audience appeal by building upon the familiar mythology of a similar author.

Both "Babylon Revisited" and *The Last Time I Saw Paris* begin with the same opening scene. Charlie Wills (or "Wales," as he is named in Fitzgerald's original) stops in at a familiar bar in Paris to gather courage by talking to old friends before heading on to his sister-in-law's home, where he hopes to recover custody of his young daughter. Here, in this early scene, Brooks sets the stage for his incorporation of biographical elements about Hemingway. In Fitzgerald's original story, the bar is one of Fitzgerald's favorite real-life watering holes, the Ritz. However, in Brooks's film, the name of the bar has been changed to the Dingo, a familiar Hemingway haunt, where the authors were first introduced to one another (Baker 145). This subtle change may be read as a gentle introduction to the concept that the two authors' lives will both be incorporated into the film.

Many other bits of Hemingway lore find their way into Brooks's film as well. For example, Charlie Wills begins the film as a low-paid reporter for the fictitious *Europa* news service, who later transfers to the *Stars and Stripes* in an effort to earn more money. Since Fitzgerald never worked as a reporter while in Europe and was fairly wealthy when he arrived there, the source of this information is most likely to have come from Hemingway's biography. Hemingway worked as a foreign correspondent for the *Toronto Star* upon first arriving in Paris and later, during World War II, wrote as a correspondent for the *Stars and Stripes*. Also, Hemingway and his first wife, Hadley, lived in an inexpensive carpenter's loft over a sawmill, which was the best that they could afford on their small incomes (Baker 122). The addition of Hemingway's biographical material makes sense for several reasons.

First, by moving the film's time setting to begin at the end of World War II, rather than in the early years of the Great Depression, the writers have no authentic biographical material from Fitzgerald's life to draw upon from that era. Fitzgerald died in 1940. Therefore, the additional material to flesh out an updated adaptation of the story must be drawn from other sources, and the life of an author closely related to Fitzgerald in the public eye is a logical choice of inspiration.

Second, inclusion of the Hemingway material would have broadened audience appeal for male viewers, since it allowed for scenes of relatable manly pursuits, such as serving in the military, arm wrestling, auto racing, and horse track betting, that were not found in the original story nor were parts of Fitzgerald's everyday life. Last, adapting the short story for screen necessitated the creation of a back story for Helen Wills, Charlie's flamboyant wife, played by Elizabeth Taylor in the film. Alluding to Hemingway opened up the possibility to draw upon worldly female characters from his early career, such as Brett Ashley and Catherine Barkley, as more rational bases for a female lead played by Taylor, who would have found little to work with as a Zelda clone or a Southern belle in the Daisy Buchanan mold.

However, Brooks also drew upon Fitzgerald's life and works to fill in the gaps left in the transition from printed story to film. On the most elementary level, changes made by Fitzgerald himself for the never-filmed screenplay *Cosmopolitan* (1940) can be found in Brooks's film. In the *Cosmopolitan* screenplay, Fitzgerald changed the name of Charlie and Helen's daughter, Honoria, to Victoria. This change reflected a changed loyalty in Fitzgerald's friendships. At the time he wrote "Babylon Revisited," Fitzgerald and Zelda were close friends with Gerald and Sara Murphy, a couple they often vacationed with in Europe. The Murphys' daughter, Honoria, was the initial namesake of Fitzgerald's character. However, by the late 1930s, one of Fitzgerald's closest friends was the screenwriter Budd Schulberg. After Schulberg's first daughter, Victoria, was born, Fitzgerald changed the character's name, telling Schulberg, "When she's old enough to understand, you can tell her that the little girl in the movie, who may be played by Shirley Temple, was named for her!" (*Babylon Screenplay* 11). Beyond these rudimentary updates, Fitzgerald made an almost complete overhaul of the storyline in his own adaptation of "Babylon Revisited" for the screen.

In Fitzgerald's screenplay, the emphasis was not on Charlie Wales, the reformed alcoholic father who feels remorse for his wife's early death and who longs to reconnect with the daughter he has lost because she represents his "only chance for a home" ("Babylon" 332). For Fitzgerald, the Charlie Wales of his original creation was a way of working out his greatest fear as a father, the possibility of losing custody of his daughter Scottie to Zelda's sister Rosalind, who blamed him for Zelda's initial nervous breakdown. Fitzgerald's screenplay shifts the focus away from the guilt-ridden father and highlights instead the viewpoint of the daughter, Victoria, while adding a sensationalist murder-for-hire subplot along the way. After reworking his story as a star vehicle for Shirley Temple, Fitzgerald wrote in his notes accompanying the screenplay:

> This is an attempt to tell a story from a child's point of view *without* sentimentality.... So who ever deals with this script is implored to remember that it is a *dramatic piece*—not a homey family story. Above all things, Victoria is a *child*—not

Daddy's little helper who knows all the answers. Another point: in the ordinary sense, this picture has no more moral than *Rebecca* or *The Shop Around the Corner*—though one can draw from it any moral one wishes about the life of the Wall Street rich of a decade ago. It had better follow the example of *Hamlet*, which has had a hundred morals read into it, all of them different—let it stand on its own bottom [*Babylon Screenplay* 190].

From this note and the author's extreme willingness to alter the plot, it is easy to discern that Fitzgerald would have been content for his original story to be adapted in any way that maintained a sense of dramatic tension while pursuing a storyline that did not attempt to moralize the situation or make the child annoyingly precocious.

The film that Brooks finally created, after purchasing the rights from original producer Lester Cowan and rewriting Fitzgerald's screenplay with the help of Julius Epstein and Philip Epstein, appears to satisfy most, but not all, of Fitzgerald's intentions. In the film created from the Brooks and Epstein twins' screenplay, Charlie Wills's struggles with his own memories create the primary conflict, with the backstory of his history with Helen told as support in a lengthy flashback that takes up most of the film's running time. The flashback sequence contains many details from Fitzgerald's actual life, including his efforts to become a writer of wealth and renown in order to acquire and hold the attentions of the woman he loves. Although this storyline would be familiar to almost anyone with even cursory knowledge of Fitzgerald's romance with his wife, Zelda, it is not included in the original text of "Babylon Revisited." Since the story remains silent on the issue of how Charlie and Helen initially met and fell in love, the decision to supplement with information from Fitzgerald folklore seems logical.

Also, the film contains many lines that allude to other biographical information and works by Fitzgerald, demonstrating that the screenwriters diligently researched their subject matter. One early sequence in the film shows Charlie bailing Helen out of jail after she was arrested for jumping in a Paris fountain. Helen defends her actions by saying that she did it for fun, and Charlie accuses her of doing it because she wanted "to get into print" (*Paris*). Biographies of Fitzgerald and Zelda contain numerous accounts of Zelda jumping into swimming pools and fountains for attention. This scene is followed by Charlie's retrieval of Victoria from the room over the Dingo Bar, where Helen has left her waiting. The little girl has fallen asleep in her ballet costume, and upon waking immediately wants to demonstrate her dancing to Charlie. However, Victoria's ballet skills are not very good, and she falls down.

This juxtaposition of Helen, who represented Zelda in the original story, pulling a crazy stunt for attention, followed by a ballet sequence, should not be read as a mere coincidence. In real life, Zelda's first mental breakdown was brought about after she failed to become a ballerina in Paris at thirty, an achievement which she had hoped would make her Fitzgerald's creative equal. Little nuances like these create a sense of Fitzgerald's presence within the film as a hypertext, which reflect an effort by its creators to maintain a consistent artistic vision with the original story and its author.

In a later scene during which Helen and Charlie argue about whether to return to America to save their marriage, Helen says, "Charlie, let's go back, before we crack up. If you love me, let's go back home" (*Paris*). This statement may be read as an allusion to Fitzgerald's series of magazine essays detailing his alcoholic breakdown in the 1930s, which were later collected in *The Crack-Up* (1945). The devolution of Charlie and Helen's marriage that follows, including the drinking, irresponsible spending sprees, and suspicions of infidelity, screen like a lightly fictionalized version of Fitzgerald and Zelda's relationship from 1924 onward. While Fitzgerald was writing *The Great Gatsby*, Zelda allegedly had an affair with French aviator Edouard Jozan (*Grandeur* 195). In Zelda's personal writings and in her semi-autobiographical novel, *Save Me the Waltz* (1932), Zelda denies that the affair ever escalated beyond serious flirtation (Cline 149–50).

On Fitzgerald's first trip to Hollywood, he began a similar relationship with the young actress Lois Moran, who became the inspiration for Fitzgerald's novel *Tender Is the Night* (1934). In the novel, Moran is written as Rosemary Hoyt, a young actress with whom Fitzgerald's alter ego, psychiatrist Dick Diver, falls in love. However, their relationship does not become a sexual affair until after Dick's wife, Nicole, leaves him for a young playboy, Tommy Barban. The Nicole/Barban plot is generally believed to be Fitzgerald's response to Zelda's Jozan affair, and the manner in which it was characterized in *Save Me the Waltz*. In real life, Fitzgerald was apparently much more interested in Moran than she was in him, going so far as to screen test in an effort to be cast in a film with her, but nothing ever came of it (*Grandeur* 255). Although Zelda was angry and suspicious as Fitzgerald had been about her affair with Jozan, both Fitzgerald and Moran claim that the affair was never consummated (*Grandeur* 255). The tension from these events, and the novels that resulted from them, culminated in the marriage between Fitzgerald and Zelda becoming "openly competitive." Zelda, believing herself to be the loser in their battle of wills, "resented the arrangement" (*Grandeur* 259–60).

The Moran and Jozan affairs became so much a part of the public consciousness surrounding the Fitzgeralds and their opposing novels that information about them appears to have provided a substantial amount of the plot for *The Last Time I Saw Paris*. In the film, Helen begins a serious flirtation with playboy tennis bum Paul Lane, portrayed by a young Roger Moore, while Charlie is working on his third unsuccessful novel. To retaliate, Charlie escalates his relationship with a wealthy, frequently-divorced socialite, Lorraine Quarl, played by a perfectly cast Eva Gabor. Although the Lorraine character appears briefly in "Babylon Revisited," their relationship is greatly expanded in the film adaptation. Also, their exploit is changed from a drunken, late-night ride on a three-wheeled butcher's bicycle in the story to a more glamorous cross-country auto race at Monte Carlo in the film. These changes most likely reflect an effort by the filmmakers to create an environment of dangerous excitement, rather than petty foolishness, to explain why Charlie would be enticed into an affair with Lorraine. Such dramatic enhancements seem to be in accord with Fitzgerald's original intentions for a nonmoralizing adaptation of the story and should be read as acceptable plot alterations.

The Paul Lane counterplot is completely absent from "Babylon Revisited," and instead parallels the real-life Zelda/Jozan affair. In the film, Charlie gets drunk and starts a fistfight over Helen with Paul at the Dingo, and has to be carried out. This action coincides with similar events in Fitzgerald's life, during which "Zelda egged him into fighting" knowing that he, after "a certain stage of inebriation, was ready to fight anyone. He believed he was—or should be—a proficient boxer. He wasn't, and his saloon brawls usually resulted in beatings for him" (*Grandeur* 258). This atmosphere of mutual agitation between Charlie and Helen mirrors the emotional climate of Fitzgerald and Zelda's relationship. In both the original story and the film, this conflict results in Charlie, who is passed out in a drunken stupor, accidentally locking Helen out in the snow. Helen subsequently catches pneumonia, which complicates her heart condition, and she dies. Helen's death scene in the hospital is especially moving, and provides a reasonable visualization of events only alluded to in "Babylon Revisited." For viewers familiar with the bedside vigils that Fitzgerald kept while Zelda underwent psychiatric hospitalization, the scene provides additional emotional resonance because of its biographical origins.

The interpretive style used in updating the time frame in "Babylon Revisited" from World War I to World War II in its adaptation, *The Last Time I Saw Paris*, has been highly criticized by Fitzgerald scholars. As Gene Phillips notes, the film "was deprived of the rich ambiance of Paris after World War I, which permeated the short story, and since the movie was likewise deprived of the hard-edged conclusion of Fitzgerald's original story, it was written off by many viewers as a classy contemporary soap opera" (*Fitzgerald* 61). Phillips's criticism of the film's updated setting shows a bias toward the faithfulness side of the film adaptation debate. Although he acknowledges that it seems "logically and artistically right that the scriptwriters should follow Fitzgerald's lead in utilizing further details from the author's life, over and above those which he had himself already put into the story, in order to flesh out the screenplay," Phillips fails to recognize that such incorporation showed an unprecedented attention to the careful balance of preserving Fitzgerald's original themes and tone while simultaneously reaching out to potential audience members who might have been alienated by a historical piece.

Although Phillips is correct to point out that the altered ending of the film adaptation veers perilously off-course toward exactly the sort of homey family story that Fitzgerald warned against, careful scrutiny of the final lines of Fitzgerald's original piece indicate that Brooks made the best concession possible to accommodate studio demands. Contrary to Phillips's reading of "Babylon Revisited," the story ends, not with Charlie's request for custody being irrevocably denied, but instead with Charlie being told by his brother-in-law "to let it slide for six months" before approaching the issue with Marion again ("Babylon" 341). Afterward, Charlie leaves, thinking to himself in the story's closing lines, "He would come back someday; they couldn't make him pay forever. But he wanted his child, and nothing was much good now.... He was absolutely sure Helen wouldn't have wanted him to be so alone" ("Babylon" 341). From these lines, it is easy to see how the adapters of "Babylon Revisited" could write into the screenplay a scene like the final one in the film, which allows Charlie to reclaim Victoria after Marion has a change of heart. Brooks and the Epstein brothers simply had to abbreviate the six months time span into a few days, before giving Charlie the resolution of reestablishing custody of Victoria.

Choosing to put the phrase "Helen wouldn't have wanted you to be so alone" into Marion's final lines, rather than in Charlie's mind, simply reworks Fitzgerald's original sentiment in a more positive light that would have been suitable for the tastes of MGM executives (*Paris*). Phillips makes a pertinent point in his book on Fitzgerald's films:

> The compromised ending of *Paris* was symptomatic of the fact that, as Richard Brooks states, many studio executives at the time had a predilection for sentimental endings of this sort. When he tried to tone down the sentimentality that tinged movies like *Paris* while he was making them, he was resisted by the front office. Studio boss Louis B. Mayer told him, You seem like a nice fellow, but if you could only make our kind of movies it would be much better. I can't blame them for their attitude, says Brooks, but he concedes, I should just not have gone along with it, when it came to sending the audience away with a smile rather than a tear at the end of a picture like *Paris* [60].

However, the process of making movies is usually a careful dance of giving concessions and making stands. *The Last Time I Saw Paris* is a testament to how that process can sometimes bring out the best in actors, authors, and screenwriters to establish balanced creative command.

Charlie Wills was the last role Van Johnson played under contract to MGM. Signed to the studio in 1943, Johnson rose to prominence after a severe car accident left him ineligible for military service, but still available to pick up many roles after MGM's usual leading men left to serve in World War II. Johnson's blond, all–American good looks and affable charm were well suited to the light romantic pictures of his early career. His easy-going personality was also well suited to the studio system. Regarding MGM as "one big happy family and a little kingdom," Johnson flourished in the studio system environment, saying, "Everything was provided for us, from singing lessons to barbells. All we had to do was inhale, exhale and be charming. I used to dread leaving the studio to go out into the real world, because to me the studio was the real world" (Harmetz, "Johnson"). Perhaps because of his complacency about his role as an MGM actor, Johnson never strove for a role that especially showcased his talents.

However, with *Paris*, Johnson seemed to tap into his closely guarded personal life to create one of his best performances. By 1954, Johnson's personal reputation was similar to that of Fitzgerald's at the time "Babylon Revisited" was written. Both were witty, midwestern men of fair complexion and high ambition, whose commercial appeal was beginning to fade with their looks as the younger audiences who had idolized them grew up. Also, both men had a history of alcohol abuse in their families. Fitzgerald and Zelda's drinking destroyed their marriage and made life difficult for their only daughter, Scottie. In contrast, Johnson's mother was an abusive alcoholic who divorced his father when her only son was still a toddler (Harmetz, "Johnson"). Perhaps this is why Johnson seems so adept at playing up the sense of psychological despair experienced by Charlie Wills as he struggled with controlling his own alcoholism in an effort to regain custody of Victoria. An actor's best performances are often created when he finds a sense of personal resonance within the storyline. Regardless, Johnson's witty, self-doubting monologues in *Paris* expose the insecurities of Charlie Wills and Scott Fitzgerald more poignantly than anything else in the Fitzgerald film adaptation canon and seem to suggest that the actor may have studied Fitzgerald's personal essays while creating the character's psychological context.

The Last Time I Saw Paris also strikes a careful balance between reflecting the historical and socio-cultural manners of Paris during the 1920s and 30s, captured in Fitzgerald's original story, and the cultural awareness of an audience that would have been more familiar with World War II than World War I. As writers of the most famous film set during World War II, *Casablanca*

(1942), the Epstein brothers would have known how small details, such as how Charlie and his future brother-in-law Claude became friends while under General DeGaulle's command, would have provided a frame of reference to draw an audience into the story. However, the device that they use to provide details about the Lost Generation is perhaps the cleverest of all.

In *Paris*, Walter Pidgeon plays World War I veteran James Ellswirth, father to Helen and Marion, who is apparently a holdover from the hedonistic Lost Generation. As Helen explains to Charlie in an early scene in which they gather liquor bottles from her father's secret stash for a V-E Day party, "Father says that after a war we should always be gay and have fun. He started after the Great War and has been celebrating ever since" (*Paris*). Upon first meeting Charlie Wills, Ellswirth asks him whether he is "one of the wealthy Willses from Maryland," to which Charlie replies that he is merely "an average Wills from Milwaukee. Does that count against me?" Fitzgerald's father's family was one of the wealthier families in Baltimore before the Civil War; however, his father lost his inheritance through a series of bad investments and he and his wife were forced to move to his mother's home in St. Paul before Fitzgerald's birth. Since the Charlie Wills of "Babylon Revisited" was from Burlington, Vermont, the most likely explanation for this exchange about Charlie's background is that it is another allusion to Fitzgerald's actual life and the sociocultural implications that surround it.

Coupling this information with further characterization of Ellswirth as a Lost Generation leftover, the overall impression to be derived from his character is that he is the combined ghost of Scott Fitzgerald and the original Charlie Wales, hovering as a spectral reminder of the adaptation's roots. This supposition gains credibility when combined with the scene in which Charlie catches up with Ellswirth several years after Helen's death. At their reunion, Ellswirth, who is approximately the age that Fitzgerald would have been had he been alive in 1954, is no longer the well-dressed middle-aged rogue Charlie remembers. Instead, he is a sad, pale old man in a wheelchair, who is under doctor's orders to give up drinking and smoking due to a series of strokes. In accordance with Fitzgerald's admonition against moralization, the audience is left to determine for themselves whether Ellswirth's carefree lifestyle was worth his early demise.

The manner in which Ellswirth is portrayed suggests that he is a cultural symbol of the wasted lives that resulted from the Lost Generation. Even down to his wilted sweater and ascot, Ellswirth looks similar to photographs taken of Fitzgerald during the months immediately preceding the author's death. After a series of heart attacks, Fitzgerald was also required to give up smoking and drinking, but to no avail. In sum, the fun-loving Ellswirth can be read as

Brooks's and the Epstein brothers' homage to the original Charlie Wales, and his similarly ill-fated author Scott Fitzgerald. In a film that was interpreted in an updated time period to gain audience appeal, inserting the character of James Ellswirth, who is not present in "Babylon Revisited," may have been their subtle way of suggesting that the audience should recall the story's original setting.

In short, *The Last Time I Saw Paris* is a frequently underrated film adaptation in the Fitzgerald canon. It represents not only one of the earliest manifestations of the Hemingerald phenomenon, but also one of the first times in which the levels of creative command among author, screenwriters, director, producer, stars, and audience come together in compromise to form a film that reflects the common interests and knowledge that most parties concerned with Fitzgerald and his works share. Although a later adaptation updated in the interpretive style, *The Curious Case of Benjamin Button*, would travel further down these same paths, this film version of "Babylon Revisited" can be credited with opening up a whole new way for filmmakers to reconsider Fitzgerald's biography as a gateway into meaningful visual portrayals of his works.

Tender Is the Night (1962)

Henry King's version of *Tender Is the Night* (1962) started a new trend in Fitzgerald adaptations. With this trend, which would continue through the 1970s, filmmakers converted Fitzgerald's original work with as few changes as possible. The result of this effort is that, except for a few deletions or alterations of potentially volatile subject matter concerning race and sexuality, the finished film represents one of the most completely consistent artistic visions in the Fitzgerald film canon.

King's adaptation maintains a level of incorporation of details about Fitzgerald's personal life that is an almost perfect replica of the original. Most critical articles on the novel discuss how Fitzgerald's inspiration came from his personal feelings regarding the dissipation of his life and marriage following Zelda's first mental breakdown and her subsequent series of lengthy psychiatric treatments, first at the Prangins clinic in Switzerland and later at Johns Hopkins in Maryland. Fitzgerald's guilt about how his own drinking might have contributed to Zelda's decline, as well as his diminishing ability to produce quality pieces of new writing, are also often cited as the sources of the novel's central conflict.

The plot of Fitzgerald's novel follows a young psychiatrist with a promising career, Dick Diver, as he falls in love with one of his patients, the wealthy, emotionally disturbed heiress Nicole Warren. Although Dick is gradually able to help Nicole overcome her mental illness, which was caused by Nicole's father's sexual abuse of her as a child, Dick gradually succumbs to the indolent lifestyle that Nicole's money provides for the couple after their marriage. Eventually, after Dick becomes an alcoholic and both he and Nicole fall into affairs with others, Nicole leaves Dick for Tommy Barban, another man whom she perceives to be more stable. The novel reads as a manifestation of Fitzgerald's worst fears about his relationship with Zelda, that cavorting with her had turned him into an alcoholic whose creativity and emotional vitality had been drained by her constant needs. In short, Fitzgerald and his hero, Diver, shared the same fear: that they had become permanently weakened by their attempts to make the women they loved strong, only to have those women leave their empty shells for stronger men.

Interestingly, David O. Selznick and female star Jennifer Jones seemed to share a similarly symbiotic marriage. When Jones first met Selznick, she was a little-known, newly-wed actress still performing under her maiden name, Phyllis Isley. However, after Jones screentested for Selznick, he signed her immediately to a personal seven-year contract. Jones's first leading role under this contract, in *Song of Bernadette* (1943), earned her an Academy Award and made her a star. The film also introduced her to director Henry King, for whom Jones would consistently perform her best acting work, including her role as Nicole Diver in *Tender Is the Night*. By 1945, both Jones and Selznick had developed a romantic relationship, left their respective spouses, and married.

As with the early years of marriage between Dick and Nicole Diver, Selznick was clearly in control of almost every aspect of Jones's life. According to Aljean Harmetz, "from 1943 until his death in 1965, Selznick made virtually all the decisions in his wife's career. He supervised her dramatic training and produced many of her early movies." However, as Jones aged, Selznick continued to take risks with his own career in order to secure desirable acting roles for his wife, an act of self-sacrifice which ultimately proved to be his undoing as a producer. Selznick's lavish production of Ernest Hemingway's *Farewell to Arms* (1957), starring Jones as Catherine Barkley, "was a critical and box-office failure and the last movie Selznick made" (Harmetz, "Jones"). After *Farewell* flopped, the man who made *Gone with the Wind* (1939) retired from every aspect of the movie business except one: bolstering Jones's career. In this aspect, he succeeded, and Jones eclipsed her husband's notoriety to remain a viable star for the next decade. Perhaps this is why the film remains so faithful to Fitzgerald's original novel. By telling the story of the Divers, and by proxy the story of the Fitzgeralds, David Selznick and Jennifer Jones were stepping inside the ouroboric circle of Fitzgerald's celebrity by folding in a veiled adaptation of themselves.

The connection between Selznick and Fitzgerald actually began during *Gone with the Wind*, when Selznick, who had long been an admirer of Fitzgerald's novels, hired the writer to polish dialogue on the film. Always in need of quick cash for the heavy expenses of Zelda's treatments and daughter Scottie's schooling, Fitzgerald hastily wrote a screen treatment of *Tender Is the Night* in hopes of capitalizing on his new Hollywood connections. Unfortunately, the treatment was seriously flawed and filled with unnecessary scenes of garish action that rendered it an unmarketable commodity for many years. Still, Selznick had been a fan of the novel since its first release in 1934, and secured the film rights. Many years later, after Jones read the novel and set her heart on playing the part of Nicole, Selznick began the process of securing funding for the film. However, in 1958, after the failure of Selznick and Jones's adaptation of a similar project, Hemingway's *Farewell to Arms*, Selznick was unable to place the project and had to sell the script, along with Jones's services as Nicole, to Twentieth Century–Fox. Selznick recalled afterwards, "It is one of the great regrets of my career that I did not make *Tender Is the Night*" (qtd. in Phillips 140).

Even though he sold the rights to the production, Selznick could not stay completely out of the project. In essence, Selznick planted his own director's chair directly in the shadow of Henry King's, offering daily doses of unsolicited advice on casting, dialogue, cuts, and staging with his choices, more often than not, leaning toward lengthening scenes that included Jones (Phillips 141–42). The end result was an adaptation that seems to drag out almost every emotional scene that contains an opportunity for Jones to give another Oscar-worthy performance, especially the scene of Nicole's breakdown in the bathroom, which is brief in the original but quite lengthy in the film. However, Jennifer Jones's portrayal of Nicole Diver should not be discounted, even if her husband permitted overindulgence. According to Aljean Harmetz, Jones "was in precarious mental health herself" while playing the equally disturbed Nicole ("Jones"). Regardless, Jones gives one of her best performances in the role. As the emotionally dependent wife of a brilliant man who had made her over, often at his own expense, Jones would have found much to relate to in Nicole Diver. Like Van Johnson in *The Last Time I Saw Paris* (1954), Jones seemed to draw on her personal struggles to create a convincing portrayal of a Fitzgerald character, which is not a surprising phenomenon. In general, Fitzgerald's characters tend to convey his turbulent relationship with Zelda, adding a sense of realism for audiences.

Years later, in an interview with Gene Phillips, Henry King made the same complaint, stating that Selznick "was working on the assumption that the more of Jennifer there was in the film, the better it would be. As much as I like and respect Jennifer, that was not the case. More was less" (142). Regardless, King went on to say that he was vetoed on many cuts that would have shortened the film and he was overridden by Fox in the decision-making process. King recalled, "the studio let Selznick have his way, because they said he had caused so much trouble during shooting that they just wanted to get the picture out into theaters as soon as possible, and be done with his meddling" (Phillips 142). The film would be the last for King, who was seventy-five at the time, and frustrated with his lack of creative control. In an odd instance of life imitating art, it appears that the Nicole Diver character drained the professional vitality of yet another man during King's adaptation of *Tender Is the Night*.

Yet, even with this flaw of well-meaning overexposure of Jones as the female lead, King's adaptation of *Tender Is the Night* remains a film text that is remarkably consistent with Fitzgerald's original artistic vision. Jason Robards is subtly effective, playing Dick Diver's slow devolution into a pitiable alcoholic with sympathetic grace and a dry wit that evokes the *mea culpa* attitude of Fitzgerald's *Crack-Up* essays. Among the supporting cast, Tom Ewell, as Abe North, is a particular standout. Ewell takes North's character beyond the simply drawn boor of Fitzgerald's creation, making his senseless decline from respected composer to washed-up drunk appear as an echoing tragedy that mirrors Diver's decline, showing that no man can escape the destructive powers of easy riches. King's choice to direct Ewell's character as a sort of Greek chorus, incessantly playing his unfinished ballad, which grows into the theme song of the film, is a particularly effective way of showing the tragedy of an unrealized potential life through music.

By using the Abe North storyline as an echoing tragedy, King deftly sidesteps the race issue in Fitzgerald's original novel, which would have been virtually unfilmable for a mass audience in 1962. In the novel, Abe North accuses an unnamed black man of robbing him, and Jules Peterson, a shoe-polish inventor of mixed African-Scandanavian descent, corroborates North's story when he gives a statement to the police against the robber. Peterson is subsequently murdered by the robber in Rosemary Hoyt's hotel room. When Diver arrives to find Peterson dead on Rosemary's bed, he fears that the scandal of a dead black man in her bedroom will ruin Rosemary's acting career. Then, Diver has the hotel manager bribe the police to dump Peterson's body elsewhere. Diver, who by this time is in love with Hoyt, nevertheless summons Nicole to bring him a blanket in which to wrap Peterson's body. When Nicole arrives, and is shaken by the sight of Peterson's dead body, Diver attempts to comfort her with a phrase that would be read as much more racially insensitive today than in 1933, saying "Look here—you mustn't get upset over this—it's only some nigger scrap" (*Tender* 110). If the scene had appeared in King's 1962 adaptation, which debuted during the key years of the African American Civil Rights movement, it could have easily incited riots for its racist theme.

Still, it would have been irresponsible to ignore the race issue that is clearly present in the novel, and for that matter, much of Fitzgerald's work. According to Robert Forrey, "On the question of race, Fitzgerald does not belong in the liberal tradition in American letters...Fitzgerald had a fondness for lost conservative causes, such as the Confederacy" (295). Forrey provides this explanation:

> On the basis of what is known from his fiction and life, it does not seem unfair to suggest that Fitzgerald believed in the inherent inferiority of Negroes. In stories in which he indulged his imagination most freely, rich whites rule in lordly splendor, catered to by Negro servants of the docile and inferior kind [295].

Forrey's interpretation of Fitzgerald's racial politics is supported by Dick Diver's reaction upon first meeting Jules Peterson, whom he describes as "a small, respectable Negro, on the suave model that heels the Republican party in the border States" (*Tender* 106). This statement, meant as a sort of backhanded compliment, does not seem natural to a doctor from upstate New York like Dick Diver. Instead, it seems much more likely to be spoken by someone like Fitzgerald, a descendant of Maryland plantation owners who tended to romanticize the Old South as a lost high point in American culture. This mindset, obviously incendiary by post–Civil Rights movement standards of racial equality, is completed when Fitzgerald describes Diver's characterization of his behavior after the incident as the pinnacle of chivalry. In Diver's opinion, his cover-up of Peterson's murder raised his standing in Hoyt's eyes, as he thought "she adored him for saving her ... and she had listened in wild worship to his strong, sure, polite voice making it all right" (*Tender* 112). In 1962, mixed-race audiences of King's film adaptation would have found nothing "all right" about Diver's antiquated racism or his cover-up of Peterson's murder.

Instead of using this scene in his film, King made the wise choice of changing the entire context of the confrontation between Abe North and his unnamed black adversary. In the film, North plays his unfinished theme at a piano in a bar with his usual refrain of drunken ramblings instead of an ending. Sensing North's difficulty in finishing his composition, an unnamed black piano player comes up and offers his assistance. Somewhat annoyed, North gets up from the piano and allows the man to play. The piano player proceeds not only to provide an excellent ending for the piece, but also to greatly surpass

North's hokey playing style by adding numerous runs and flourishes that clearly display extensive classical training and musical sophistication. Angered at being shown up by the other musician, North takes a swing at the black piano player, starting a fight which ends with North being ejected from the bar. Diver and Rosemary, who had also been at the bar, leave and Diver returns Rosemary to her room. Afterward, Diver goes down to the bar at his hotel where he sees Collis Clay, a young Yale man from Georgia with a deep Southern accent who is in love with Rosemary. The two men discuss why neither will ever have Rosemary, and in the following scene the discussion evolves into a fistfight between the two. When Rosemary reappears to break up the fight, paparazzi catch Diver and Rosemary together and publish their story as the scandal of a young actress tempting a married man. Upon returning to his hotel room with Nicole, Diver learns that North returned to the bar and was killed.

The overall effect of the juxtaposition of these altered scenes in King's adaptation expresses a racial theme that would have been much more acceptable to audiences in 1962 than that of Fitzgerald's original novel. White men who resisted integration of African Americans in the 1960s often feared two things would happen if black men were allowed equality: black men would surpass them in the professional fields and also charm white women, leaving resistant white men without careers or potential spouses. The confrontation between North and the black piano player demonstrates the fear that a white man could be surpassed by a black man in his chosen vocation if the black man were allowed equal opportunity and education. Also, by situating Diver's struggle for Rosemary's affections against the younger white Southern gentleman, Clay, between the two scenes of North's confrontations with a younger, more talented black musician, King's film seems to suggest that a sophisticated black gentleman could prove more adept at securing the affections of a white female than either Diver or Clay. For viewers choosing to see it, King's substitution of these scenes in place of Fitzgerald's less-relevant originals might be read as a subtly brilliant commentary on the state of race relations in the 1960s, added into an otherwise historically faithful film set in the 1930s.

King also makes a brilliant decision in his choice of staging for another potentially scandalous scene, in which Nicole's sister, Baby Warren, reveals that Nicole was raped as a child by their father, a crime which is cited as the source for Nicole's mental illness. In Fitzgerald's original novel, Devereux Warren, Nicole's father, comes to the clinic to confess directly to Dr. Dohmler, Diver's supervisor, that he had committed incest with Nicole. Mr. Warren described the situation as if Nicole had become a substitute for her mother, and that to all outward appearances, they were the ideal father and daughter, until one day their relationship went too far. As Warren says, Nicole and he "were just like lovers—and then all at once we were lovers—and ten minutes after it happened I could have shot myself—except I guess I'm such a God-damned degenerate I didn't have the nerve to do it" (*Tender* 129). Although it was possible for an author in 1933 to write about incest, it would have been completely impossible, according to the Production Code still in place in 1962, for an actor to portray such a character on camera without scandal. Even Stanley Kubrick's adaptation of Vladimir Nabokov's *Lolita* (1962), in which the incest between a step-father and daughter forms the main plot, was severely toned down but nevertheless caused a major scandal upon release. Making the incest plotline a major feature of an adaptation of *Tender Is the Night* would not only have caused a scandal, but also possibly alienated audiences of Fitzgerald films, who generally wanted their author's works romanticized.

For these reasons, Henry King and his screenwriter, Ivan Moffat, chose to stage the revelation scene of Nicole as an incest victim through a series of awkward pauses expressed in a conversation among Baby Warren, Diver, and Dohmler at the clinic. The sequence is well played by the three actors, who break off just short of stating that incest has occurred and allow the audience to fill in the unavoidable details. Mr. Warren never appears on screen. By making the act of incest so unspeakably horrible that the characters never actually name the crime, and eliminating the presence of Nicole's attacker, King creates an atmosphere of horror about the incident that captures the tone of Fitzgerald's original without stating its facts.

Also, King wisely omits the detail that Rosemary Hoyt, the young actress with whom Diver eventually has an affair, is filming a picture called *Daddy's Girl* when she first meets Diver. One inference that can be drawn from Diver's falling for Hoyt is that he is the sort of man who is attracted to spoiled socialites who live charmed lives. This interpretation gains support when one considers that Nicole is the rich heiress of Devereux Warren. Audiences can also infer from Diver's relationship patterns that he tends to see the emptiness behind the facades of such women, and becomes attracted to them in the role of their caretaker and protector. However, the inference that would have been impermissible to many film audiences in 1962 is that both Rosemary and Nicole tend to view Diver as a father figure. Knowing that Nicole was sexually exploited by her father, coupled with the belief that she viewed Diver as a father figure, could have caused audiences to believe that Diver was continuing to exploit, rather than helping her as a psychiatrist, by stepping into the abusive father role. This same unflattering inference could be extended to Diver's relationship with the much-younger Rosemary, skewing the dynamic of their affair and making Diver appear like an exploiter of both women. Since the point of the film adaptation is to focus on the central plot from Fitzgerald's original—

the rise and fall of Diver's relationship with Nicole—Henry King makes a smart choice by eliminating the name *Daddy's Girl* from the film. By placing Rosemary in Rome to film an unnamed project, King removes all possible connections between Diver and Nicole's exploitive father that could have alienated audiences in 1962.

However, King does not eliminate all scenes of potentially controversial discussions of sexuality in his film adaptation. In one vignette from Fitzgerald's original novel Señor Pardo, whom Fitzgerald describes as "a handsome iron-gray Spaniard, noble of carriage, with all the appurtenances of wealth and power," comes to Diver's clinic and rages that Diver must do something to cure his son, Francisco, of being a homosexual (*Tender* 243). Diver listens patiently, withholding his disgust, as Pardo tells him that he had another psychiatrist attempt to cure Francisco of homosexuality by giving him injections of cantharides and taking him to a bordello. When the supposed cure proved ineffective, Pardo whipped his son mercilessly.

Both in the novel and in the film Diver is much more sympathetic to Francisco, questioning the young man about whether he is happy with his sexuality and advising him on ways to live with it other than through excessive drinking, which had been Francisco's preferred coping method until their meeting. Fitzgerald describes Señor Pardo's issues with his son's sexuality as hilariously overreactive and offers Diver's opinion that "often the sheer hysteria of the family representative was as interesting psychologically as the condition of the patient" (243). King's adaptation adds a homophobic accusation from Señor Pardo directed at Diver's attempts to tell him the truth about Francisco's sexuality, when Pardo says that Diver's "affection for my son may indicate that you are the same sort of swine that he is" (*Tender*). This wild claim achieves its desired effect, by making audiences side with Francisco and acceptance of his sexuality rather than with his father, a concept that was still radical in 1962. This scene demonstrates King's attempt as a director to push the envelope of social equality as far as he dared, within the confines of then-present cinematic moral standards, in order to remain consistent with as many of Fitzgerald's original themes as possible.

In his excellent book, *Fiction, Film and F. Scott Fitzgerald*, Gene Phillips emphasizes the effect of Catholicism and the ritual of confession on Fitzgerald's repeated use of his personal life as a basis for his fiction. Concerning *Tender Is the Night* and the *Crack-Up* essays, Fitzgerald's chief works of the mid–1930s, Phillips claimed that the works "reflect the spiritual values that his Catholic education had afforded him" and that these works "embody a public examination of conscience which testifies to the fact that, as noted, the Catholic faith had a firmer hold on Fitzgerald than he was aware of" (136).

In King's adaptation of *Tender Is the Night*, it appears that Fitzgerald's Catholic tendency toward confession is contagious to filmmakers as well. As director, King used the otherwise faithful conversion of fiction to film as a platform to subtly push a social agenda that is decidedly pro-racial integration and anti-homophobia. The film's first producer, David Selznick, and his wife, lead actress Jennifer Jones, became attached to the project possibly as a way of expressing the true dynamic of their relationship. Given the success of King's adaptation among Fitzgerald scholars and audiences, one might say that Catholic-style confession can easily be absorbed into the film adaptation ouroboros.

• TWO •

Screening the American Icarus, Part Two
Film Adaptations of Fitzgerald, 1974–2013

During the 1960s and 1970s, the conversion style dominated Fitzgerald-based cinema, as filmmakers attempted to create adaptations that were faithful representations of the author's originals. *The Great Gatsby* (1974) and *The Last Tycoon* (1976) were successes at the box office and in release to video audiences; however, critical opinions on these films remain mixed. Jack Clayton's *The Great Gatsby*, often maligned because of its slow-paced plotline, deserves reconsideration for its visual manifestation of Fitzgerald's forays into Bergsonian philosophy. *The Last Tycoon* is possibly the most underrated Fitzgerald adaptation, if for nothing else than director Elia Kazan's excellent choice to incorporate themes found in the author's other works to enlarge Fitzgerald's take on Hollywood's mythmaking powers, including the creation and maintenance of the American capitalist mythos as a whole. Only one revisionist adaptation of a Fitzgerald work, Richard Wolstencroft's *The Beautiful and Damned* (2008), has appeared in recent years. Unlike Elia Kazan's *The Last Tycoon*, which limited directorial editorialization on Fitzgerald's role in latter-day popular culture to the scope of Fitzgerald's original texts, Wolstencroft's film serves as a cautionary tale against allowing too much of a director's own socio-political viewpoint to overpower a film adaptation. As with the first forty years, the interpretive style has proven to be the most successful means of transferring a Fitzgerald text to film. David Fincher's interpretive adaptation, *The Curious Case of Benjamin Button* (2008), strikes an excellent balance among incorporation of autobiographical details, Hemingerald phenomena, and original text to create a film of lasting resonance. Fincher's adaptation demonstrates, yet again, that film adaptation works best as a fully balanced collaborative process.

The Great Gatsby (1974)

Jack Clayton's adaptation of *The Great Gatsby* (1974) is perhaps the most faithful conversion of the novel to film currently in existence. According to Gene Phillips, Clayton paid painstaking detail to the historical accuracy of the film's costumes and setting, using 1920s vintage clothing and automobiles arranged around authentic mansions in Newport, Rhode Island's Miracle Mile, all in an effort to recapture the lost opulence of Jazz Age New York. Also, "to top it off, some of the extras who played Gatsby's crass menagerie of roistering party guests were actually members of Newport's first families" (Phillips 121). Clayton's adaptation is also careful to convey Fitzgerald's main themes, exploring through the voiceover of Nick Carraway's inner monologue issues of race, class, gender, romance, and the American dream as Eden that linger in Fitzgerald's Bergsonian understanding of the suffocating power of memory.

However, critics of Clayton's film claim that it fails in one important aspect: pace. Blaming Clayton for this fault, Gene Phillips writes, "It must be conceded that all of the interpolations which Clayton made in the screenplay, taken together ... result in a motion picture that in the last analysis seemed at times slow paced and overlong" (120). Truthfully, Fitzgerald's original novel is a remarkably taut piece of prose. In fewer than two hundred pages, Fitzgerald captures both the failure of an epic romance and the hedonism of the 1920s. In contrast, Clayton's film sprawls to an epic length of 144 minutes. The main reason for Clayton's extended treatment of the work is his persistent choice to dwell upon developing the personalities of Fitzgerald's characters, making the lives of each member of the novel's two love triangles a tragedy in its own right.

The languid pace of the film might be defended in two ways. First, Fitzgerald intended the novel partly as a commentary on the wasteful lives of the idle rich. An adaptation which takes such a leisurely stroll through the mixed psychologies of the characters reflects the tone of repulsion from overindulgence that was intended to ground audience sympathies against these people living the so-called good life. Also, critics of the film tend to overlook the impact of Bergson's theory on the duration of memory that permeates not only *The Great Gatsby*, but all of Fitzgerald's work. Bergson's duration theory concentrated on the power of moments that the Romantic poets would have referred to as "spots of time," or incidents in a person's life that haunted his or her very existence and influenced all major decisions. Fitzgerald's novel clearly demonstrates the influence of this Romantic connection between memory and quest in the overleaf, written by his *nom de plume*, the fictitious poet Thomas Parke D'Invilliers, declaring:

> Then wear the gold hat, if that will move her;
> If you can bounce high, bounce for her too,
> Till she cry, "Lover, gold-hatted, high-bouncing lover,
> I must have you!" [*Gatsby* 1].

Clayton's film dwells upon this sort of Bergsonian image, allowing scenes intended for special impact to linger like dreams in celluloid, in hopes that they will persist in the audience's collective memory.

This Bergsonian presence of memory in the film begins with its opening lines, converted directly from Fitzgerald's original novel through voiceover by Nick Carraway:

> In my younger and more vulnerable years my father gave me some advice that I've been turning over in my mind ever since. "Whenever you feel like criticizing anyone," he told me, "just remember that all the people in this world haven't had the advantages that you've had." He didn't say any more but we've always been unusually communicative in a reserved way and I understood that he meant a great deal more than that. In consequence, I'm inclined to reserve all judgments, a habit that has opened up many curious natures to me and also made me the victim of not a few veteran bores [*Gatsby* 5].

By choosing to open the movie with Fitzgerald's opening lines about long-remembered advice and its impact on Nick's current character, Clayton establishes a meditative pace in his adaptation that allows audiences to ruminate on the characters Nick meets, reserving judgment upon them, as if they had met them personally.

Clayton not only continuously relies upon inner monologue and voiceover to indicate points of character meditation for audiences, but also uses many visual metaphors to convey ideas expressed in Fitzgerald's novel that would not otherwise translate well to film. During the aforementioned opening monologue, Nick, dressed in a spotless white suit, attempts to guide a small, uncontrollable motorboat across the bay. This image begins the visual metaphor that will continue throughout the film until the final lines of Fitzgerald's original novel, that all men are voyaging dreamers, who will "beat on, boats against the current, borne back ceaselessly into the past" (*Gatsby* 189). Although Clayton's film uses more of Fitzgerald's original dialogue than any previous adaptation, his persistent use of visual metaphor effectively extends Fitzgerald's themes even further, creating a truly consistent artistic vision between original author and director.

Clayton also remains remarkably consistent with Fitzgerald's original in conveying the author's ideas about race and gender within the historical context of the 1920s. Instead of softening Tom Buchanan's blatant racism to suit post–Civil Rights movement sensitivities, Clayton makes the bold choice to trust that his audiences will hate Tom without the help of directorial editorialization. Through Bruce Dern's excellent portrayal of Tom as a blustering bully, audiences are able to laugh at him, along with Daisy and the others, as he rambles on about the potentially dangerous rise of what he calls "the colored empires" (Clayton). Counting on his audience to intelligently view Tom's racism as reprehensible, Clayton continually incorporates Tom's exact statements from Fitzgerald's original in most confrontation scenes, in an effort to direct audience sympathy toward Tom's opponents. During the climactic scene with Daisy, Gatsby, and Tom in a New York hotel room, which is replicated almost identically from the novel in Clayton's adaptation, Tom rants about the decline of family, saying:

> I suppose the latest thing is to sit back and let Mr. Nobody from Nowhere here make love to your wife. Well, if that's the idea you can count me out.... Nowadays people begin by sneering at family life and family institutions and next they'll throw everything overboard and have intermarriage between black and white [*Gatsby* 137].

By connecting Tom's racism to his rage about Daisy's affair with Gatsby, Clayton garners audience sympathy for the adulterous couple, even though mainstream sensibilities would normally be against them. Adding a touch of irony to the film that is not present in Fitzgerald's original, Clayton also allows a black eyewitness to come forward to identify Gatsby's car at the scene of the accident in which Myrtle is killed. The inference to be drawn in the scene is that Tom, who claims to be an upholder of traditional family values, is actually a hypocrite because he is having an affair with Myrtle, a woman from the lower classes whom Tom, only hours earlier, decried as the worst sort of person with whom to violate marriage vows. By permitting a black man to tell Tom the true story about the incident, Clayton effectively conveys the message that Tom's ideas about both race and marriage are completely inaccurate and potentially dangerous.

Further, Clayton's choice to consistently juxtapose scenes depicting Tom's difficult relationships with Daisy and Myrtle forces audiences to consider the linkage of financial status and social independence on gender relations that is integral to Fitzgerald's original novel. In most critical accounts, Fitzgerald is considered a champion for the rights of flappers, both rich and poor, to use their feminine wiles as tools in order to subvert the social order. As Ruth Prigozy states, Fitzgerald "shows clearly that they have become victims of a social order that values youth, beauty, and wealth" while their "destructive behavior simply mirrors the intense conflict these young women experience in an era that has removed the old boundaries and has not offered them the alternatives that the feminist movement would help make available for their granddaughters in future decades" (141). In both Fitzgerald's novel and Clayton's film, women are put at an economic disadvantage. While upper-class women such as Daisy were allowed some degree of relief through affairs that could provide them with the emotional satisfaction they often lacked in their marriages of financial need, lower-class women like Myrtle were forced to use their sexuality merely to attain a greater standard of living, often without receiving psychological fulfillment from either lovers or husbands.

Two scenes in Clayton's film show the comparative state of psychological oppression between Daisy and Myrtle. In an early scene with Jordan Baker, Daisy describes how she almost changed her mind on the day before her wedding, even throwing away the expensive strand of pearls from Tom, all because she had received a letter from Gatsby telling her that he loved her. However, after listening to persuasion from friends and family about her financial future, Daisy "married Tom the next day without so much as a whimper" (Clayton). This scene shows Daisy as a woman with freedom of choice in her decision about marrying Tom.

In contrast, Myrtle claims to have been deceived by George, who told her he had money to provide for her, even though she later finds out that "he didn't even own the suit he was married in" (Clayton). This scene suggests that Myrtle, if offered the truth about her choice, would not have chosen George as a husband. Outraged over the deception, Myrtle becomes progressively more dangerous and physically violent. This violence escalates throughout the film, beginning with Myrtle knocking on a window so hard as to break it and cut her hand and ending with her death after trying to flag down what she believed to be Tom's car. Also, Myrtle engages in role-playing to imitate rich women like Daisy when she dresses up and acts haughtily in the party at the New York getaway flat she shares with Tom.

However, when Myrtle speaks the name of his upper-class wife, Tom breaks her nose as a physical demonstration of his power. This party scene shows that Tom thinks no more of Myrtle than the female puppy, who is passed through the window of the car in the exact same manner that Myrtle clambers in only a few moments earlier in Clayton's excellent shot parallel. The cumulative meaning of Clayton's juxtaposition of these scenes is clear. Even though upper-class women suffered many disappointments because of gender pressure, they were still thought enough of to be told the truth. Lower-class women, on the other hand, were forced to rely on falsehoods when making their own choices and ordered around as if they were, in Tom's parlance, "bitch" dogs.

Interestingly, the scenes of Tom's violent affair with Myrtle move swiftly in the film, whereas the love scenes between both Daisy and Gatsby and Daisy and Tom move at an almost excruciatingly slow pace. Most likely, Clayton's choice to speed up the scenes of spurious hookups in contrast to genuine love affairs was intentional, and constructed to produce the effect that romance causes time to stand still—to evoke the sense of Bergson's *duree* memory. One of the most influential philosophers on states of consciousness in the 1920s, Bergson described the development of human passions as a gradual, cumulative process:

> An obscure desire gradually becomes a deep passion. Now, you will see that the feeble intensity of this desire consisted at first in its appearing to be isolated and, as it were, foreign to the remainder of your inner life. But little by little it permeates a larger number of psychic elements, tingeing them, so to speak, with its own colour and lo! Your outlook on the whole of your surroundings seems now to have changed radically. How do you become aware of a deep passion, once it has taken hold of you, if not by perceiving that the same objects no longer impress you in the same manner? All your sensations and all your ideas seem to brighten up: it is like childhood back again. We experience something of the kind in certain dreams, in which we do not imagine anything out of the ordinary, and yet through which there resounds an indescribable note of originality [8].

The effect of reading the great philosophers, such as Bergson, while at Princeton had a profound effect on Fitzgerald. As a young writer, he was especially concerned with the concepts of free will and how man chooses either to exercise it or become bound by history (*Grandeur* 75). Many such philosophers, including David Hume, who appears as an overstuffed armchair into which a beautiful girl appears in front of a young scholar in Fitzgerald's early story "Head and Shoulders," were evoked by Fitzgerald's works in order to explain the complex impact of early love on the lives of serious-minded young men (312).

Fitzgerald's use of Bergson in this manner is perfectly captured in Jack Clayton's slow staging of the evolution of the relationship between Gatsby and Daisy after their reunion. As with all the scenes that include Gatsby and Daisy, Clayton swathes their reunion in whites and softly lit pastels, to evoke the dreamlike quality of their relationship. To further the Bergsonian connection, Clayton picks up the line from Fitzgerald's original novel in which Nick prods Gatsby to stop "acting like a little boy" and finally enter the room at Nick's cottage where Daisy waits. The lingering reluctance of their approach to one another in the cottage scene contains the haunting resonance of recaptured childhood mentioned in Bergson. Clayton's choice to frame the close-up of Gatsby's face with an expensive silver tea set in the meeting scene just before he sees Daisy demonstrates how Gatsby attempts to create a barrier of wealth between his past feelings of insecurity and his current mental state. However, when Daisy enters the room and the two come together for the first time, Clayton frames the shot in a simple, white woodframe mirror. As Clayton's camera lingers on Daisy's close-up, the audience seems invited to compare the uncomplicated beauty of this love rediscovered in the more pastoral setting of Nick's small cottage as preferable to Gatsby's attempt to make an unnatural display of his urban wealth in an attempt to impress Daisy.

This sensibility builds throughout the film, from the scene in which Gatsby tosses his vast collection of sorbet-colored shirts into the air, causing them to float to the ground like so many butterflies, to his last lingering kiss with Daisy relaxing by the koi pond, each childish, pastoral dream lingering longer than the last, like living pictures in Gatsby's well-maintained scrapbooks. The scrapbooks are an addition to the film outside the scope of Fitzgerald's original novel, and seem to demonstrate Clayton's knowledge of, and attempt to incorporate, then-current trends in Fitzgerald literary scholarship. In 1974, the year of Clayton's adaptation, Fitzgerald's daughter, Scottie Fitzgerald Smith, released a pictorial autobiography of her parents gleaned from their voluminous scrapbooks. For the first time, this book allowed audiences access to the lives of the Fitzgeralds simultaneously in three types of media: fiction, photographs, and a film adaptation of one of Fitzgerald's most personal works. When considered together, Clayton's lingering shots of Gatsby's scrapbooks in his adaptation and the contemporaneous release of Fitzgerald's own photographic recollections provide the final connection of ouroboric linkage, incorporating Fitzgerald's actual life, his writing, and film adaptations of his works into one complete idea.

Returning specifically to the film, as the pair attempts to re-create the innocence of their youthful romance, Daisy at last admits that Gatsby is even more "sentimental" than she when he admits to keeping, and then models, his uniform, after she admits to having tossed away the dress she wore to their first meeting (Clayton). These scenes, with their animal imagery and soft coloring, create a sense of natural ease and calm reflection between the two about their relationship that best evokes Fitzgerald's latent Romanticist sensibilities. They provide a stark contrast to the swifter confrontation scenes of the rest of the film. In short, Clayton's drawn-out love scenes are necessary breaks in the plot's pace to show how the seductive power of memory can pull a person into endless self-reflection.

Clayton's slow-paced love scenes also serve the important function of demonstrating that such excessive reflection can dull the senses so that one is not aware of potential dangers. In Gatsby's death scene near the end of the film, he lounges in the pool, lost in dreams of Daisy, while George Wilson sneaks up from behind and shoots him in the back. As a member of the organized crime community, Gatsby would normally have been aware of threats to his personal security, attested to by the constant presence of his bodyguards in the film's early scenes. Later on, out of fear for the discovery of his relationship with Daisy, Gatsby fires all his servants, effectively eliminating all his usual safety barriers against the outside world. Through slowly showing Gatsby's declining interest in his personal security and business affairs, Clayton captures an important aspect of Fitzgerald's original novel that other filmmakers miss, that one "can't repeat the past," at least, not in a purely constructive way. The irresistible allure to do so is futile, no matter how innocent or recoverable it may appear in later circumstances.

Clayton's adaptation also captures, in sensitive visual details, the second of Fitzgerald's major themes portrayed in the original *Gatsby* novel that is often neglected on film: the author's persistent characterization of the American dream as Eden. In the scene during which Nick and Gatsby meet for the first time, a picture of a colonial tall ship is on display behind Gatsby's desk. The presence of this painting, although not described in the novel, can be interpreted as a visual representation of Gatsby's belief in the American dream, and his self-characterization as a ship tossed in the waves toward what he hopes will be the fulfillment of his lifelong desires for wealth, power, and the hand of Daisy Fay. Read as such, the scene shows a heavy influence of the adaptation's chief screenwriter, Francis Ford Coppola.

While on break between the first two installments of his *Godfather* trilogy, Coppola wrote the screenplay adaptation for *Gatsby*. He has complained loudly in critical circles that the screenplay of *Gatsby* was "interminable" and "not what I had set up in the beginning" after the re-addition of certain scenes by Clayton into Coppola's initially shorter screenplay (Phillips 119). However, Clayton's final product does retain the stamp of Coppola's work, particularly the opening of Coppola's original *Godfather* film, in Don Corleone's ominous, dimly-lit office, into which Bonasera comes to ask Don Corleone for a favor. Bonasera's initial line, "I believe in America," is the first spoken in the film; however, the remainder of the scene shows progressively how little faith Bonasera still has in the American dream of equal justice and opportunity for all (Coppola). Clayton's meeting scene between Gatsby and Nick is similarly staged in a dark, opulent office filled with Gatsby's intimidating entourage, and conveys the same message of a man who tries to cling to his belief in the American dream despite the obvious knowledge he has of its falsehood.

Clayton's pursuance of Fitzgerald's theme about self-made men and their growing sense of disillusionment with the American dream is furthered by a later visual detail that is not included in the original novel, but which makes sense in the context of Fitzgerald's Romantic-era leanings. Just after Gatsby reunites with Daisy and Nick walks out of the house to give them some privacy, Nick spots a dead, white seabird washed up on the beach. Since the earliest records of seafaring lore, dead albatrosses have been signifiers of sailors lost at sea, and of the hopes and dreams that perished with them (Eyers 12). A quick line of inference can be drawn from Gatsby's dead bird to the albatross in Coleridge's *Rime of the Ancient Mariner*. The albatross's killing marks the beginning of the mariner's nightmare journey, whereas Gatsby's attempt to erase all emotional record of Daisy's marriage to Tom signals the opening of the lover's pentagram that will later consume all three of the novel's characters of lower-class origin: Gatsby, Myrtle, and George. Although both Gatsby and the mariner embark on their respective voyages with the best intentions, they are forced to cling to flagging faith as they are presented with mounting obstacles to overcome on their journeys. However, as most viewers of Clayton's adaptation will already know when they see the film, Gatsby can never shake the albatross of ill-gained wealth from his neck. The dead bird foreshadows the inevitable end of Gatsby's self-made version of the American dream, washed up dead on the rocks of reality.

Two other pastoral scenes from Clayton's adaptation further support his characterization of *Gatsby* as Fitzgerald's Romantic meditation on the paradoxical loss of innocence that many suffer on their way to achieve the happiness promised by the American dream. First, just following the hotel confrontation scene with Daisy, Tom, and Gatsby, Clayton places another scene of dialogue in which Nick and Gatsby stand on the front porch of Nick's cottage overlooking the sound and discuss the first settlers of New York. Nick says to Gatsby, "Can you imagine what this island must have looked like to those Dutch sailors when they first saw it? Fresh green. Like a dream of the new world," and Gatsby replies, "They must have held their breath, afraid it would disappear before they could touch it" (Clayton). For viewers familiar with the history of the American Revolution and the Romantic literary movement that paralleled it, this scene does much to establish a sense of Gatsby's America as a new Eden, designed to allow love to be produced as the naturally meritorious result of persistence and determination fostered by his German immigrant heritage, Midwestern upbringing, and Lutheran work ethic.

Second, it is no accident that, in Clayton's film adaptation, the director adds a small gift from Gatsby to Daisy of an emerald ring. This green emerald is intended to symbolize the natural connection of their hearts through rekindled love; however, Daisy refuses to accept the gift, and Gatsby dies wearing it on his pinky finger. The gleam of this emerald ring, which swings out from under the sheet on Gatsby's hand as his body is carried away on a stretcher, is then reflected in the green light at the end of Daisy's dock that Nick sees in the final scene as he recites in monologue the lines from Fitzgerald's original text, "I thought of Gatsby's wonder when he first picked out the green light at the end of Daisy's dock. He had come a long way to this lawn. And his dream must have seemed so close, that he could hardly fail to grasp it. He did not know that it was already behind him" (189). In addition to being a symbol of fresh hope and the type of organic Romanticism coupled with desire for success in a new Eden that encouraged settlers to come to America, Gatsby's emerald ring shares an obvious connection to Fitzgerald's insecurity about his Irish roots in the "Emerald Isle" that should not be ignored. Clayton's addition of Gatsby's failed gift of the emerald ring is one of the most powerful blended metaphors in the film, incorporating Fitzgerald's impressions about America and its inability to fulfill its promises, especially to ambitious immigrant sons.

The final impact of Clayton's adaptation can be read then not just as a Bergsonian mediation on the allure of memory, but more deeply as an indictment of the class distinctions at the heart of Fitzgerald's original novel. Both the film adaptation and the novel ultimately force the audience to ponder the questions of what happens to a self-made man from humble beginnings and whether he can ever stay true to his originally honest intentions after making the inevitable sacrifices necessary to get ahead. Clayton's adaptation develops possible solutions to these questions throughout his film, causing the audience to question such themes. Through reading Robert Redford's facial expressions during tortured retellings of Gatsby's story, viewers can easily sympathize with a man who is ashamed of his past, without condoning the actions that Gatsby himself already condemns.

Also, Clayton's excellent attention to details of the general "ugliness" of business with a man like Meyer Wolfsheim, who wears cufflinks made of human molars in both the book and the film, is well intended to garner the appropriate amount of sympathy and revulsion for Gatsby (Clayton). By choosing to show, rather than tell, his audiences how they should judge Gatsby's overall character, Clayton mirrors the temperament of Fitzgerald's narrator Nick, who ultimately refrains from expressing his opinion on Gatsby until the end of the work, when he suddenly exclaims, "They're a rotten crowd. You're worth the whole damn bunch put together" (Clayton). For three specific reasons, the placement of this statement as the final words between the two friends provides an excellent coda to Nick's interactions with Gatsby.

First, Clayton has already prepared his audience for Nick's pronouncement with his characterization of Tom as a racist hypocrite. Second, he follows the statement with a confrontation scene after Gatsby's death in which Nick admonishes Daisy for her hypocritical "retreat back into [Tom's] money" so soon after her declaration of love for him (Clayton). Last, Clayton's choice to include the scene with Mr. Gatz near the end of the film, rather than omitting it as in the 1949 version, provides a final capstone to his increasingly sympathetic portrayal of a young dreamer who wanted to accomplish "big things," but who still remained "very generous" with the family he had left behind (Clayton). By closing with Mr. Gatz as a symbol of steadfast Midwestern family values, shown in sharp contrast to Gatsby's fair-weather friends who do not even attend his funeral, Clayton invites audiences to pass final judgment against the wealthy as unworthy of their station, to which many Americans aspire. This approach is far more effective than the too-often critically acclaimed 1949 adaptation of *Gatsby*, which has a much heavier, moralizing tone that is completely out of sync with Fitzgerald's original text.

Little else remains here, other than to discuss briefly the possible causes of the overall sense of animosity that many Fitzgerald enthusiasts have for Clayton's generally well-made film. Even Fitzgerald's daughter, Scottie, who praised the film for its adherence to historical background, expressed a preference for Coppola's original, shorter screenplay, "which she read in advance" and found "excellent in every detail" (Phillips 122). Although slow pacing and choice of Clayton, a British director not known for high emotionalism in his films, are the most common complaints made against the piece, evidence has been offered here that Clayton's goals for the film may be read in a manner validated by Fitzgerald's original artistic vision. Also, some critics, again including Scottie Fitzgerald, have complained about the choice of Redford for the lead. This position is untenable because at the time the film was cast, Redford was a natural fit. Following his roles in the nostalgic tearjerker *The Way We Were* and his Depression-era period piece *The Sting*, both in 1973, the waspishly good-looking Redford was certainly in every position as an actor to capitalize on America's parallel memories of Fitzgerald as another golden boy from a bygone era.

Perhaps the most accurate criticism against Clayton's adaptation can be levied against the choice of Mia Farrow as Daisy. Farrow, a native Californian from a famous acting family, had little in common, either personally or through previous acting roles, with Fitzgerald's Southern heroine, Daisy. As Scottie Fitzgerald explains, Daisy was modeled on her mother, Zelda, and intended by Fitzgerald to be "intensely Southern," while Farrow, "fine actress though she is, failed to project this aspect of Daisy's personality" (qtd. in Phillips 122). Farrow's decision not to attempt a Southern accent or mannerisms in the role of Daisy results in the loss of the innate sense of infatuation with the mysteries of Southern women that pervades much of Fitzgerald's work, including *The Great Gatsby*. By choosing instead to concentrate on portraying Daisy more simply as a shallow, *noveau riche* social climber rather than a Southern woman who married up but still recalled her roots, Farrow's performance lacks the warmth of Fitzgerald's original character, making love scenes between Daisy and Gatsby seem forced despite Clayton's persistent attempts to create warmth through soft coloring and natural imagery.

Also, Farrow chooses to portray Daisy's reactions to highly emotional situations, such as the confrontation with Tom and Gatsby, as consistently overwrought, whereas smaller, tenderer scenes that normally would have required a more nuanced performance are often played too coolly to generate any emotional chemistry between the two lead actors. As a result, audiences must struggle to remember Fitzgerald's original characters, while Redford attempts valiantly to solicit genuine romantic emotion from his costar. Farrow's failure in the role serves as a reminder of the important balance of intentions among actor, director, and original author in forging the tenuous linkage of adaptation for audiences from page to screen.

In short, Clayton's adaptation of *The Great Gatsby* is an excellent conversion of the original historical, psychological, and socio-cultural aspects of Fitzgerald's original novel, which has probably been judged too harshly in the past by critics due to its languid pacing and faulty performance choices made by its lead actress. Despite persistent derision by critics, Clayton's *Gatsby* found enough acceptance by general audiences to gross over $26 million, more than four times its shooting budget of $6.5 million, during initial box office release (IMDB.com). These statistics, coupled with the film's market presence as the only adaptation of the novel currently in wide release on DVD, perhaps serve as the best argument to claim that Clayton's *Gatsby* deserves a more positive reconsideration by critics.

The Last Tycoon (1976)

Since the creation of Virgil's *Aeneid*, great writers in emerging cultures have attempted to establish value systems through creating series of myths, explained in the most then-current forms of artistic expression. As a writer always concerned with the effects of the American dream in all its permutations, it comes as no surprise then that F. Scott Fitzgerald, by the time he reached his mid-forties while living in Hollywood, would choose to write a novel that encapsulates the value system of American mythology as depicted through film. On its most basic level, Fitzgerald's *The Last Tycoon* can be read

Two • Screening the American Icarus, Part Two

as an attempt to legitimize Hollywood's place in the American landscape as the Mount Olympus of popular culture, where stars and filmmakers weave epic tales of romance and adventure onscreen, while simultaneously living even more intriguing lives offscreen, shaping their personas as cultural icons.

What complicates this relatively simple task is the fact that filmmaking is an ouroboric art form, fed not only by the desire to create motion pictures that present life as realistically as possible, but also to inversely create lives that measure up to the standards set in such pictures, until the line between fantasy and reality becomes so blurred that it is impossible to tell where one begins or another ends. This meditation on the effects of erasing boundaries between the real and the imaginary is at the heart of *The Last Tycoon*. However, since existential crisis is difficult to describe on the printed page, and even more impossible to film, Fitzgerald, and later-adapting director Elia Kazan, couch these ideas in three different, easier to understand contexts: the romance, the Western, and classical mythology. These three approaches combine to make *The Last Tycoon* Fitzgerald's most deeply intellectual work, as well as and his most significant contribution to the explanation and furtherance of the American cultural mythos.

Fitzgerald's original novel begins squarely in the realm of romance. As the book opens, the narrative is told from the point of view of Cecelia Brady, daughter of movie producer Pat Brady. Cecelia, a junior on school break from Bennington College, is in love with her father's partner, a young phenom producer named Monroe Stahr. Most critics agree that Fitzgerald modeled Stahr on the boy-wonder Irving Thalberg and Brady on MGM's legendary mogul Louis B. Mayer. In contrast, Cecelia represents a blend of Mayer's daughter, Irene, "who in her biography admits she had something of a crush on Thalberg," as well as two Communist-sympathizing sons of studio executives, Budd Schulberg and Maurice Rapf, with a touch of Fitzgerald's daughter, Scottie, a Vassar girl at the time of her father's writing, thrown in (Rapf 78).

Cecelia identifies with the romantic side of Hollywood from her first admission, which forms the opening line of the novel, "Though I haven't ever been on the screen I was brought up on pictures. Rudolph Valentino came to my fifth birthday party—or so I was told" (*Tycoon* 3). This statement sets the tone that pervades the remainder of Fitzgerald's original text, that Cecelia is to be the voice speaking like a Greek chorus for all Americans who have been "brought up" on the romantic notions begun by Hollywood's golden age of cinema and have absorbed them so completely into their collective psyche that they are no longer separable from any individual sense of identity. In short, from the bobby-soxers of Cecelia's generation forward, Americans have grown up with their sense of romantic love shaped by the movies, fostering a collective, yet unrequited, teenage crush on men like Monroe Stahr, who shaped these images.

However, telling the story from Cecelia's point of view would have been a hard sell in a mainstream motion picture adaptation of the novel, since films based around the feelings of girls in their early twenties tend to be attended only by people from that same demographic. Most likely, screenwriter Harold Pinter changed the point of view of Fitzgerald's original text from Cecelia's perspective to the third person in his adaptation at least in part to reach a wider market. This wise choice opens Fitzgerald's romance into a broader context, to include not just a young woman's fascination with a handsome, dynamic executive, but more broadly, as Stephen Matterson describes it, to focus on "the power of the cinema as a romance, on its capacity to magically transform mundane reality, to enrich and enlarge individual experience like any other art form" (50). In the opening scenes of Pinter's adaptation of *The Last Tycoon*, the audience sees clips of dailies from several different films in rapid succession through the eyes of Monroe Stahr in his screening room. The intention is not only to make the viewer fall in love with Monroe Stahr for the same reasons that Cecelia did—for his intellect, energy, and intensity—but also to fall into love with the process of making movies as a romantic, artistic endeavor. Collectively, this is the effect desired by the filmmakers as the viewer is allowed into the inner workings of Stahr's thought processes during the opening scenes from the screening room.

Fitzgerald would have found much to identify with in Thalberg's character, thereby providing a logical first step away from his usual pattern of incorporating novels out of thinly veiled autobiographical elements. Like Fitzgerald, Thalberg was both ambitious and precocious, gaining success in his early twenties, while working as Carl Lammele's personal secretary fresh out of high school and rising meteorically by his wits to executive producer over Universal City by age twenty-one (TCMDB.com). Once firmly established as a force to be reckoned with, first at Universal and later at MGM, Thalberg developed a signature style of high-quality pictures, chiefly focusing on literary adaptations of classic texts, which he tested rigorously with audiences in post-production previews. Thalberg's concern with audience reception of his films supported his ability to produce prestige pictures that retained a high level of commercial appeal in a manner similar to the way in which Fitzgerald, during his early years, was consistently able to write critically successful novels and stories that were wildly popular with his readers. Fitzgerald's choice to incorporate his personal experiences with Thalberg's into the character of Monroe Stahr can be read as a conscious effort to enlarge his persistent vision of himself as a romantic hero, and also expand what a romantic hero was capable of in his novels.

Yet, the romance of Monroe Stahr in the eyes of the audience, as a modern-day epic hero or, as John Callahan refers to him, an "Icarus in executive dress," is not the only type of romance present in either Fitzgerald's original novel or the film adaptation (208). The actual romance between Stahr and his deceased wife, Minna Davis, as well as Stahr's subsequent attempt to romance Minna's Irish-rose look-alike, Kathleen Moore, together form a second layer of intrigue that adds considerable depth to Stahr's otherwise strictly-business demeanor. The Stahr/Davis plotline is partially based upon the real-life relationship between Irving Thalberg and his wife, actress Norma Shearer. The marriage between Shearer and Thalberg was unlike so many in Hollywood, idyllic, producing two children and mutually advancing the careers of both until Thalberg's untimely death from pneumonia in 1936 at the age of 37 (TCMDB.com). Since Shearer outlived Thalberg, one must wonder about the source for Fitzgerald's inspiration to create the young widower.

As usual, Fitzgerald's chief source of inspiration to fill in the blanks of character was his own life. By the time he had begun work on *The Last Tycoon* in 1939, Zelda had been institutionalized with a series of mental health issues for almost a decade. With Zelda unable to leave the mental hospital and his work requiring him to live across the country in Los Angeles, Fitzgerald found himself in the awkward position of constructive widower. However, he was not without companionship. Fitzgerald's last romantic relationship would form the basis for the interactions between his lead characters in *The Last Tycoon*.

In 1937, Fitzgerald first saw Hollywood gossip columnist Sheilah Graham at the Screenwriter's Ball in Los Angeles, the same event in which Monroe Stahr and Kathleen Moore first strike up acquaintance in *The Last Tycoon*. Also like her fictional counterpart, the English-born Graham was in a relationship with a titled man, the Marquess of Donegal, just before she met Fitzgerald. According to Matthew Bruccoli, the Marquess "had come from England to propose" to Graham on the night that she met Fitzgerald (*Grandeur* 423). In another biographical parallel that he incorporated into *The Last Tycoon*, Fitzgerald did not catch Sheliah's name at the ball, but instead was forced to track her down afterward based solely upon her resemblance to Zelda and the fact that she had been wearing a silver belt (*Grandeur* 425). However, the similarities between the fictional Kathleen Moore and the real-life Sheilah Graham begin to diverge beyond such coincidences.

As a self-made, once-divorced woman, Graham was far more secure and independent than the unemployed Kathleen Moore. Graham's syndicated column, "Hollywood Today," ran in 178 papers at its peak, nearly double those of her chief rivals, Louella Parsons and Hedda Hopper. Still, despite her success,

Graham was a woman who felt insecure about her humble beginnings and inadequate education in a Jewish orphanage. Over the course of their three-and-a-half-year relationship, Fitzgerald would prescribe intellectual readings for Graham in what the pair came to call her "College of One." They had planned to culminate with her reading Spengler's *Decline of the West*, exactly as Kathleen Moore describes doing with her former lover in *The Last Tycoon* (*Grandeur* 441). In return, Graham worked diligently to help Fitzgerald maintain sobriety, which he finally achieved, albeit too late, a year before his death.

When incorporated, these double-blended biographical inspirations for Fitzgerald's original characters in *The Last Tycoon* demonstrate a maturation of literary sensibilities. For the first time in his career, Fitzgerald was constructing, at the time of his death, a novel that used the techniques of romance to go beyond literary solutions to his own personal concerns. Instead of continuing merely to build upon the romance of his life as *F. Scott Fitzgerald*, tragic literary figure of high aspirations and devastating reversals of fortune, Fitzgerald reached beyond his own experience to write what Matthew Bruccoli has called in his preface to the authorized version of the text "one of the few American novels with a convincing and compelling businessman hero" (*Tycoon* vii). In short, by the time he created *The Last Tycoon*, Fitzgerald was still a Romanticist; however, he was no longer the often self-absorbed romantic egoist displayed in his earlier writings. Perhaps this is the reason why Fitzgerald chose to create a hero who was a movie producer. Only a man on the business side of entertainment could continue to appreciate the beauty of illusion even after he saw the workings that maintained it.

The scene in Elia Kazan's adaptation that most perfectly captures this sense of Fitzgerald's maturation as a romantic writer is the often-reviewed "nickel for the movies" sequence. In the scene, Robert DeNiro, playing the part of Monroe Stahr, uses monologue and pantomime to act out a scene that seems to be straight out of a stock film noir piece. The English writer, Boxley, based on Aldous Huxley, who had only moments earlier completely dismissed film as an inferior medium of expression for conveying depth of emotion, is drawn in by DeNiro's riveting performance, carefully absorbing every detail of his action and description. When DeNiro brings the performance to an abrupt close without explaining why a nickel is left on the table, Boxley betrays the fact that, despite his earlier discounting of the medium, he was drawn into emotional engagement with the scene by inquiring about the nickel. DeNiro grins like a delighted little boy performing a trick and replies, "The nickel is for the movies" (*Tycoon*).

In this instant, the audience sees exactly what Boxley realizes. In the hands of a masterful actor and director, film is a medium that can make even the most mundane details marvelously fascinating, just as romantic love with someone can transform every movement into a performance and every utterance into a song. In this scene, we see through DeNiro's performance both why Irving Thalberg/Monroe Stahr literally worked himself to death to create movies, and why Fitzgerald felt that, without writing, he was nothing. The power to draw disbelieving others in, to perceive reality from romantic illusion, is the closest modern man will ever come to performing magic. The joy of achieving this masterful feat of illusion evokes a sense of wonder normally known only to children and validates filmmaking as an art form equal to literature. In sum, both Kazan's film and Fitzgerald's original novel can be read not only as the romantic life of Stahr, a man who makes movies, but also as a romance of the movie industry itself, in which Stahr plays a role.

The move from classic romance to Western is a logical step for any American writer, since the elements that comprise a Western are essentially the same as those of a romance, only more clearly delineated. Whereas in a romance, the hero may have to overcome virtually any sort of adversary, including himself, in order to reach different goals or desires, the Western fills in these vague circumstances with specificity. The full title of Fitzgerald's novel, *The Love of the Last Tycoon: A Western*, suggests that the author was aware of the conventions of the Western genre and intended to manipulate them to suit his purposes. Yet, if one is to read *The Last Tycoon* as a Western, two questions arise. First, why exactly did Fitzgerald seek to utilize the conventions of the Western genre to flesh out his mediation on filmmaking as American mythology? And second, to what extent does Kazan's adaptation also use these embedded conventions from Fitzgerald's narrative to assist in creating a visual representation of his work?

The easiest answer to the first question is that Fitzgerald, as a screenwriter who had seen the success of Western genre films' ability to create memorable characters of mythic proportions, viewed the conventions in a broader and deeper sense than most others of his day. Like a jazz musician who uses standard chord progressions not as a way to bind his music into a formula, but rather as a way to lull audiences into certain expectations, only to offer a surprise break from them, Fitzgerald seems eager to reinterpret the conventional expectations of the Western genre in his novel.

In order to see how far *The Last Tycoon* actually goes beyond the expectations of a typical Western, one might compare both the original novel and its film adaptation to the classic Western film *Stagecoach* (1939), which came out during the year that Fitzgerald began his novel. In *Stagecoach*, John Wayne plays the hero, a fugitive named the Ringo Kid, who falls for Dallas, the typical prostitute with the heart of gold, as they ride with a motley crew of travelers across the dangerous Indian territory from Tonto, Arizona, to Lordsburg, New Mexico, in 1880. Among their companions are several stock Western genre players, including a schoolmarm, a drunken doctor, a Southern gambler, and several criminals, all of whom are superficially more socially acceptable than the fugitive Ringo Kid, but turn out to be far more morally reprehensible as the journey progresses. The real threat to the Ringo Kid is Luke Plummer, another fugitive, whom Ringo ultimately kills in a shootout before riding off into the sunset with Dallas.

In contrast, Fitzgerald's hero, Monroe Stahr, is a businessman, not a gunslinger. However, as a New York Jew on the West Coast, Stahr shares with Ringo his position as a skilled outsider thrust into the role of protector, whose presence is tolerated only because he performs a desirable service. Whereas Ringo protects the stagecoach full of travelers from Indians and outlaws with his strength and marksmanship, Stahr protects his studio from financial ruin by managing a series of more modern disasters, ranging from on-set floods caused by earthquakes to offering psychological counseling to actors with impotency problems. Both Ringo and Stahr fall for the same type of women with questionable pasts. Dallas was an actual prostitute whereas Kathleen was merely a woman who engaged in a sort of *de facto* prostitution, living with a wealthy man whom she didn't love out of necessity before meeting Stahr, and then marrying yet another rich man afterward, while still holding feelings for Stahr.

Fitzgerald shows his willingness to thwart the expectations of a conventional Western as Kathleen, ostensibly a damsel in distress, refuses rescue by the hero, Stahr. This failure to win the girl who is the object of his affections is the first clue that Stahr, who is set up to be a Western hero, either is not fit for the role or that modern society has changed in such a way that it is no longer possible to present a Western hero in the classic sense. Next, Fitzgerald writes Stahr as a failure in both of his two defining conflicts. First, Stahr fails in his effort to get rid of the Union organizer Brimmer, who represents an outside threat to the financial security of the studio system in a manner similar to the way in which Luke Plummer represents a threat to the physical security of the people of Lordsburg. Whereas Ringo dispatches with Plummer easily in their shootout, Stahr becomes drunk and is knocked out with one punch by Brimmer, in front of the schoolmarm character Cecelia. Stahr's failure to maintain his composure with Brimmer or to hold his own in a physical confrontation, especially in front of a female, marks the beginning of the end of his reign as a prince of Hollywood deal-making diplomacy and his failure as a Western hero.

In Kazan's film adaptation of the novel, the Brimmer incident also sets up Stahr's final expulsion from the studio. This addition to the text was made by playwright Harold Pinter and represents a logical extension of Fitzgerald's systematic thwarting of Western genre conventions throughout the novel. In a conventional Western, after the foe is vanquished, the hero is embraced by the locals and either becomes one of them or rides off into the sunset in search of new adventures, as Ringo does in *Stagecoach*. However, by allowing Stahr to fail in his attempt to run Brimmer and the Union organizers out of Hollywood, either by using his legendary business savvy to play power politics or by a show of physical force, Kazan and Pinter necessarily set up Stahr's rejection by the studio brass and expulsion from the studio in disgrace.

Although Fitzgerald's original novel was left unfinished due to his premature death, the ending depicted in Pinter's screenplay completes the story arc established by Fitzgerald's attempt to use the generic conventions of the film Western to demonstrate that, in the modern American business world, it is no longer possible for a hero to win the girl or triumph over adversity. In all likelihood, that was why Fitzgerald viewed Monroe Stahr as "the last tycoon." Like many other romances, which depict the last cowboy or the last hero, Stahr is a man whom Fitzgerald perceives to be of a dying breed, an executive with integrity in an industry that he saw as trading on emotions, but without any actual heart of its own. As such, it is only fitting that Kazan ends his visual depiction of Stahr's narrative with Stahr defeated, walking into the lonely abyss of an empty soundstage. The dark soundstage serves as a reminder of Stahr's failure as a generic Western hero and also represents a reversal from the brightly lit sunset into which so many victorious Western heroes ride. Read in this manner, Kazan and Pinter's ending provides appropriate closure to Fitzgerald's inversion of the Western in a modern context.

Critics of the Kazan/Pinter adaptation are divided about the decision to end the adaptation in this manner. Some, such as Lloyd Michael, see its open-endedness as purposeful, "an appropriate analogue for the aura of possibility left behind by Fitzgerald's unfinished manuscript" (117). Others see it, and the scene of Stahr's dismissal leading up to it, as incurably flawed, overlong, and melodramatic, feeling instead that, given Stahr's hit record at the studio, "a bonus, rather than a dismissal, would have been more believable" (Atkins 110). Additionally, most of the scene's critical detractors seem as if they would have preferred an approach that attempted to convert the remainder of Fitzgerald's unfinished work faithfully from his notes. However, no critic addresses the issue of the ending as a possible attempt by Kazan and Pinter to purposefully extend Fitzgerald's exploration of Western genre tropes in a modern context. To paraphrase the adage about Homer, it is on this point that critics nod off, while the perfectly balanced team of Pinter, Kazan, and DeNiro continue

Fitzgerald's artistic dream of creating, from a tale based in the Hollywood Western and romantic genres, a cohesive sense of American cultural mythos on a scale of Greek epic proportions.

The final theme that Kazan and Pinter explore in their adaptation of *The Last Tycoon* is Fitzgerald's continual employment of stories from Greek mythology to explain the creation of American mythology in the motion picture industry. Almost every critic of the film adaptation has made a passing reference to Fitzgerald as "both the sarcastic and truthful mythologist" who explores the mythos of America's universal hero, the self-made man, not only in *The Last Tycoon* but also in *The Great Gatsby* (Marsh 105). However, no critics have actually worked through exactly how Fitzgerald manipulates the classics to serve his thematic purposes, even though a completely separate dissertation could be made from these efforts alone.

Fitzgerald's formal grounding in the classics began during his teenage years at the Catholic Newman School, in Hackensack, New Jersey, where he studied Virgil, Cicero, Latin, and ancient history, and continued at Princeton, where he took the required curriculum in Greek and Latin literature, which included intensive study in Livy, Sallust, and Cicero again (*Grandeur* 36–67). Further, Fitzgerald's lifelong study of the romantic poets, particularly John Keats, began at Princeton. Specifically, the young writer's obsession with Keats's "Ode on a Grecian Urn" caused him to endeavor "to become a prose Keats, imitating the poet's rhythms and enriching his own style with lush Keatsian imagery" (*Grandeur* 70). As a result of his love for the poem, which melded classical sensibilities with Romantic style, Bruccoli writes:

> Keats became an enduring presence in Fitzgerald's life, providing him with a model of creative sensibility. Like Keats, Fitzgerald was painfully responsive to the mutability of beauty and the evanescence of youth. Both yearned for immortality through art, and Keats's early death imbued Fitzgerald with a sense of urgency. Above all, Fitzgerald identified with the Keatsian archetype—the handsome youth acclaimed for his genius. Literature was a glamorous thing for Fitzgerald. He aspired to early triumph and the fame that went with it [*Grandeur* 71].

From this background, it is easy to see how, in Fitzgerald's mind, the circle of immortality was drawn, using Greek mythology to connect artistic achievement as a Romantic endeavor with his aspirations for immortality. In all likelihood, the character of Monroe Stahr was born out of this ouroboros, and therefore represents the culmination of Fitzgerald's mediation on this theme.

Close reading of Fitzgerald's description of Stahr in his original text reveals Fitzgerald's attempt to create an American mythological hero in the classic model. As the allegedly blind Greek cameraman Pete Zavras describes him in the novel, Stahr is "the Aeschylus and the Diogenes of the moving picture ... also the Asclepius and the Menander" (*Tycoon* 61). The ever-playful Fitzgerald engages in this moment of classical name-dropping with the purpose of describing Stahr as the embodiment of the goals of the American motion picture industry, and, in turn, the American mythmaking ethos.

Aeschylus, the oldest of the trio of Greek tragedians that included Sophocles and Euripides, signifies Stahr's role as supreme purveyor of meaningful emotion in an industry and nation full of fluff. Stahr's constant mission to convey truthful emotion that assists Americans in understanding their collective feelings, so prevalent in the "nickel for the movies" scene already described, in which he warns against actors who perform "violent movements," speak "cheap dialogue," and make overwrought "facial expressions," is invoked by Fitzgerald's passing mention of Diogenes (32). Diogenes, who carried a symbolic lantern of truth through the darkness in his relentless search for an honest man, could be equated with Stahr's ritual in Kazan's adaptation of sitting in his darkened screening room alone, with only the flickering light of his projector illuminating his quest to pull true human emotion out of actors. By invoking the name Asclepius, the Greek god of medicine, Fitzgerald conveys Stahr's role as a healer, and, in turn, the cathartic role that motion pictures play in the American consciousness as a medium for collective vocalization of aspiration and resulting emotional release. Last, by naming Menander, the father of Athenian comedy, as Stahr's final classical parallel, Fitzgerald effectively claims that the laughter provided by lighter, humorous films, often played during Stahr's screening room clips in Kazan's adaptation, is just as important as tragedy for its healing powers and also in creating a balance within the overall American cultural psyche.

The total effect of Zavras's description is summed up in Stahr's brief line, "I'm the unity" (*Tycoon*). Spoken in the meeting scene among the studio brass, screenwriter Harold Pinter wisely transfers this line directly from Fitzgerald's original novel. In both the novel and film adaptation, Stahr stands for a perfect unity of artistic emotion in American filmmaking that is also in sync with the collective emotional needs of a nation, a unity that has been striven for since the very beginnings of narrative with the Greeks. In short, Stahr represents the culmination of the classical unities written large for the American cinematic stage.

Further, it is no accident that this description of Stahr is given by a Greek cameraman, whose career is jeopardized by a vicious rumor of his impending blindness before Stahr saves his reputation by sending him to an oculist and correcting the rumor. Fitzgerald, a Catholic writer of poetic sensibility who loved to play with words and names and had a classical education, could have intended symbolic meaning for Pete Zavras's name as a combination of St. Peter, who holds the keys to the Kingdom, and Zephyrus, the Greek god of the fructifying west wind who in mythology was thought to bring love and spring. This reading of Zavras's name is the key to Fitzgerald's use of classical symbolism and is supported by Zavras's statement in the novel that Stahr is an "oracle ... the solver of Eleusinian mysteries" (*Tycoon* 61). The Eleusinian mysteries, in Greek mythology, are part of the cult of Demeter and Persephone, and connect the mysteries of the passing of the seasons with the transition to the afterlife. Anyone who solves the Eleusinian mysteries is supposed to unlock the secret to immortality. Therefore, the ultimate significance of cameraman Pete Zavras's presence in Fitzgerald's original novel can be read to signify Stahr's abilities as a sort of Hollywood oracle, who has divined the secret of immortalizing stars, and the characters they portray, through film.

The secondary symbol of blindness, coupled with immortality, is also significant to a complete interpretation of Stahr's character. Although Stahr is able to immortalize in celluloid the stars of his motion pictures, he is powerless to preserve the life of his beloved wife, Minna Davis. As a result, Stahr remains purposefully blind to the possibility that another woman, Cecelia Brady, could offer him the emotional comfort he so desperately needs. Further, Stahr's blindness to anything other than the physical resemblance of Kathleen Moore to Minna Davis prevents Stahr, otherwise an impeccable judge of character throughout the novel, from seeing that Kathleen is emotionally unavailable and that Cecelia would be a far better mate.

Once again, Fitzgerald plays with name symbolism to support this inference, since Cecelia is a name of Latin origin signifying one who finds a way for the blind. Cecelia continually takes on this motherly role toward Stahr, culminating in Fitzgerald's novel with the final completed scene that he wrote, in which Stahr becomes so drunk that he blacks out after a fight with Brimmer, the Communist organizer. Kazan's film picks up in this moment with original material, putting Cecelia in the role of caretaker as she nurses Stahr's hangover and his ego, allowing him to maintain his delusion that he knocked Brimmer out, rather than the opposite, which is the actual truth. Read in consideration of the symbolism behind Cecelia's name, Kazan's staging of this scene makes clear Fitzgerald's intention. Cecelia may have been the only woman with a realistic chance of helping Stahr overcome the destructive blindness to the motivations of others that he has suffered from ever since falling for Kathleen.

To complete the exploration of Fitzgerald's implementation of classical mythology in his tale of Stahr as an American mythmaker who becomes ouroborically consumed by his own mythos, one must consider the possible classical parallels behind Stahr himself. When Stahr first sees Kathleen, she is "on top of a huge head of the god Shiva" having "found sanctuary along a scroll of curls on its bald forehead" and is "floating down the current of an impromptu river" made by the breaking of water pipes on a film set after an earthquake (*Tycoon* 26). This striking image is no doubt a symbolic gesture. Shiva is the Hindu god of destruction and rebirth, from whose hair Hindus believe the waters of the Ganges River flow, representing immortality. Stahr is immediately struck by Kathleen's resemblance to his dead wife, Minna. Fitzgerald describes the scene through Stahr's point of view:

> Smiling faintly at him from not four feet away was the face of his dead wife, identical even to the expression. Across the four feet of moonlight the eyes he knew looked back at him, a curl blew a little on a familiar forehead, the smile lingered, changed a little according to pattern, the lips parted—the same. An awful fear went over him and he wanted to cry aloud. Back from the still sour room, the muffled glide of the limousine hearse, the falling concealing flowers, from out there in the dark—here now warm and glowing. The river passed him in a rush, the great spotlight swooped and blinked—and then he heard another voice speak that was not Minna's voice [26–27].

In this passage, Fitzgerald uses Kathleen's arrival, on the head of Shiva, to symbolize how Stahr's memory of Minna makes her not only immortal, but also larger than life, like a goddess. Kazan's adaption furthers Fitzgerald's use of Shiva symbolism by including tiger-skin rugs in Stahr's home and office. Since tiger skin is an often-used symbol of the lustful side of Shiva's presence, the tiger skins can be read to represent Stahr's ongoing internal struggle with sexual desire both for his dead wife and elusive girlfriend. Kazan's set decoration in his adaptation furthers this theme, by adding portraits of Minna looming over Stahr's shoulder in every scene of his quiet reverie about Kathleen. These additions to the set go a long way to further the viewer's sense that Stahr's feelings for Minna, and later, Kathleen, have surpassed mortal love and crossed over into the realm of religion.

Of course, the use of love and art to cross the borders between mortality and divinity is a pervasive theme in Greek mythology. Fitzgerald's inclusion of a small detail, replicated in the costume design for Kazan's adaptation, gives the audience a clue as to which mythological character Stahr is supposed to parallel. When Stahr begins his search for Kathleen, he does not know her name. He only remembers that her face looked like Minna's and that she wore "a silver belt with stars cut out of it" (*Tycoon* 54). The Greek mythological character most closely associated with a belt of stars is Orion, the great hunter, who pursued the seven sisters of the Pleiades, until Zeus turned them all into stars, destined to roam the heavens for eternity in an unrequited romantic quest. A well-read man who knew his mythology, Fitzgerald could easily have been inspired to create a powerful producer named Stahr, whose judgment is blinded by his love for a woman wearing a starred belt, from the mythological story of Orion, a mighty hunter who is struck blind in pursuit of unattainable females, and whose constellation is a belt of stars.

Further, the faintest and westernmost of these stars in Orion's belt, Mintaka, is supposed to represent Merope, the most beautiful and graceful of the seven sisters with whom Orion is especially infatuated. Interestingly, Mintaka is a double star, meaning that it is actually made up of two stars, one brighter and one dimmer, revolving in an eclipsing orbit around the same center point. Considered in this context, the names of Stahr's two women, wife Minna and girlfriend Kathleen, might have had a combined inspiration, in Fitzgerald's ever-inventive mind, in the name Mintaka, the most unique star in the Orion/Pleiades constellation. Such an interpretation makes sense when considered in conjunction with the fact that the dramatic sea cliff location of Stahr's unfinished home is in Santa Monica, a town named in honor of one of the Three Marys, which is an alternate name for the major stars in the Orion's Belt constellation. Kazan's choice to film these scenes on the actual Santa Monica seashore, where the stars seem so close that the actors could almost reach out and touch them, offers a breathtakingly beautiful backdrop that promotes the inference of Stahr's proximity not only to Hollywood stars, but to actual ones, and the immortal tales represented by their constellations that most likely inspired Fitzgerald.

This mythological information allows viewers to appreciate not only Fitzgerald's original novel, but also Kazan's carefully constructed adaptation. Critics have complained that the film adaptation of *The Last Tycoon*, like Clayton's *Gatsby*, is too long and slow-paced, saying that Pinter's screenplay is "too filled with long awkward pauses" and that Kazan "is not a director noted for great sensitivity or depth of feeling" (Atkins 110). However, it is virtually impossible to watch the tasteful and poignant lovemaking scene in Stahr's unfinished house and not be moved by DeNiro's performance as a man whose calm wonder at finally consummating his love for Kathleen clearly depicts Fitzgerald's sense from the novel that Stahr was a man in love with a dream of a woman, and of the life that they would share in the still-unfinished house, more so than the actualization of the dream itself. Pinter's use of dramatic pauses, combined with Kazan's sensitive staging, and DeNiro's unhurried approach to delivering Stahr's lines, give the film an overall meditative quality of a love affair whose every moment must be savored because its participants are all too aware of the fleeting nature of such times.

Fitzgerald's original text seems ready to defend the adaptation's languid pace. In his description of their first meeting, which Kazan smartly stages as a balcony scene reminiscent of *Romeo and Juliet*, complete with an overhanging crescent moon, Fitzgerald writes, "Stahr's eyes and Kathleen's met and tangled. For an instant they made love as no one ever dares to do after. Their glance was closer than an embrace, more urgent than a call" (*Tycoon* 64). Looks of love such as these fill Fitzgerald's original novel, and cannot be hurried along without destroying their significance.

The ultimate effect produced is not one of an unnecessarily slow film, but instead a piece that evokes memories of Fitzgerald's reverence for Keats's "Ode on a Grecian Urn," a poem that conveys the same message as Fitzgerald's prose ode to Hollywood. Art, whether it is in the form of a Grecian urn, an English poem, an American novel, or a Hollywood film, has the power to capture and immortalize beauty and the love that so often is inspired by it. However, art will always remain, as Keats referred to it, a "cold pastoral" whose "silent form dost tease us out of thought / As doth eternity" (lines 44–45). Here, Keats's poem articulates the reason why Stahr can never be content by merely surrounding himself with cinematic images of Minna, and instead chooses to pursue the shadow of her presence in Kathleen. Although Stahr may be able to capture the essence of Minna's physical beauty in cinematic art, the actual presence of her inner beauty, however fleeting or difficult it is to procure, remains tantalizingly valuable. In his pursuit of Kathleen, Stahr hopes to recapture the happiness that he found only in real life with Minna.

Always respectful of Fitzgerald's thematic vision in his conversion of novel to screen, Kazan faithfully represents these effects of the author's leisurely approach, allowing his audience time to ponder each Bergsonian moment of recognition and romance in order to appreciate the balanced artistic vision among original author, director, screenwriter, and actors. By using a manner of adaptation that maintains historical accuracy in its incorporation of the same level of biographical detail included in Fitzgerald's original novel, Kazan and his collaborators are able to bring to life an adaptation that conveys the same psychological complexity of Fitzgerald's original novel, calling attention to the minor theme of fame's effects on male sexuality by casting Tony Curtis in the small but important role of the nerve-wracked, impotent leading man, Rodriguez. Also, Kazan explores the socio-cultural significance of the motion picture industry in American culture by utilizing liberal amounts of Fitzgerald's original dialogue, as well as casting actors, such as Robert Mitchum in the role of Pat Brady, whom audiences would recognize as living embodiments of fame created within the Hollywood system. Kazan even calls attention to Fitzgerald's minor political theme of America's anti–Communist anxiety, mirrored and magnified by the Hollywood community, by casting high-profile actor

Jack Nicholson as Brimmer, the Communist organizer. Each of these supporting actors use their considerable screen presences to create remarkably nuanced performances of Harold Pinter's carefully wrought screenplay. As a result of these combined efforts, Elia Kazan's *The Last Tycoon* remains one of the best film adaptations of a Fitzgerald work to date.

The Curious Case of Benjamin Button (2008)

David Fincher's film version of F. Scott Fitzgerald's short story "The Curious Case of Benjamin Button" is a rare example of an adaptation that not only represents a consistent artistic vision of the collaborators, but also demonstrates a keen sense of how to interpret stylistically that text to make it relevant for an entirely new generation of readers. In the table of contents for the collection in which "Button" was released, Fitzgerald dedicated "these tales of the Jazz Age into the hands of those who read as they run and run as they read" (802). Fincher's adaptation team seems to take this dedication as a motivational point. His Benjamin Button is a man of perpetual motion, which is a fitting portrayal of a man whose life runs backward, as if in flight from death, even as he inevitably moves toward it. The film's heavy incorporation of many locations and circumstances paralleling the life of Benjamin's globe-trotting creator, Scott Fitzgerald, prompts audiences to explore further into the author's life and works. Relying on historical and socio-cultural updates, Fincher creates new levels of psychological depth in Button's character that were only hinted at in Fitzgerald's original.

Fitzgerald was a writer immensely concerned with the issue of aging. According to Alice B. Toklas, Fitzgerald met with Gertrude Stein on his thirtieth birthday and said it was "unbearable for him to have to face the fact that his youth was over" (*Grandeur* 232). The short story most concerned with the process of aging that Fitzgerald wrote was "The Curious Case of Benjamin Button." First published in *Collier's* magazine and then collected into *Tales of the Jazz Age* in 1922, "Button" was an ironic and darkly humorous story about a man born looking physically old who aged backward into infancy. Fitzgerald wrote his own abbreviated source study for the story in the annotated table of contents for *Tales of the Jazz Age*:

> The story was inspired by a remark of Mark Twain's to the effect that it was a pity that the best part of life came at the beginning and the worst part at the end. By trying the experiment upon only one man in a perfectly normal world I have scarcely given his idea a fair trial. Several weeks after completing it, I discovered an almost identical plot in Samuel Butler's *Notebooks* [800].

According to Andrew Crosland, Fitzgerald learned of Twain's odd observation about the aging process from reading Albert Bigelow Paine's three-volume biography of Twain, in which Twain supposedly thought that "if all men were born old, they would be happier" (137). Apparently, Fitzgerald, worshipper of youth that he was, took issue with Twain's comments and decided to try them out in a story that became a mockery of the idea, focusing the reader's attention on the "incongruities which result from the fact that Button's way of maturing runs counter to that experienced by other people" (Crosland 137).

From its first publication in *Tales of the Jazz Age*, critics seemed aware of the odd mix of both ironic humor and deeper concerns such as morality and the meaning of life that Fitzgerald had in mind when writing "Button." An unnamed critic writing in 1922 for the *Portland Evening Express* commented on the humor in both *Tales* in general and "Button" in particular, but also noted that the reader "chuckles again, but on a different note" with this story, which perhaps made the reader "yield to emotions he had not been very sure he possessed, and is left with the impression that there is, after all, more even in his own drab world than he supposed" (Inge 145). The *Express* critic's take on the story may have been the most insightful reading of the "Button" story until the creation of David Fincher's 2008 film rendering, *The Curious Case of Benjamin Button*, starring Brad Pitt and Cate Blanchett. Fincher's adaptation seems to capture, through the added perspective of generational hindsight, many layers of nuanced meaning deeper than the original.

Fincher's interpretive film version, although in many aspects a radical departure from Fitzgerald's original text, conveys in a 21st-century context the social issues that Fitzgerald lampooned in his original version in a straightforward way, made more easily digestible for contemporary audiences. In this manner, Fincher creates a valid interpretation of the "Button" story by incorporating many common themes from Fitzgerald's longer works as well as numerous aspects of the author's biographical history. Ultimately, Fincher's film portrays the greater, yet more highly obscured, themes about love and mortality that Fitzgerald, who was only twenty-six at the time "Button" was written, may have subconsciously recognized but repressed behind a protective veil of humor, due to a youthful lack of authorial perspective and maturity regarding the consequences of aging.

Button's journey from page to screen would become a long one. According to the DVD of supplemental materials included with the Criterion Collection edition of *Button*, in 1992 screenwriter Robin Swicord was hired to create a screen adaptation of the "Button" story by the newly formed Kennedy/Marshall production company, with Steven Spielberg set to direct and Tom Cruise selected to star. With this setup of a high-profile, all–American cast and crew,

Swicord's vision for the storyline centered on making the cinematic adaptation a semi-retelling of Fitzgerald's life as an American icon, with heavy reliance on a jazz soundtrack to subliminally suggest the connective ouroboric cycle among original author, text, and work. As director David Fincher recalled, "It was a beautiful world, but a very different one from our film. It was much more about the Jazz Age: Benjamin as a stand-in for Scott Fitzgerald. But for me it required the audience to know too much about jazz" (James 28). Spielberg dropped out of the project after the fervor following *Jurassic Park*, and Cruise passed on the role. Unwilling to give up on the project, Kennedy and Marshall commissioned a rewrite by Eric Roth, who read the original story and the major Fitzgerald biographies to re-create a screenplay that was a darker meditation about love, death, and the value of human experience in his 2002 update (*Supplements*). What resulted was a film of epic proportions, a complete reinterpretation of Button as a sensitive, adventurous, modern-day hero, who had more in common with Indiana Jones, another Kennedy/Marshall creation, than F. Scott Fitzgerald.

Still, even with this expanded scope, the film depends on Fitzgerald's often-used sense of Bergsonian meditation to bring an overall feeling of calm to what could have otherwise been a ludicrously-paced romp through American history. Credit for this approach should be given to David Fincher, who loved the Roth rewrite of the script and recommended his recent collaborator from *Fight Club*, Brad Pitt, for the leading role of Benjamin. Pitt, who envisioned the storyline of the screenplay as a romantic tragedy, felt the role would be an opportunity for him to show a more subtle side of his acting abilities by playing Benjamin at many different ages (*Supplements*). Pitt wisely plays Benjamin as a quiet, soft-spoken man of deep feeling, bringing his natural standard of quiet intensity to the role and causing audiences to ponder his carefully chosen words.

David Fincher's final addition to the creation of the screen interpretation of *Button* was widening the ouroboric cycle of authorship to incorporate not only Fitzgerald's customary inclusion of autobiography, but also some of his own personal history. By choosing to direct Pitt's Benjamin as a man reminiscent of his own recently deceased father, a "journalist" and "wallflower," who was "very cautious" and "didn't want to engage with things until he really understood them," Fincher incorporated his personal history into Fitzgerald's original tale (James 28). Fincher claimed that the goal of his collaboration with Roth on bringing the screenplay to life was to make a film showing a real man with real regrets about the fleeting quality of youth and love, regardless of how he aged, because such concerns were universal. As Fincher told Roth, "Eric, if we're not making a movie about regret, then we're not making a movie about life" (James 28). After learning about the intricacies of this carefully constructed project that represents such a unified collaborative effort on the part of all parties, not to mention the expenditure of hundreds of thousands of dollars in Academy Award–winning CGI effects to portray accurately and naturally the aging process of Pitt and Blanchett in the film, it is difficult to find that the film is not an artistic work worthy of addition to the Fitzgerald canon.

Yet, some critics have found grounds to dismiss the project completely. At the 2009 meeting of the F. Scott Fitzgerald Society in Baltimore, scholar John L. DiGaetani wholeheartedly expressed his disdain for the film, concluding his lecture about what he perceived to be unforgivable deviations from the Fitzgerald *oeuvre* by saying that Fincher's film "is a failure on all levels." In the discussion portion following his lecture, DiGaetani appeared to focus his displeasure with the film on the casting of Brad Pitt, whom he felt was "much too old" for the role, and Fincher and Roth's adaptation, which he felt strayed too far from the original text, mostly because the setting was moved from Baltimore to New Orleans.

Given the all-too-common tendency of literary scholars to dismiss film adaptations that are not "faithful" to their printed originals, DiGaetani's disdain for Fincher's interpretive adaptation of *Button* is not surprising. However, it is important to remember that Fitzgerald was extremely open to significant alteration of his works for the screen, even doing so himself with the *Cosmopolitan* revision of "Babylon Revisited." Also, given Fitzgerald's proclivity for admiration of those he perceived to be of social standing, he would most likely have been excited about the possibility of a prestigious cast and crew taking such pains to make his words translate to a new, younger audience.

Fitzgerald's primary concern, during his early career when "Button" was written, was that his writing was timely and appealed to young people:

> My idea is always to reach my generation. The wise writer, I think, writes for the youth of his own generation.... Granted the ability to approve what he imitates in the way of style, to choose from his own interpretation of the experiences around him what constitutes material, and get the first-water genius [*Grandeur* 137].

From this statement by Fitzgerald, one can derive that the author would have considered a rendering of any story, even his own, in a way that was not directly relevant to the youth of the generation reading or viewing it as an ineffective writing product. According to Fitzgerald, it would have been valid for Roth and Fincher to take the base concept of "Button" and reinterpret it to reflect both the current social climate and their own personal experiences, which included their reactions to Fitzgerald's own tragic biography. Fitzgerald's most often articulated fear was to become a forgotten anachronism, out of touch with youth culture and taste. Therefore, to dismiss a film adaptation of an original Fitzgerald text chiefly because it was carefully adapted to suit the sensibilities of the 21st-century moviegoer would actually be a departure from the author's original intentions for the public reception of his works.

Perhaps even more important, Brad Pitt, because of his similar social standing to Fitzgerald, was the perfect actor upon whom to paint the visual canvas of the backward-aging Button. The handsome, blond Fitzgerald, who became an overnight celebrity at twenty-four with the publication of *This Side of Paradise*, can be seen as a Brad Pitt of the 1920s. Both men's lives have been ceaselessly documented by a constant barrage of paparazzi, who have meditated on their looks and personalities much more than on their respective works, especially after their marriages to high-profile females (Zelda Sayre and Angelina Jolie) who possessed scandalous reputations and questionable records of sanity. Also, both men, by the time they turned forty, become objects of female desire. Each waited pensively to see whether his respective audience would continue to embrace him after his youthful glamour faded.

Unfortunately for Fitzgerald, the Jazz Age audience he had cultivated proved fickle, and he died believing himself a failure. However, Pitt seems to have fared much better. If audiences for *Button* can be considered an indicator, Pitt's viewers appear to be more than willing to pay to see their idol spend over half of a movie as either a wrinkled old man or a child. As proof, the film adaptation of *Button* was the number two movie of the record-earnings 2008 Christmas weekend, bringing in $39 million in four days (Semuels). Also, reprints of Fitzgerald's original short story have skyrocketed since 2008, with new editions of "Button" appearing as the cover story in numerous mass-market Fitzgerald compendiums, such as Penguin's *The Curious Case of Benjamin Button and Other Jazz Age Stories* (2008).

Perhaps most intriguing about the phenomenal number of reprints inspired by the film's success is the public interest in Fitzgerald that such editions have reawakened. One need only peruse the customer comments on Amazon.com to find that many Fitzgerald fans rediscovered the author because of Fincher's adaptation and the reprint phenomenon that it sparked. Most of the comments read like those of Connecticut's Marjorie Bachand, who claimed that she was "enjoying this book so far, I forgot how much I used to enjoy Fitzgerald's stories, it has been a long time since I read him" (Amazon.com). Other readers chose to analyze the connection among Fitzgerald, the reprints, and the film adaptation more deeply. Wesley Mullins from Kentucky wrote a particularly long response about his reaction to rediscovering Fitzgerald:

> Longer than a short story, shorter than a novella, "The Curious Case of Benjamin Button" was destined to be lost to everyone except the most ardent F. Scott

Fitzgerald fans until Hollywood rescued it and turned it into a film. Intrigued by the trailer, I looked for the story to read before seeing the film.... From what I have seen of the trailer, the film and story differ greatly.... Fitzgerald speaks of Benjamin in almost fairy tale tones.... It's full of the same quirks that have caused the movie to be one of the most anticipated this year.... The story is tricky, poignant and sad, It was impossible to not see Brad Pitt in the role and impossible to not think about how they are going to show him as 80 years old or (sorry Brad) as a teenager. I don't think reading this spoiled anything about the movie for me. If anything, it only makes me want to see it even more [Amazon.com].

The fact that Mullins's review was for the Kindle edition of the reprint points to the important fact that the technologically savvy reader, with a youthful mindset, finds Fitzgerald's work to resonate for today's popular culture through its connection with Brad Pitt in the film adaptation, showing that the film has expanded and extended the story's shelf life.

Perhaps most important, a customer from Long Island, using the name "Long Island Momma Abigail," wrote that the reprint and film not only renewed her interest in Fitzgerald but also encouraged her son to read his work as well:

I read this story before seeing the movie starring Brad Pitt. The story is great and worth reading. It is only 20+ pages, but really interesting. I saw the movie yesterday, and highly recommend the movie. The movie has taken some liberties from the book, but still excellent. Movies are always a little different from the book. I recommend you read this story before seeing the movie. I gave the book to my 19 year old son to read, and he enjoyed it too. We went to the movie together, and both enjoyed the movie. It was a nice mother/son date. I am an avid reader, but my son normally only reads for school or Harry Potter books, so it was nice that he enjoyed this story too, and wanted to see the movie with his mother. Pick up the book and share it with your family, you might be surprised how much they enjoy reading it too [Amazon.com].

Abigail's review is important because it shows how the average consumer of entertainment products can use a film adaptation in support of an original text to encourage a younger generation of readers to become interested in Fitzgerald and to read more in general. This is the best possible outcome that a film adaptation of a classic text can achieve.

Although it might seem odd to consider customer comments about a literary work in a serious critique, such analysis is warranted here to establish the validity of Fincher's film as instrumental in reviving an interest in Fitzgerald studies. Fitzgerald was interested in consumer reactions to his stories, even choosing to put a reader's letter into the entry for "Button" in his Table of Contents for *Tales of the Jazz Age*. Always interested in pleasing his audience, Fitzgerald took an amused approach to what he describes as a "startling letter from an anonymous admirer in Cincinnati" and then reprints the letter, complete with mechanical errors:

> Sir–
> I have read the story Benjamin Button in Colliers and I wish to say that as a short story writer you would make a good lunatic. I have seen many peices of cheese in my life but of all the peices of cheese I have ever seen you are the biggest peice. I hate to waste a peice of stationary on you but I will [*Fitzgerald: Novels and Stories* 801].

This entry from Fitzgerald demonstrates how the author's eagerness to entertain his target audience was coupled in his early career with a sense of humor about the public reception of his works. Throughout his career, Fitzgerald worked in both the popular media of magazines and film, as well as the serious medium of literary writing, and would have known the value of public reputation. As an artist who stood astride these two worlds, Fitzgerald, in all likelihood, would have delighted in the resurgence of interest in his life and works as Fincher's film adaptation brought the ouroboric cycle of Fitzgerald's fame into the age of digital media.

The Roth/Swicord script of the Fincher film plays off the audience's ability to connect the cycle of Fitzgerald's fame as a public author in the early 20th century with Brad Pitt's similar celebrity status as an actor in the 21st. As EW.com's Lisa Schwartzbaum observes:

> Pitt, a comely actor, is no longer the golden surprise he was in *Thelma and Louise*. What he is, though, is a phenomenon of heightened celebrity. And that rarified status, combined with good grooming and exquisite digital effects care, produces the exact force field of fame needed to take our breath away in that first moment on screen when, rid of gray hair, Benjamin is bathed in sunlight that honors the movie-star beauty Pitt is. Was. Is.

The connection between a 21st-century understanding of the transitory nature of movie star celebrity and actual accounts of Fitzgerald's mid-twentieth century fall from the heights of international fame is an easy one to make. This theme is also a valid one to pursue in a film adaptation of "Button," a story which places its primary concern on how a man is alternately embraced or negatively stereotyped by his culture because of his apparent physical age.

This additional connection of a meditation on whether Brad Pitt's fame is lasting actually enhances the underlying themes of Fitzgerald's original story, while simultaneously inviting the ironic comparison to the author's own tragic biography. Any critic who hastily discounts the validity of an interpretive film adaptation of a Fitzgerald work primarily on the basis of a lack of faithfulness misses the entire point of Fitzgerald. He was a writer who deliberately sculpted his life into a work that he perceived to be of epic proportions, and then wrote about it, only to find that his work began to take on a life of its own, eerily predicting, fulfilling, and documenting his own inevitable demise, in an ouroboric circle of celebrity. The real irony of "The Curious Case of Benjamin Button" was that the elliptical nature of the story's plotline reflected the elusive reciprocity of life and art in Fitzgerald's world.

With this understanding of how the "Button" story was created, it is now necessary to look at how some specific details of the story were translated into a film suitable for 21st-century sensibilities. First, the setting of the film in New Orleans, Paris, and New York is drastically different from that of the original story, which was Baltimore. Fitzgerald's choice to set his tale in Baltimore was most likely related to his family history with the city. Fitzgerald's full name, Francis Scott Key Fitzgerald, reflected his father's pride in the family's Old South lineage traced to the founder of Maryland, Philip Key, Fitzgerald's grandfather of four generations back, and to Francis Scott Key, who was Fitzgerald's second cousin (*Grandeur* 13). Throughout his entire lifetime, Fitzgerald considered himself a Southerner and a Confederate sympathizer who "became convinced that his father had never recovered from the Civil War and that its disappointments had sapped his ambition" (*Grandeur* 13). Fitzgerald's father, Edward, was a former member of the Southern gentility who was a failure at every business enterprise he attempted. From these circumstances, Fitzgerald held a mixed view of the antebellum South as partly a fairytale land of aristocracy to which he, by birthright, should have been a part, and alternatively a pitiful, self-deluding disaster that collapsed upon the men who had been the pillars of its society before the war. Fitzgerald turned this inward meditation about the cultural lineage that Southern fathers leave their sons into a humorous send-up of the morals and values of the Old South in the text of "Button," his only story set not only in Baltimore, but also in the antebellum South.

Although Fitzgerald's choices of time and place setting would have been easily relatable to his Jazz Age readers, who very possibly could have endured many long-winded stories from their own fathers and grandfathers about the supposed glories of the Old South lifestyle, they would have been too remote for 21st-century audiences. The negative association of racial prejudice with the Old South and regional profiling of Southern stereotypes would have alienated many potential moviegoers, even if they recognized the society that Fitzgerald was attempting to lampoon in his original story. Instead, what was needed to modernize Fitzgerald's story was the selection of a different Southern city, which had a better reputation for racial equality, but that still maintained the classic ambiance of a Southern harbor town.

New Orleans was the city selected by Fincher's production team after much debate as to the best reconciliation of all these concerns. Contrary to the belief of some critics who sought to dismiss the film as pandering to the sympathies of Americans after Hurricane Katrina, New Orleans was actually chosen several months before the hurricane, a situation which became a huge production obstacle around which the film crew had to work. Both Fincher and Pitt firmly believed that New Orleans was the ideal setting to house their vision of a film in which old and new were so closely juxtaposed. The film took on added metaphorical and cultural significance as set pieces such as streetcars and classic homes were restored by the film crew, some of the first signs of rebirth in the storm-ravaged city (*Supplements*). Also, the film's chronological setting of Benjamin's birth was moved forward to begin on World War One Armistice Day 1918, rather than in 1860. This move was another accommodation for audiences, who would have been more familiar via personal experiences of talking with elderly family members and friends about World Wars One and Two than the Civil War, making the film more personally resonant while retaining ties to America's military history.

Last, the choice of setting the film in early 20th-century New Orleans allowed the filmmakers to grapple with issues of race, class, and social status that would be understandable to 21st-century audiences. In Fincher's film, Benjamin's father, upon seeing what he perceived to be his newborn son's deformity, runs away with the baby and leaves him on a doorstep in the "colored" section of town. The baby, Benjamin, is discovered by Queenie, the African American manager of a nursing home for elderly whites, and her long-term boyfriend, Mr. Weathers. Instead of judging Benjamin for his impairment of early-onset old age, Queenie takes Benjamin in and raises him as her own child, and after his marriage to Queenie, Mr. Weathers becomes a father figure to Benjamin. Over the course of the narrative, the audience learns that Queenie is a hard-working, generous woman of true Christian faith, while Mr. Weathers, who works as a cook, is actually highly self-educated, even reciting Shakespeare to Benjamin as he works.

These two morally sound characters stand in stark contrast to Benjamin's true father, whom Benjamin first meets in a brothel, and who never acknowledges Benjamin as his son until shortly before his death. As a result, the audience sees that the highly romantic, optimistic, and hard-working Benjamin learned these virtues from his African American adoptive parents, prompting the inference that audiences should reconsider the contributions made to American history by the nation's black population, who worked only in the shadow of whites during the early twentieth century. By the end of the film, when Queenie dies, Benjamin is clearly moved by the loss of his adoptive mother much more than that of his biological father, whose portraits he sells along with the house and business he inherits from Mr. Button. Finally, when Benjamin and his great love Daisy become old, they return to the nursing home where he began his life as Queenie's son, suggesting that others should return to rebuild and repopulate New Orleans. As the film ends with Daisy's death in the hospital while floodwaters sweep away Mr. Gateau's clock, audiences are prompted by a montage of all the historical events and people Benjamin has known to consider how much history could be lost if New Orleans were left in ruins. The ending of the film then becomes an ironic meditation not only on the significance of one human life that was allowed the possibility of being relived, but also on the possibility of what New Orleans, and the rest of America, could have been had all of its people been given equal opportunity to succeed.

The overall tone of the film differs from the tone of the story for one primary reason. Fitzgerald was a witty writer who often used ironic humor to create biting social satire in his works. However, social satire of a literary nature is extraordinarily difficult to translate to the screen, especially when the satire is made of a culture over a hundred years out of date. Screenwriter Eric Roth, who also transformed Winston Groom's Southern satiric text *Forrest Gump* into more palatable mass market film fare, chose wisely when he decided to make the message of the *Button* film more straightforward than satirical. Although Fitzgerald's primary concerns about aging and the mutability of love over time are still present in Roth's screenplay, they are not obscured by Fitzgerald's poignant, yet anachronistic, witticisms.

One plot device that is completely new in the film adaptation of *Button* is the story of Mr. Gateau and his clock. The film opens with a sequence about a blind clockmaker who, heartbroken over the death of his only son in World War I, builds a clock for the new train station that runs backward instead of forward, saying, "I made it that way ... so that perhaps the boys that we lost might stand and come home again" (Roth and Swicord 12). Although this element is not present in Fitzgerald's story, the symbolism of Gateau's clock serves as a visual reminder of two themes important to the adaptation. First, a chief underlying theme of both the story and the film is that time can never be reversed. No matter how much sentimentality and worry are wasted, the fate of every person will continually unfold steadily and inevitably. This idea is furthered by the sequence in which the events of the day of Daisy's career-ending accident are unfolded in slow motion. Narrated by Benjamin, the sequence shows how, because of the sum total of small mishaps that befall numerous people in Daisy's world, she is fated to arrive in the spot where a car strikes her, shattering her leg. Daisy's ruined ballet career calls to mind the circumstances of Fitzgerald's biography, in which Zelda also failed as a ballerina, mostly because she began too late in life. Gateau's clock, with the ridiculous oddity of its reverse timekeeping, is a visual symbol of this futility, which calls to mind the last line of *The Great Gatsby* that people are merely "boats against the current, borne back ceaselessly into the past" (Fitzgerald 189). Second, the death of thousands of young men in the unprecedented bloodbath of World War I was the event that defined Fitzgerald's Lost Generation. The inclusion of World War I's end early in the film, as the moment from which time should be made to run backward in order to erase the mistakes of the past, is a valid choice, based upon biographical incorporation from Fitzgerald's life.

Also, the circumstances of Benjamin's early life are different in the original story than in the movie, but these differences often serve to clarify or make more rational the events surrounding his birth. In the film, Benjamin's mother dies in childbirth, whereas in the short story, the mother is simply not mentioned again after she delivers Benjamin. Death of the mother as a result of complications from childbirth is acceptable considering the respective times in which Benjamin might have been born. The biblical Benjamin's mother, Rachel, died after giving birth to him, creating a possible symbolic context that Jewish screenwriter Eric Roth might have built upon in his adaptation (Gottheil). Further, it is possible that Fitzgerald intended to allude to the legend of the Wandering Jew in his tale, using Benjamin metaphorically in his farce as a symbol for the collective consciousness of man as an eternally restless species.

This possible allusion is made clear in the short story, when one of the Yale students mocks the gray-haired freshman, Benjamin, by yelling out, "He must be the Wandering Jew!" ("Button" 965). As Joseph Jacobs has noted, "The figure of the doomed sinner, forced to wander without the hope of rest in death until the millennium, impressed itself upon the popular imagination, and passed thence into literary art, mainly with reference to the seeming immortality of the wandering Jewish race" ("Wandering Jew"). Fincher's film illustrates this concept by showing a montage of Benjamin on a journey of self-exploration in his later life, during which he roams all over Europe, Asia, and the Middle East, after he realizes that, because of his aging condition, he will never be able to behave as a true husband for Daisy or father to their daughter, Caroline. Instead, Benjamin sends her a series of letters and a diary, chronicling his adventures and wishes for her to live a fulfilling life in which she "always seeks out people with different points of view" to challenge opinions that she may hold (*Button*). Again, the inference in the film embraces Fitzgerald's penchant for self-exploration, but broadens it to an overall sense of cultural exploration befitting 21st-century sensibilities.

Often in his work, Fitzgerald showed concern for the place of the Jew in early 20th-century America as a metaphor for the universal plight of humanity. In his final, unfinished novel, *The Last Tycoon*, Hollywood film producer Monroe Stahr is a Jewish executive who overworked himself while building a career that created no sort of meaningful existence for him. When Stahr at last slows down enough to allow himself the opportunity to find love, he becomes frustrated and depressed, realizing that he has waited too late to learn to enjoy the things in life that should bring the most meaning (*Tycoon*).

In short, the message conveyed by Monroe Stahr in Fitzgerald's final novel is not unlike the one proposed by Benjamin Button, in both the film and original story versions. Life is not the sum total of aspirations and achievements, but is instead measured by the added values of earned experiences and personal relationships to create a balance within the whole equation of human existence. Fitzgerald's personal life reflected a similar lack of aptitude for this sort of algebraic method of life's true worth, and that same theme pervades two of his longer works, *The Great Gatsby* and *The Last Tycoon*. Like their author, the heroes of both these novels allowed the allure of fame and wealth to become their rulers. Fitzgerald was widely known for incorporating specific elements of his life into his characters, and Fincher's adaptation follows his lead.

Further in-depth study of potential motivations behind the adaptation choices of the *Button* filmmakers might be pursued to uncover even more insights that add meaning to a careful rereading of the original short story text. One example of this approach could be an exploration of the relationship between Hildegarde, called Daisy after Gatsby's heroine in Fincher's film, and Benjamin, compared to the relationship between Fitzgerald and Zelda. In the film adaptation, Daisy is a headstrong young ballerina with an independent personality very much like Zelda's; however, in the story, Hildegarde is a long-suffering wife who indulges her husband's whims for years before finally leaving him and going to Europe. Fitzgerald's original heroine might be read as an expression of the worst fears he had for Zelda living a life in his shadow, while Fincher's adaptation is more likely a speculative, biographical reflection on the ballet career that Zelda might have had, and/or the life that the fictional Daisy might have led, as an independent woman, had she been born a generation afterward and married later in life.

Another direction of inquiry that might be pursued is the possible incorporation of biographical parallels not only to Fitzgerald's life, but also Hemingway's, that Fincher's adaptation appears to utilize. In the film, Benjamin takes part in World War II in an unusual way, by joining the crew of the Irish Captain Mike's tugboat. Captain Mike is a Hemingwayesque character of overtly masculine personality who is given to alternating displays of bravado and debauchery that call to mind numerous exploits of Hemingway and the fictional Scotsman he created for *The Sun Also Rises*, Mike Campbell. Among his many military exploits, Hemingway was known for using his fishing boat, the *Pilar*, to help the Allies in World War II. Also, Benjamin's unique romantic relationship with the sophisticated British diplomat's wife, played by British actress Tilda Swinton, whom he meets in Murmansk during World War II, seems very similar to the relationship between Jake Barnes and British Lady Brett Ashley in *The Sun Also Rises*. Only through further interviews with the filmmakers involved in the *Button* adaptation can these connections ever be solidified as definite examples of the Hemingerald phenomenon in Fitzgerald film adaptation.

Still, the major themes in Fitzgerald's original story survive into Fincher's film adaptation in expanded, thought-provoking form. Fitzgerald said, in his working notes for *The Last Tycoon*, "There are no second acts in American lives" (qtd. in "Second Acts"). Yet, Fitzgerald's short story "The Curious Case of Benjamin Button" clearly has enjoyed a more popular second act over eighty years after its first. Benjamin Button's revival followed many years after the initial Fitzgerald revival in the 1960s, when this quotation was used in a 1968 *Time* magazine piece about Americans finding their avocations in second careers: "Any American who seeks self-renewal by serving others can almost certainly find a way today" ("Second Acts"). Brad Pitt's on-screen characterization of Benjamin epitomizes this new-found mid-life optimism of the 1960s, when Benjamin says through his diary to his daughter, Caroline, "It's never to late, or in my case too early, to be whomever you want to be.... I hope you live a life you are proud of, and if you're not, I hope you have the courage to start all over again" (Roth and Swicord 252). Although this statement is a clear departure from the cynical humor of Fitzgerald's original text, it cannot help but make those familiar with the author's biography wonder if his screenwriting career might have actually been a positive turning point in his life. If Fitzgerald had gained sobriety early enough in his Hollywood career to write out the sentiments that others have found percolating just beneath the smug veneer of protective humor in his early works, "Button" might have become a masterpiece in Fitzgerald's otherwise lackluster screenwriting career. Instead, David Fincher's adaptation of *The Curious Case of Benjamin Button* stands as a monument to the exciting potential for additional depths of meaning that Fitzgerald's works can have, if carefully interpreted for a new generation by a balanced group of collaborative writers, actors, and filmmakers.

The Beautiful and Damned (2008)

Richard Wolstencroft's independent, revisionist adaptation of F. Scott Fitzgerald's *The Beautiful and Damned* (2008) has never been the subject of scholarly review. This fact is not surprising, considering the chilly reception that the film received at its debut screening for the Tenth International F. Scott Fitzgerald Conference in Baltimore on October 2, 2009. Wolstencroft's adaptation prompted large scale walkouts, with Fitzgerald scholars mumbling comments from the polite, such as "I have better things to do with my time," to the obviously dissatisfied and disturbed. At subsequent screenings after the conference, Wolstencroft's adaptation has produced mixed reviews, the most positive of which originated in his native Australia. Reviewer Jack Marx sums up the Australian critics' position best, saying:

> Fitzgerald's classic may have found a spiritual home in the hands of Wolstencroft. An independent filmmaker working on a peasant's budget, Wolstencroft could be similarly assailed for 'careless' construction, his adaptation of *The Beautiful and Damned*, like his two previous feature films (*Bloodlust* in 1990 and *Pearls Before Swine* in 1999), notable for the sorts of technical deficiencies that are par-for-the-course when it comes to micro-budget cinema. But these are not the more remarkable aspects of Wolstencroft's *B&D*—it's what's being filmed that is guaranteed to kick a few crickets where the General Public is concerned [news.au.com].

Marx is certainly correct to point out the film's low production values, which include shoddy camera work and porn-style staging, yet it seems to be the alterations in content from Fitzgerald's original that are more likely to raise the ire of Fitzgerald scholars in the future.

Although Wolstencroft's revisionist adaptation captures the rebellious, hedonistic spirit of youth culture from Fitzgerald's novel, he neglects the trademarks that made the book quintessentially Fitzgeraldian, such as muted commentary on racism, purposeful linguistic playfulness, open discussion of fate versus determinism in American capitalist society, and an overall romantic approach to gender relations. Instead, Wolstencroft replaces these themes with a plot that is tailored around his own personal interests, such as film censorship, the corrupting power of wealth, and the devaluation of meaningful sexual relationships in the 21st century. These discrepancies demonstrate an imbalance of creative control that improperly favor the director and serve to make Wolstencroft's adaptation a noncohesive cautionary tale for all future filmmakers seeking to adapt Fitzgerald's works for mainstream audiences by incorporating their own autobiographical lives.

To be fair, Wolstencroft's adaptation does begin with a title screen that quotes Fitzgerald's title page for the novel, "The victor belongs to the spoils" (*Beautiful and Damned* 435). However, immediately in the following screens, Wolstencroft states that the adaptation, from his production company, Ontological Pictures, is to be "An Ereignis by Richard Wolstencroft." Wolstencroft, a self-proclaimed serious student of Heideggerian philosophy, appears to make plain his intention here to create a revisionist adaptation that focuses on his own philosophical commentary about the state of youth culture in the 21st century, rather than to interpret Fitzgerald's 20th-century views on the subject for a new generation.

In the first full scene of Wolstencroft's adaptation, there is an attempt to make the protagonist's morning ritual relevant and appallingly decadent for today's audiences. In the novel, readers are supposed to be amazed by the lavishness of what Fitzgerald dubs Anthony Patch's "reproachless apartment" and appalled at Anthony's choice to wallow lazily in bed while his English servant, Bounds, serves his breakfast and makes "deprecative" comments (*Beautiful and Damned* 444, 446). In his adaptation, Wolstencroft captures Anthony's lavish home in the opening scenes, but adds two girls, referred to by the derogatory moniker "the Hoover sisters," as Anthony's bed companions. One girl is openly topless and another strategically placed to conceal most of her toplessness. After Anthony is up and dressed, Bounds tells Anthony that he is "paid very well to be a PA two days a week, but some days I feel like a fucking housemaid" and asks whether he "should call the lost dogs society," to dispose of the girls, to which Anthony replies, "Just make them breakfast and be sure they leave, preferably without any of my possessions" (Wolstencroft). As Anthony leaves, Bounds dismisses the girls by pulling off the covers, fully revealing their nakedness, and barking the one word command, "Out!" (Wolstencroft). This scene, which has no parallel in Fitzgerald's novel, is the first example of alteration to the plot and style of dialogue from the original.

Nowhere in Fitzgerald's entire published canon does the author ever use the word "fuck," although the epithet is one of many frequently used in Wolstencroft's adaptation. Also, there is never a mention of a threesome in Fitzgerald's work. Instead, Fitzgerald tended to leave women of easy virtue as objects of interest and speculation to his fictional young men like Anthony Patch, who finds such girls, "for all their vulgarity ... faintly and subtly mysterious" (*Beautiful and Damned* 456). One might read this scene, then, as an early example of Wolstencroft's choice to depart from Fitzgerald's worldview and impose his own on the adaptation.

Wolstencroft's autobiography factors largely into his creative choices for the film. In 1992, Wolstencroft opened The Hellfire Club, a controversial S&M nightspot in Melbourne. According to Australian nightlife reporter

Michelle Griffin, "for years, he was the public face of the leather and lace-up crowd, generating headlines with calls to loosen pornography laws, and ill-advised plans for Nazi dress-up nights" (theage.com). Then, in 2000, Wolstencroft started the Melbourne Underground Film Festival, mostly as a reaction to the larger Melbourne International Film Festival's refusal to show films that displayed controversial amounts of sex, explicit language, or drug use. In an interview with Jack Marx, Wolstencroft acknowledges his connection to a life of drugs and dangerous sexuality as providing the genesis of his revisionist version of Fitzgerald's novel:

> When I ran the Hellfire Club I pretty much lived the Beautiful and Damned lifestyle. I had lots of money, a beautiful girlfriend, and I was friends with all these trust fund kids who didn't work, who all lived in mansions, who partied for five days in a row.... I wanted to make a film about that whole milieu. Then I read *The Beautiful and Damned*, about a young couple who destroy themselves through excess. And I realized it was in the public domain. So I took it and laid it over my own experience. You'd be surprised—about 70 per cent of the dialogue in the film is Fitzgerald's [news.au.com].

Although Wolstencroft's assessment that a majority of the dialogue in his adaptation comes from Fitzgerald's original is an exaggeration, his statement that the novel was a secondary overlay to his own experiences in creating the film appears accurate. Many scenes from Wolstencroft's adaptation include large amounts of cocaine use, group sexuality, pornography, and even date rape, which simply are not present anywhere in the Fitzgerald canon, but in all likelihood were witnessed by Wolstencroft as part of his everyday existence as an S&M club owner. As a result, the film is quite clearly Richard Wolstencroft's *The Beautiful and Damned*, not Fitzgerald's. Still, what remains is to discuss exactly how Wolstencroft's personal life and directorial choices work within Fitzgerald's text, in order to determine whether this approach adds any relevance to the classic tale for today's audiences.

First, the issue of language use must be considered. According to Madeline Glaser, Fitzgerald uses wordplay in the novel "in the form of inverted semantic elements that disclose issues on which the plot revolves. This semantic reordering is an intentional reversal of the word order of a familiar quotation or common saying, which reorders meaning in the text" (238). The overall intention of Fitzgerald's witty turns of phrase, according to Glaser, is to create the sense in readers' minds that Anthony "lives in a society where cause and effect have been reversed" because "the rational concept of causal effect is challenged in the Jazz Age and is illustrated by chaos" (238). Therefore, the aforementioned quotation, "The victor belongs to the spoils," represents not just a clever turn of phrase, but instead a deliberate effort by Fitzgerald to demonstrate how

Anthony's wealth "possesses him rather than frees him" (Glaser 238). This type of wordplay, intended to convey a reversal of meaning, was rightly placed in the context of Fitzgerald's era, during which the world's value system had recently been inverted by World War One and Prohibition.

In Wolstencroft's adaptation, this type of wordplay is almost wholly omitted, and is instead replaced with a more hard-edged, 21st-century linguistic sensibility that reflects the current state of youth culture's need to express a tough, aloof approach to the world by using large amounts of profanity, particularly the word "fuck." In his commentary after the film's debut at the Fitzgerald Conference, Wolstencroft claimed that one of his inspirations in creating authentic dialogue that represented current youth culture was Bret Easton Ellis, whose novel *Less Than Zero* takes a similar approach. The argument could be made that Wolstencroft's profanity-spewing youths are reacting to the same needs as Fitzgerald's more wittily-spoken characters, in that both are attempting to reflect a cool, nonchalant reaction to the chaos of everyday modern life. Read in this context, Wolstencroft's choice to alter Fitzgerald's linguistic sensibilities in the adaptation could be partially justified as an attempt to revise the emotional state that such phraseology was originally intended to convey.

In Fitzgerald's time, the social mores might have been turned upside down, but they were still identifiable enough that young people could identify and hold fast to basic emotions, such as aspiration, love, and sexual desire. However, Wolstencroft seems to be saying that in the 21st century, conventional values are not simply inverted, but have become fragmented beyond recognition. Therefore, Wolstencroft, who wrote the screenplay for his adaptation in addition to directing and producing it, might be suggesting, through his continual employment of repetitive profanities like "fuck," that every possible avenue of romantic endeavor or intellectual aspiration for young people today has been irretrievably perverted and that individuals are reduced to merely fulfilling the simplest of desires. In short, Wolstencroft's characters' repeated use of the word "fuck" may indicate not only that they consider their lives "fucked" in every possible way, but also that the very term "fuck" has been divorced from its sexual connotations, because even sex itself has become meaningless and devalued in the 21st century. Considered in this context, one could infer that Wolstencroft uses explicit language to reflect his belief that today's youth culture faces an emotional wasteland even more barren than that of Fitzgerald's Lost Generation.

This reading is justified by Wolstencroft's frequent tirades against censorship in the press and in his "Manifesto for Ontological Cinema," which is posted on his blog. In Wolstencroft's "Manifesto," which is similar in many ways to the Dogme 95 manifesto, he claims that his philosophy of filmmaking is an attempt "to apply the ideas of Martin Heidegger and others to cinema" (IdeaFix.com). Wolstencroft's most clearly stated directive in the "Manifesto"—"Be honest when you make a film; do not lie. Uncover the truth of Being, do not observe it as an object"—seems to be the goal he is seeking in his adaptation of *The Beautiful and Damned*, which appears to be an attempt to convey the truth about life as Wolstencraft has experienced it, far more than it seems to be a reflection on Fitzgerald's novel (IdeaFix.com). Although incorporation of a director's personal experiences is inescapable and in some ways necessary in order to achieve a balanced collaboration of creative voices in the filmmaking process, it can be a fault when the director's personal experiences do not closely parallel those of an adapted text's original author. Wolstencroft's worldview, which is far more sexually explicit and pessimistic than Fitzgerald's in this early work, often overshadows the themes present in the original novel.

Yet, according to Wolstencroft, his role as a director of supreme authority over his project is intentional. According to Wolstencroft's "Manifesto," "Cinema is in some senses inherently fascist at a deep level. The role of the director is fascism at its purest, a dictator of a cinematic world, with total power. But it should be noted that many, many directors are not tyrants or authoritarians and are truly and deeply transcendental fascists" (IdeaFix.com). "Transcendental fascism" is a term created by Wolstencroft to describe a political system that he advocates, which allows a benevolent dictator to rule with absolute power, but that does not include hatred of, or action against, any ethnic or sexual minority groups. This philosophy, which he discusses at length on his blog, has garnered much criticism in the Australian press, where it has been connected with other neo-fascist groups that Wolstencroft claims are completely unrelated to his beliefs. Regardless, Wolstencroft's ideology that the director should be a supreme authority over his films is clearly at odds with the six-question approach to film adaptation advocated throughout this dissertation, because it represents the direct opposite of cohesive artistic vision among all collaborators, which is the goal of such inquiry.

Still, it is important to understand Wolstencroft's transcendental fascist approach to ontological filmmaking in order to discuss some of the more unusual choices he makes in adapting *The Beautiful and Damned*. One scene, near the exact chronological center of the film, depicts Wolstencroft as a friend of Anthony Patch who is visiting Patch's home. Patch enters the room to see Wolstencroft's character watching a vivid and explicit pornographic film of himself date raping a woman who is asleep after being slipped some rohipnol. Patch is disgusted by the graphic film and the delight in which Wolstencroft's character and the other men seem to take in watching it. This scene is apparently intended to be the most morally revolting display of sexual deviance in a film that contains many such acts.

As a filmmaker working under his own "Manifesto" of transcendental fascism, Wolstencroft is under a duty of obligation to personally oversee this key commentary about his opinion on the true state of modern Being as it relates to sexuality. By putting himself in the role of a filmmaker who is engaging in sexual exploitation of a woman that is clearly reprehensible even under current, relaxed standards, Wolstencroft suggests that natural sexual desire has reached a complete state of depravity in today's youth culture, and the few who attempt to hold on to traditional connections of emotion and sexuality, as exemplified by the relationship between Anthony and Gloria Patch, are actually outside the mainstream. This questioning of traditional beliefs about what are considered acceptable exercises of sexuality and visual depictions of sexual behavior is at the heart of Wolstencroft's film, and also of his particular worldview, which makes it fitting that his character is the one depicted in the scene. In Wolstencroft's cinematic world, sexuality is almost completely divorced from emotion, and he, as the director, must be present to oversee the proceeding.

However, once again, this scene has no thematic parallel to Fitzgerald's original novel. Instead of making a statement about the divorce of sexuality from emotion as the new standard of modern society, Fitzgerald appears to suggest that sexuality can only produce meaning as a natural extent of romantic emotion and that it is natural for society to move toward this goal. Fitzgerald's Anthony Patch continually bemoans "The Meaninglessness of Life" as a wealthy, bored, Ivy League–educated young playboy, but his life seems to gain a sense of focus when he meets the love of his life, Gloria Gilbert (*Beautiful and Damned* 479). Fitzgerald describes the way in which Anthony Patch perceives Gloria's role in his life:

> Out of the deep sophistication of Anthony an understanding formed, nothing atavistic or obscure, indeed scarcely physical at all, an understanding remembered from the romancings of many generations of minds.... The sheath that held her soul had assumed significance—that was all. She was a sun, radiant, growing, gathering light and storing it—then after an eternity pouring it forth in a glance, the fragment of a sentence, to that part of him that cherished all beauty and all illusion [*Beautiful and Damned* 494].

Although Anthony's life would later devolve as his party lifestyle pushes him further into excess, alcoholism, and even an adulterous relationship outside his marriage to Gloria, Anthony's love for her never ceases to be the best part of his character. As Fitzgerald describes the situation, even though Gloria slowly falls out of love with Anthony over the course of the novel, Gloria remains Anthony's "sole preoccupation.... Had he lost her he would have been a broken man, wretchedly and sentimentally absorbed in her memory for the remainder of his life" (*Beautiful and Damned* 659). Anthony's ability to love Gloria before he consummates a relationship with her creates a sense of longing that makes the sexual acts which occur between them later more poignant. This story of a man who is so capable of love and devotion to one woman, but who then alienates himself from that woman's affections, thereby rendering his existence meaningless, creates a romantic sensibility that makes Anthony Patch's tragic downfall incredibly pitiable in Fitzgerald's original novel.

However, by surrounding Anthony constantly with images of debauched sexuality that is completely devoid of emotion both before, during, and after his relationship with Gloria begins, Wolstencroft's adaptation loses the sense of tragic romance present in Fitzgerald's original. In what comes across as his zeal to make a blanket statement about how film censors should be more open about allowing graphic sexual scenes in films in order to convey society truthfully, Wolstencroft loses the sense that Fitzgerald's narrative is the story not of any generation as a whole, but instead as one particular couple, and their existence within a generation.

Although Fitzgerald's novels today are widely regarded as voices that speak generationally to the hedonistic youth culture of the 1920s, one must always remember that those novels began as thinly-veiled fictional accounts of the biographical lives of two specific people, Scott Fitzgerald and Zelda Sayre. Almost all of the events in the novel that involve the interactions between Anthony and Gloria have autobiographical parallels to the turbulent early years of petty jealousies and personal insecurities in the relationship between Scott and Zelda. To take away the individuality of these characters, in an effort to make them seem more like behavioral models for any group of young people, is to remove the sense of authenticity derived from their closely autobiographical authorship, rendering them ineffective, and their story meaningless. In Fitzgerald's novel, even if society as a whole loses meaning, individual relationships still matter. Yet in Wolstencroft's adaptation, this Fitzgeraldian illusion, of finding happiness in a small, cathartic oasis of romance amid a desert of wealth, is lost.

Also lost in this adaptation are subtle sociopolitical commentaries on racism and capitalism that are present in Fitzgerald's original work. For example, many critics have noted that Fitzgerald's portrayal of Jewish-Americans changed dramatically over the course of his career, from the highly stereotypical and unflattering depiction of Meyer Wolfshiem in *The Great Gatsby* to the almost saintly description of Monroe Stahr, the Jewish hero of his final novel, *The Last Tycoon*. Alan Margolies has noted that Fitzgerald's description of Joseph Bloeckman, the Jewish film producer in *The Beautiful and Damned*, reflects Fitzgerald's mixed opinions about Jews during his early career.

Indeed, Fitzgerald's description of Bloeckman as "a stoutening, ruddy Jew of about thirty-five" who "introduced himself with a little too evident assurance" while "emitting two slender strings of smoke from nostrils overwide" is certainly unattractive (*Beautiful and Damned* 511). Also, Gloria's choice to "relentlessly pun on his name" results in the unfortunate nickname "Blockhead," foreshadowing her treatment of Bloeckman as an older man whose attraction to her is never taken seriously, but instead constantly manipulated for her benefit (*Beautiful and Damned* 515). Still, even though Patch refuses to recognize the Jewish Bloeckman as a legitimate rival for Gloria's affections, Fitzgerald makes a point of having Patch get beaten up after drunkenly raving against Bloeckman for being a "Goddamn Jew" (*Beautiful and Damned* 785). According to Margolies, this incident is "dramatically acceptable since Fitzgerald is demonstrating how despicable Anthony has become" (78). Fitzgerald's depiction of Bloeckman, who has by midpoint in the novel changed his name to the Anglicized "Joseph Black," as "a dark, suave gentleman, gracefully engaged in the middle forties," provides a stark contrast to Patch, who has aged out of his early handsome appeal through years of drunken debauchery (*Beautiful and Damned* 754). This change in physical description demonstrates that Bloeckman's appeal as a potential mate for Gloria is greater than Patch's by the novel's end, and recognition by Fitzgerald of his own racial insecurities about Jewish men, if allowed to be romantic equals.

Yet, Wolstencroft's adaptation reflects none of this sentiment about male Anglo-American insecurities when faced with the potential of more stable, Jewish rivals. Instead of gaining appeal over the course of his film's narrative, Bloeckman comes across as increasingly villainous, culminating in a scene during which he tricks Gloria into taking off her clothes for a pornographic screen test after she mistakenly believes she is auditioning for a role in a mainstream film. This scene stands in stark contrast to the gracious manner with which Bloeckman treats Gloria for the screen test at his production company, Films Par Excellence, in Fitzgerald's novel. When Bloeckman tests Gloria, he acts professionally, and after determining she is too old for the role, offers her a smaller character part, which she declines because her vanity will not allow her to accept anything but a leading role. Additionally, Bloeckman's wardrobe in Wolstencroft's film consists entirely of gold chains and open-collared, chest-hair-revealing shirts which, combined with his heavily hair-gelled comb-over, convey the overall sense that he is a sleazy, exploitive producer of adult films. Rather than demonstrating, as Fitzgerald does in his original text, that Jewish men can quickly and easily overcome racial stereotypes to surpass Anglo-American men in social standing through hard work and good grooming, Wolstencroft's adaptation suggests that Jewish businessmen are willing to stoop to the lowest possible standards to make money. This portrayal of Jews in Wolstencroft's film reinforces the kinds of racial stereotypes that Fitzgerald discarded as his maturity as a writer progressed, and thus represents a serious thematic departure from the spirit of the original text.

The final and perhaps most serious thematic discrepancy between Wolstencroft's adaptation and Fitzgerald's novel is the absence of any sense of the battle between free will and determinism in American capitalist society that is present in the original text. As Ronald Berman explains, Fitzgerald had a tendency to describe America "as an idea rather than a land or a people" (43). Throughout his career, Fitzgerald continued to work through this conception of America as a capitalist ideal versus what Berman characterizes as the chief threat to that ideal, which he calls "the Idea of Regress" (42). Berman explains the aim of the novel:

> Fitzgerald's major work of 1922, *The Beautiful and Damned*, uses a generational sequence to satirize something a good deal larger and more interesting than the follies of great wealth. It gains momentum because it sticks to the great subjects of the Civilization debate, the loyalty of Americans to the idea of progress and the manifestation of those energies that Fitzgerald so much admired in life. This novel's language describes the downward trajectory from great moral energies of the past to inertia and unconsciousness in the present [45].

This characterization of Fitzgerald's novel as a meditation not only on the devolution of a young couple's lives into decadent ruin, but also on the parallel deconstruction of American idealism when confronted by the harsh realities of 20th-century capitalist stagnation, is on point because of its universal incorporation into all of Fitzgerald's major works.

Fitzgerald continually returns to the theme of a past that almost coexisted within the present, haunting young men in particular with the possibility that they will never fulfill the promise of the dreams that their ancestors began. In the *Beautiful and Damned*, Anthony Patch is constantly plagued by the fact that he is the grandson of the great business tycoon Adam Patch, and that he has done nothing to further that legacy or even to equal the achievements of his other Ivy League-educated friends like the writer Dick Caramel, of whom he is extremely envious. Yet, even by the end of the novel, when he becomes involved in a common barroom brawl, Anthony seems to want to draw strength from his heritage, as he calls out to his attackers, "I'll fix it with you. My grandfather's Adam Patch of Tarrytown" (*Beautiful and Damned* 787). This outcry demonstrates that no matter how low Anthony sinks, he maintains a sense of pride and awareness that he is descended from good stock, and that this lineage will eventually rescue him.

However, there is no such reverence for history, or the tragedy of its loss, in Wolstencroft's adaptation. Instead, the film serves as an extended exploration of the idea that Anthony's grandfather, depicted as a wealthy anti-drug reformer in the revision, is a laughable old man, completely out of touch with the interests and concerns of Anthony's generation. After he dies, Anthony engages in the struggle to hold on to his grandfather's fortune, just as he does in the novel, but he fails to grapple with the loss of his grandfather's other legacies, namely his highly esteemed business and social reputations.

Wolstencroft's elimination of the burden of American industrial and social history from his piece cannot be excused because of his choice to set the film in Australia, since that country also experienced growth from colonialism into an independent national presence as a result of the determined efforts of its industrial pioneers. In fact, Wolstencroft has spent most of his career to date arguing against what he finds to be archaic moralism left over in Australian society from this earlier, Protestant work ethic-imbued era. By choosing to craft his adaptation in a way that caters only to what he perceives as the need of young people to forget the past, Wolstencroft negates the possibility of creating a meaningful mediation on the struggles produced by the very generation gap that he so clearly identifies and combats in his public protests.

In Fitzgerald's original text of *The Beautiful and Damned*, the writer Dick Caramel ironically decries the state of literature in the 1920s:

> You know these new novels make me tired. My God! Everywhere I go some silly girl asks he if I've read *This Side of Paradise*. Are our girls really like that? If it's true to life, which I don't believe, the next generation is going to the dogs. I'm sick of all this shoddy realism. I think there's a place for the romanticist in literature [773].

Although his friend Anthony Patch mocks him for making such statements after writing a sensationalist novel like *Demon Lover*, Dick Caramel does make a good point about the place of entertainment in society. In almost every age, the literature produced by youth culture is perpetually derided for being frivolous and amoral. Yet, also in every era, a few voices genuinely capture not only the spirit of that generation, but also the place of that spirit in the line of previous youth cultures that preceded it. The potential danger in adapting a text that speaks to the particular sensibilities of one generation is that it is all too easy to weigh that adaptation down with the burden of editorialization about the differences between that culture and the present one. In the best revisionist adaptations, a careful creative balance is struck between the themes contained in the author's original work and the interests of the director, screenwriter, and cast creating the adaptation. Due to its excessive emphasis on furthering the philosophical and ideological aims of its director to the neglect of themes present in Fitzgerald's original novel, Richard Wolstencroft's *The Beautiful and Damned* fails at its task of adaptation.

The Great Gatsby (2013)

If the popularity of certain classic novels might be used to diagnose the health of the nations that produce them, then F. Scott Fitzgerald's *The Great Gatsby* might be considered America's national thermometer. Since its initial appearance at the height of the Roaring Twenties, *Gatsby* has tended to rise in public esteem during periods of time in which public anxiety about money has reached fever pitch. As Fitzgerald critic Matthew Bruccoli has said, "An essential aspect of the American-ness and the historicity of *The Great Gatsby* is that it is about money. The Land of Opportunity promised the chance for financial success" (*Gatsby* x–xi). And yet, what is a film director to do when faced with the situation of producing a new adaptation of the quintessential American novel about money during the Great Recession, when confidence in the monetary miracles that might be wrought by the American Dream are at an all-time low? The temptation would be strong either to ignore the current financial situation and produce a faithful, conversionist adaptation, or to rebel completely against the capitalist system to create a revisionist adaptation that is a scathing critique of all that has and could in the future be wrong with America. However, the most difficult stylistic choice would be to take an interpretive approach, starting with a text written in the best of economic times and re-creating it for jaded, 21st-century eyes in such a way to make audiences long for the orgasmic energy of America as it had been, when it was still a young, exuberant nation in which anything was possible. This challenging approach is the one chosen by Baz Luhrman in his adaptation of the novel. With the assistance of a stellar cast, Luhrman makes the most of his trademark lavish set designs and an almost mind-boggling array of top-quality musical performances to create a work of cohesive cinema that encircles another generation in the Fitzgerald ouroboros.

From the first scenes of his adaptation, it is clear that Luhrman has done significant research into Fitzgeraldian lore, allowing a large number of biographical details from the author's life to become incorporated into the film. The opening camera shot swoops across foggy water, passing through the green light that is the novel's most enduring symbol, as the audience hears the wistful voice of Nick Carraway reciting his father's warning to "Always try to see the best in people. As a result, I have been inclined to reserve all judgments, but even I have a limit" (Luhrman). Of course, Nick is speaking to his therapist, Dr. Perkins, from inside the Perkins Sanitarium. Although the location is not included in the original novel, it retains thematic significance. Maxwell Perkins, for whom the facility is likely named, was Fitzgerald's editor, the man who helped take the raw manuscript that had once been called "Trimalchio of West Egg" and transform it into one of the most iconic novels of the twentieth century. Also, any audience member who possesses even a cursory familiarity with Fitzgerald's life knows that both the author and his wife, Zelda, were under psychiatric care for significant portions of their lives. Luhrman's choice to create a frame around the Gatsby narrative, making Nick's penning of the novel that will become *Gatsby* result from a suggestion made by his therapist, is genius. By incorporating Fitzgerald's psychological background, Luhrman reaches out to a new generation, many of whom grew up considering therapy a common part of everyday life. Also, by making Fitzgerald's story seem to flow from a therapy session, Luhrman establishes Nick as a character who is trustworthy. After all, therapy is the modern-day equivalent of Catholic confession, and Fitzgerald was Catholic. Confession is a place where there is little incentive to lie because the listener is supposed to be a person offering assistance, and as such he or she needs to hear the truth. This simple addition of a narrative frame is the first of many attempts by Luhrman to make his adaptation relevant for younger viewers.

Another technique that Luhrman uses to relate to a younger audience is his choice to streamline much of the novel's dialogue in its transference to film. For example, the film's opening line, quoted in the previous paragraph, is quite wordier in Fitzgerald's original, reading:

> In my younger and more vulnerable years my father gave me some advice that I've been turning over in my mind ever since. "Whenever you feel like criticizing anyone," he told me, "just remember that all the people in this world haven't had the advantages that you've had." He didn't say any more but we've always been unusually communicative in a reserved way, and I understood that he meant a great deal more than that. In consequence I'm inclined to reserve all judgments, a habit that has opened up many curious natures to me and also made me the victim of not a few veteran bores [Gatsby 5].

In an age in which many moviegoers are more accustomed to texting and/or reading on digital computer screens with limited space than with reading on physical pages, it makes sense that the dialogue from a novel would need to be clipped to hold their attention on film.

Luhrman's film also uses all four contextual manners of adaptation in order to transfer Gatsby to the screen. Perhaps the most obvious manner of adaptation Luhrman uses is psychological. Not only does he include a biographically-based narrative framing device in reference to Fitzgerald's history with psychological clinics, but Luhrman also repeats certain psychological themes very clearly in the film. The most notable is Luhrman's repetition of Nick's phrase "I was within and without" as he traveled in the blended socio-economic climate of New York City. The first time Nick uses the phrase, he and Tom are traveling through the Valley of Ashes, which may be interpreted from the film to be a lower-income, post-industrial area of Queens. Put in the awkward situation of knowing that his friend Tom is having an affair with Myrtle, a woman of lower social class, while still married to his upper-class cousin, Daisy, Nick is a reluctant voyeur. He knows intellectually that the lower classes, particularly women, are exploited on a daily basis in the city, but he struggles with having such intimate knowledge of a particular situation of this type that he seems to wish himself away, into an introverted world beyond knowledge of such vulgarity.

On a different level, Nick, a man of middle-class, Midwestern means and sensibilities, is acutely aware that his socio-economic background puts him in a completely different moral framework from people who are either excessively rich or poor. Good Midwestern men and women go to work every day and do not cheat on their spouses. However, in New York, Nick discovers that men who are rich enough not to have to work and women who are desperate to aspire to such a situation both regularly cheat on their spouses, out of boredom and desperation. Thus, even though Nick is welcomed within many levels of New York society, he remains a moral outsider.

The second time that Nick uses the phrase about being "within and without" is when Gatsby uses Nick's cottage to stage his reintroduction to Daisy. Nick remains outside the cottage in the rain while Gatsby and Daisy become reacquainted, and only rejoins their company as Gatsby leads them both across the lawn to his mansion. The situation is especially awkward for Nick, since it appears from the text that he has never been as seriously in love or obsessed with a woman as Gatsby is with Daisy. Therefore, even though he is "within" the circle of conspiracy to help another man win his true love, Nick is "without" a love interest of his own. For some reason, Luhrman chooses to downplay the secondary plot from Fitzgerald's original text in which Nick becomes infatuated with Jordan Baker. This is a significant flaw in the film, because it is not thematically consistent with Fitzgerald's tendency to show a maturation of Nick's emotions throughout the book. By the end of the novel, readers can sense that Nick has learned what it means to be part of so-called sophisticated high society, and deciding that he wants no part of it, chooses to move back

West. However, Nick displays little sense of such realization in Luhrman's adaptation. Instead, the film shows a Nick who has become completely overwhelmed and unable to cope with the shallow selfishness of New York's upper classes, as they "retreat into their money and their vast carelessness," leaving the good-hearted Midwesterner Nick no option but to go insane (Luhrman). Perhaps this discrepancy is an editorialization on Luhrman's part that in the 21st century, a man faced with Nick's situation would resort to psychiatric treatment rather than self-coping, which is reasonable, given his choice to adapt interpretively. However, to leave out the effects of that fateful summer on how Nick approaches relationships with the opposite sex is a flaw in the film, and a waste of the talents of Elizabeth Debicki, the actress who portrays Jordan Baker, in too few scenes of the film.

Although Luhrman underutilizes some thematic elements of Fitzgerald's plot, he does an excellent job of contextualizing the social and historical issues concerning race that percolate beneath the surface of the original novel. Even as Tom Buchanan's tirades against what he calls the "rise of the colored empires" sound incredibly outdated to today's more liberal, post-integration ears, his railing against the "intermarriage of black and white" still resonates as a social concern facing certain vocal elements of today's more conservative culture (Luhrman). Watching the film, audience members cannot help but wonder whether American society remains more uncomfortably close to racist ideologies of the past than most are ready to admit.

Also, Luhrman's choice to have the creation of the film's soundtrack supervised by African American hip-hop music mogul Shawn "Jay-Z" Carter shows creative consistency with his overall vision of the film to represent a synthesis of old and new cultures. Too rare are the occasions in which popular cinema has deliberately demonstrated the contributions that African American artists have made to influence trends in American music and youth culture. Yet, Jay-Z's *Gatsby* soundtrack is filled with new songs, remakes, and mash-ups that foreground these important connections. The most obvious example of this stylistic blending is Beyonce Knowles and Andre 3000's remake of Amy Winehouse's "Back to Black." Other songs that represent this artistic choice to mix musical styles include "A Little Party Never Killed Nobody" by Fergie and "Over the Love" by Florence and the Machine. Even the other major songs on the soundtrack that have a genre-specific style, such as Jay-Z's hip-hop "$100 Bill," Lana del Rey's electro-pop "Young and Beautiful," and Jack White's hard rock "Love Is Blindness," demonstrate the readiness of collaboration among all creative forces to juxtapose as many elements of today's musical society as possible. F. Scott Fitzgerald was America's premier Jazz Age writer. Traditionally, jazz and its musical descendants, such as rap, rock, and hip-hop, are styles in which the foundations were laid by African Americans, but enjoyed by all races. Hip-hop, in particular, is the musical genre most concerned with chronicling how monetary success is the key to unlocking the capitalist American Dream of enhanced social status. Therefore, it is fitting that a successful hip-hop producer like Jay-Z would be able to produce a collaborative soundtrack based in this genre that represents the whole of a racially blended American culture.

Of course, in any critique of a Baz Luhrman film, one must address the issue of Luhrman's tendency to, for lack of a better word, "Luhrmanize" a text. Perhaps more than any other director working in the major studios today, Luhrman is known for the over-the-top, lavish-bordering-on-obscene scale of his productions. The stylistic consistency of Luhrman's films is due in part to the director's ongoing collaboration with screenwriter Craig Pearce, who penned other Luhrman hits such as *Strictly Ballroom* (1992), *Romeo and Juliet* (1996), and *Moulin Rouge* (2001). Yet, who better to produce an adaptation of a novel critiquing the sometimes hideous excesses of new money than a director known for flash? Luhrman seems to demonstrate a consciousness that film critics would attack his natural tendency to make larger-than-life movies by deliberately including bits of historic interest that they might ignore, almost daring them to say that his style has no substance. For example, the neon billboard behind Nick and Jordan, as they discuss Gatsby's unbelievable past, is an ad for Arrow collared shirts with a picture of a man who looks like Scott Fitzgerald. A common critique of Fitzgerald during his time was that he couldn't produce serious literature because he was too handsome, and looked like an Arrow collared shirt ad. Also, the building on top of which Nick and Jordan have dinner in the same scene is currently the home of the Times Square branch of Ripley's Believe It or Not Museum. Fitting, considering that Gatsby, the man whom they are discussing, is almost a fiction worthy of display in such a place. The way in which Luhrman appears to deliberately drop in such references gives the film almost a post-modern effect. His directorial eye is similar to Dr. T.J. Eckleberg's, always watching in anticipation for film critics who are quick to call his spectacle frivolous, only to show them that they are unable to see the rich depth of research that went into the production when it is clearly placed in front of their own eyes.

Regarding the actors who bring Fitzgerald's characters to life, Leonardo DiCaprio is the one most commendable for the caliber of his performance. For many years, DiCaprio has been one of America's most bankable romantic leads, playing Jack Dawson in *Titanic* (1997) and Romeo in Baz Luhrman's *Romeo and Juliet* (1996). In recent years, DiCaprio has taken on darker, more psychologically challenging roles in films such as *The Departed* (2006),

Revolutionary Road (2008), *Shutter Island* (2010), and *Inception* (2010). DiCaprio seems to bring elements of all of these films to his portrayal of Gatsby. From his character in *Titanic*, DiCaprio displays Gatsby's joyful, boyish side, as he showers a myriad of expensive shirts down from his immense closet into Daisy's waiting arms, demonstrating not only his wealth, but his love for her. His character in *Revolutionary Road*, which might be viewed as a later mirror piece to *Titanic*, gives DiCaprio a chance to explore the opposite emotion as a man falling out of love with his wife once the youthful excitement and wide open promises of the future are past. In the remaining films mentioned above, DiCaprio continues to build upon his unique ability as an actor to allow quiet anger to boil over into fuming rage, making the scene in which he finally confronts Tom about his love for Daisy feel truthful and terrifying.

Last but not least, DiCaprio's experimentation in previous roles with various types of accents lends a unique twist to his interpretation of Gatsby's lines. If one listens closely enough, it is possible to hear DiCaprio's Gatsby relax his rich and heavy "old sport" accent into a calmer, more Midwestern tone when he speaks to people with whom he feels that he can trust to be himself, such as Daisy. However, he turns it on more thickly with people he wants to impress, such as Tom or Nick. Particularly interesting is that, despite the fact his work in *Gangs of New York* (2002) proves that DiCaprio can clearly speak in a New York accent, he instead chooses an accent that sounds more like a Boston Brahmin when trying to impress. The effect of this choice shows that Gatsby is merely attempting to imitate an accent that he has heard rich people use, and that he is simply a newly rich man with boyish dreams trying overly hard to impress others. DiCaprio carries this feeling through in every gesture made with his character, most notably with the sequence which begins with his laughably perfect and awkward pose in an overdone suit on Nick's sofa as he waits to meet Daisy, only to run outside and become drenched in rain because he is so intimidated by her arrival, and then finally spoiling the effect entirely by knocking over Nick's clock. This scene, so perfectly executed, is key to garnering audience sympathy for Gatsby that might have been lost due to his lack of veracity. Also, its presence, among so many other well-acted scenes by DiCaprio in the film, demonstrates a solid understanding both between director and actor, and also actor and character, that defines the best adaptive work.

Whereas DiCaprio's performance as Gatsby might almost be considered a master class in acting technique, Tobey Maguire's portrayal of Nick Carraway is also effective, but in a completely different, more natural way. Maguire had a difficult childhood, not unlike the one that Luhrman invents for Gatsby in his film montage of the character's past. The child of teenaged parents who divorced soon after his birth, Maguire grew up poor and was shuffled amongst families of relatives throughout his childhood. According to British movie journalist Dominic Wills, there was one good thing about growing up a loner with few friends who was constantly on the move. Such circumstances gave Maguire time that all actors need to become observant. According to Wills, the young Maguire "spent his time watching people, wondering what made them tick. This was partly because he had no one to talk to, partly to see if he could trust the watchee. In the future, it would make it easier for him to inhabit a character's skin." This description of how Maguire became an actor also explains what appears to be an almost lack of acting in his portrayal of Nick Carraway.

Carraway, both in the novel and in its adaptation, is a constant observer. This personality trait is partly attributable to his aspiration to become a writer and also simply just a part of his nature. In the novel, Fitzgerald says that Carraway's choice to remain a neutral observer, refusing to pass judgment on friends, caused him to be "unjustly accused of being a politician, because he was privy to the secret griefs of wild, unknown men" (*Gatsby* 5). In contrast, Luhrman's film actually shows the audience what kinds of secret things these wild men did. One particularly well-shot scene takes in a crazy party thrown by Tom and Myrtle in the apartment which they let to carry on their affair. As a trumpet solo plays the era-appropriate song "Ain't Misbehavin'," Tom accuses Nick of being too priggish to get in on the fun, asking, "Do you want to stand on the sidelines and watch like you did in college, or do you want to play ball?" (Luhrman). Shamed into taking part in what becomes an orgy of drinking, drugs, and sex, Nick lets go for a dizzying party sequence, reminiscent of the Ecstasy-trip scene from Luhrman's earlier film *Romeo and Juliet*. Eventually, Nick tires of drinking gin from pimp cups and having his lap danced upon by Myrtle's sister, who is costumed, appropriately, like a green absinthe fairy. When Nick walks away from the party, he looks out the window and sees that the apartment across the street is filled with poor black people, who are living much more somber and sober lives. Nick thinks, once again, "I was within and without. Enchanted and repelled by the inexhaustible variety of life" (Luhrman). The reality hits Nick that, though he and Tom are in the poor part of town happily slumming with Myrtle and her friends, for many New Yorkers this is an actual lifestyle, without amusement, from which there is no escape.

Interestingly, just as Nick became repelled by the carnivalesque quality of parties among the upper classes, both large scale at Gatsby's mansion and small scale in Tom's apartment, so did Tobey Maguire become disgusted with the hedonism of Hollywood life. Early in his career, Maguire became close friends with Leonardo DiCaprio. As DiCaprio's star rose faster than Maguire's, Tobey became like a real-life Nick Carraway to DiCaprio's Gatsby. The two were constantly photographed together at trendy parties all over the globe, as Tobey became Leo's best friend and confidant. However, even though DiCaprio often helped his friend land roles in films that would feature the two of them, the ambitious Maguire took it hard that his friend earned success more quickly. Eventually, Maguire developed a drinking problem, and in 1995 was kicked off the set of the movie *Empire Records* (Wills). This event became a turning point in Maguire's life. Seeing that he could easily lose everything that he had worked for, Maguire entered rehab, quit drinking, and landed the role of Spiderman against a competitive field of other top actors, which included DiCaprio. Empowered by this success, Maguire extended the role into a franchise of three Spiderman movies, got married, and left the Hollywood party scene for good.

    This personal history between the two actors makes their performances as Nick and Gatsby all the more believable, and only serve to add constructively to the ouroboros of adaptation. Audience members who are fans of the two actors and have followed their personal lives offscreen are able to nod in laughing amusement when certain scenes are played only as they could be by two real-life best friends. DiCaprio, who remains single and part of the Hollywood nightlife scene today, despite years of numerous relationships with various supermodels, seems to have had the exact opposite reaction to Hollywood's world of excess than Maguire. How fitting, that in the scene in which DiCaprio's Gatsby brings legions of servants, dozens of flowers, and overflowing carts of food into Nick's tiny living room, he appears almost trapped and unable to move. Sitting stiffly on the sofa and peering around the abundant bouquets, Gatsby asks Nick, "Do you think it's too much?" to which Nick replies, "It's ... it's what you want" (Luhrman). The knowing smile exchanged between the two actors cements their friendship, both onscreen and off. Both have achieved exactly the effects that they want from their lives and careers. The truthfulness of their relationship, expressed in this scene and many others, serves to reinforce for audiences the nature of the bond between Nick and Gatsby, making their unlikely friendship all the more real for a new generation.

    With the bond of friendship so strong between the two male leads, it is little wonder that one of the strongest criticisms of Luhrman's adaptation is that there seems to be little genuine emotional connection between DiCaprio's Gatsby and Daisy, played by Carey Mulligan. Although Mulligan's performance is perfect in regards to delivery and technique, and the actress is clearly stunning in Daisy's many elaborate costumes, the fact remains that she is an

English actress who looks English, and whose reactions betray her natural English reserve. Mulligan, who made her film debut in a BBC remake of Jane Austen's *Pride and Prejudice* (2005), seems somehow miscast as Daisy Buchanan, a spoiled, very Southern belle from Louisville, Kentucky. Mulligan tends to react to Gatsby's advances with the utmost sincerity, her expressive eyes glowing with tears as she looks at him wistfully. The problem, of course, is that Daisy Buchanan is not a very sincere person.

Readers of Fitzgerald's novel will remember that Daisy was fickle enough not only to desert Gatsby once because he was poor, but also to leave him emotionally destitute a second time when she chooses him over Tom because of a silly memory about a punch bowl, and finally for a third time when she allows Gatsby to take the blame for her carelessness in running over and killing Myrtle Wilson. Even though Gatsby is blinded by love, generations of readers have come to the understanding that the depth of his devotion is wasted on Daisy, a woman who seems incapable of loyalty. After all, Daisy's two most strongly expressed lines in the film are, "Daisy's changed her mind," in which she means that she is still in love with Gatsby but will marry Tom anyway, and "You want too much. I loved him but I loved you too," when Tom and Gatsby attempt to make her choose between them (Luhrman). Whether the incorrect choice to play Daisy as a straightforward love interest instead of a fickle woman unworthy of Gatsby's love was made by Mulligan herself, or if she was instructed to do so by Luhrman, is a matter that will have to be taken up with biographers at a later time. Regardless, the emotional mismatch between Gatsby and Daisy remains one of the weakest points in an otherwise strong adaptation.

The final point to address when considering the Luhrman adaptation is whether his use of 3D effects is proper and warranted under the circumstances. To begin with, Fitzgerald's original text, like much of his work, is filled with visual details that seem like a desire of the author to break down the fourth wall between reader and page. For example, the iconic eyes of Dr. T.J. Eckleberg, one of the most memorable mental images from the novel, are "blue and gigantic," with "retinas one yard high" "brooding over the solemn dumping ground" of Queens with a "persistent stare" (*Gatsby* 27–28). Yet, few readers are aware that this immortal image was actually inspired by Spanish-born artist Francis Cugat. According to Bruccoli, Cugat "had designed posters and movie sets in New York before he became an art designer in Hollywood for Douglas Fairbanks. His painting ... is the most celebrated and widely disseminated jacket art in twentieth-century American literature" (*Gatsby* 196). The cover to which Bruccoli is referring is the one in which the sad eyes of a woman peer out of a dark blue sky while a single, shimmering green tear flows down her cheek. Bruccoli goes on to say that "the artist's image *preceded* the finished manuscript and Fitzgerald actually maintained that he had written it into his book ... that is to say, one symbol *evolves* into another" (197). This rather unique circumstance of cover art actually influencing an author's final work represents that a strong sense of balance in the collaboration between creative forces was embedded in *The Great Gatsby* from the very beginning. In essence, the book was destined to become both America's text and tablet, upon which audiences and other creative forces could write the stories of their own lives and compare the results accordingly.

Taken in this context, Luhrman's choice to film Gatsby in 3D is completely appropriate. In his "Author's Apology" for *This Side of Paradise*, Fitzgerald claimed his whole theory of writing was that "an author ought to write for the youth of his own generation, the critics of the next and the schoolmasters of ever afterward." Given Fitzgerald's generally expressed willingness to reach out to his audiences over generations, it is likely that he would have embraced a 3D interpretive adaptation of his most well-known work. In the film's 3D effects, Daisy's hands literally reach out to caress the faces of the audience when she tries in vain to catch the pieces of Gatsby's letter as they break apart in the water. Fireworks explode over the crowd as Gatsby appears for the first time like Oz stepping from behind the curtain, raising a toast in salutation to a sea of old sports. Finally, Fitzgerald's closing words float out and over the heads of the audience, "like boats against the current, borne ceaselessly back into the past," while the green light beams its last, and then goes dark (*Gatsby* 189). Are the 3D effects necessary? Perhaps not, but they certainly add a new dimension of involvement and interaction between author, audience, and filmmakers that insures the Fitzgerald authorial ouroboros will continue to turn, gathering in at least one more generation.

• THREE •

Papa's Grace Under Genre Pressure, Part One
Hollywood Adaptations of Hemingway, 1932–1952

In the most recent reissue of his autobiography, *A Moveable Feast*, Ernest Hemingway waxes poetic about the universal immortal spirit that imbues his memories of Paris. He says:

> There is never any ending to Paris and the memory of each person who has lived in it differs from that of any other. We always returned to it no matter who we are nor how it was changed nor with what difficulties nor what ease it could be reached. It was always worth it and we received a return for whatever we brought to it [*Feast* 236].

Hemingway's fond words about Paris, and the city's tendency to continue to live within and change the lives of those who have visited it, could also apply to most of the filmmakers who have chosen to adapt his works. With almost every film made from a Hemingway volume, one or more members of the production team appear to have a personal reason for attaching themselves to the project, blending their own stories into Hemingway's celebrity literary persona.

In the best cases, this level of engagement with the text brings out their best work from actors, directors, and screenwriters, resulting in a furtherance of Hemingway's original themes in new and interesting ways that add to audiences' understanding of both texts. This case is clearly made by careful screening of John Garfield's two leading turns in Hemingway works *The Breaking Point* (1950) and *Under My Skin* (1950). In both films, Garfield builds upon stress in his personal life to create the dogged men against the world who come alive in these plotlines.

However, far more problems occur when Hollywood attempts to make Hemingway's works conform to the strictures of stock genres. For example, even though *The Killers* (1946) and *To Have and Have Not* (1944) are considered Hollywood classics, these otherwise great films suffer critically as adaptations due to their overreliance on film noir tropes. Also, other problems such as Hays Code censorship cause some early Hemingway adaptations, like *A Farewell to Arms* (1932), to lose much of their original thematic significance. Instead of relying too heavily on genre, the Hemingway adaptations that choose to focus on filling in the gaps left by the transition from page to screen with extra details from the author's colorful life and canonical works seem to fare much better. Two films that use this approach to great effect are *For Whom the Bell Tolls* (1943) and *The Snows of Kilimanjaro* (1952).

In short, solid Hemingway adaptations, at least during the first two decades of Hollywood's attempts at the task, stay not so much close to the text as close to the author himself. Perhaps this is a clue to why Hemingway's works have continued to endure over time. Filmmakers and their audiences discovered what Hemingway readers have known all along: that the author and his works are very much like Paris. Collaborators take away from his or her interaction benefits in proportion to the amount of themselves they bring to the project with an open mind toward the realities of what is present beneath the surface of the story.

A Farewell to Arms (1932)

In 1932, Frank Borzage directed the first film adaptation of a Hemingway novel, *A Farewell to Arms*. Almost immediately, the film was rejected by Hemingway, who was unhappy with the thematic and content revisions made by Paramount. After receiving a telegram offering to send advance prints of the film from Paramount to the author, Hemingway replied:

> Use your imagination as to where Paramount can put two prints unexpectedly available of the Borzage version of *A Farewell to Arms*, but do not send them here. If the book lasts and motion pictures also endure a real film will eventually be made of that novel. Meanwhile, although Paramount bought picture rights and the chance to make a great picture, they did not buy the right to make me look at a silly one [qtd. in Leff 177].

Although Hemingway's tone in this wire is insulting, his irritation is justified. Prior to Paramount's request for an advance screening, film reviewers all over the nation anticipated Hemingway's negative reaction to the adaptation. Some, such as Regina Crewe of the *New York American*, even scolded Hemingway and the art of fiction writing in general in their overly lavish praise of Borzage's film. In her review of Borzage's adaptation, Crewe writes:

> And please, Mr. Hemingway, don't make yourself ridiculous by finding the slightest of faults with Paramount's production of your tale, for in Frank Borzage's picturation there lies a thousand times more than you, or any of you, will ever put in the sterile, colorless black and white of type and paper [qtd. in Leff 177].

For Hemingway, an author who had already wrestled for months with Maxwell Perkins and others at Scribner's over his use of language in the original novel, this undermining of what remained of his authorial presence in the project was the final insult. Hemingway tended to view *A Farewell to Arms* as a highly autobiographical account of his experiences in Italy during World War I that later shaped his entire liberal worldview on issues ranging from freer sexuality and unnecessary marriage to the ineffectiveness of religion and the futility of war. In contrast, Borzage's adaptation told Hemingway's deeply personal story from a completely opposite perspective that stressed the importance of religious faith, sexual chastity, marriage as an institution, and strict adherence to military discipline. It would be overly simplistic to argue that Hemingway's original text was sanitized in adaptation strictly because it was produced during the Hays Code era. Instead, a more nuanced reading of the adaptation reveals that the film's oddly inconsistent artistic vision results from a split between an original author who advocated social change and a director and cast who sought to uphold traditional, middle-class, conservative values.

The sanitation of *A Farewell to Arms* for the screen most likely began with the film's director, Frank Borzage. Borzage, raised in Utah as part of a conservative Roman Catholic family, retained a sense of religious reverence throughout his film career. The most obvious thematic deviations that Borzage makes from Hemingway's novel *A Farewell to Arms* center around Borzage's seeming insistence to reassert the importance of the Church amidst the chaos of World War I. Perhaps the best example of this circumstance is the scene in which Catherine Barkley is "married" to Frederick Henry by a lingering priest, who murmurs the marriage service over the couple as they embrace in Henry's hospital room. Ironically, this scene is directly opposed to the corresponding scene in Hemingway's original novel.

In the novel, Frederick and Catherine have already begun a sexual affair when he starts worrying that she might become pregnant. When Frederick expresses this concern to Catherine, and asks her to marry him, she replies, "What good would it do to marry now? We're really married. I couldn't be any more married" (*Farewell* 115). As Frederick continues to press the issue, out of concern for her reputation and the possible future of their child, Catherine explains her reasoning further: "There's no way to be married except by church or state. We are married privately. You see, darling, it would mean everything to me if I had any religion. But I haven't any religion.... You're my religion. You're all I've got" (*Farewell* 115–116). From Catherine's responses to Frederick's worried inquiries, it is easy to deduce that Hemingway most likely intended Catherine's love for Frederick to culminate not in a traditional Christian marriage ceremony, but instead as an informal, non-religious, marriage of souls. This sense of true emotion transcending the bounds of religious convention to create meaning in romantic relationships is the central sociocultural theme of Hemingway's original novel. However, this progressive viewpoint is completely eliminated in Borzage's adaptation. Instead, Borzage substitutes his trademark brand of cinematic romance, albeit within the confines of mainstream Christian morality, in place of Hemingway's modern interpretation of love.

Borzage's Christianized revision of *A Farewell to Arms* is reinforced by Helen Hayes's performance as Catherine Barkley. Hayes, also a devout Catholic and a Republican, would have been a natural choice for Borzage simply for her conservative reputation. However, Hayes's slight five foot frame and large, innocent, dark eyes made her physically a perfect fit for a typical Borzage leading lady. Critics have noted that Borzage tended to cast leading actresses who closely resembled his first wife, actress Rena Rogers. Although Borzage doted on Rena, she did not express similar emotion toward her husband, claiming to her sister-in-law, "I respect him, but I don't love him" ("Flesh and Desire"). After enduring twenty-four years of marriage in which his wife aborted their child without his consent and continually engaged in extramarital affairs with both sexes, Borzage finally divorced Rena, but spent the rest of his career:

> Funnel[ing] his gentle romantic feelings into his films. His men, many of whom look like him, are confident and pretty, but always impaired in some way, fake-tough or childlike. His women are small and will o' the wisp but emotionally resilient, believing unreservedly in the power of two people against the world. The Borzage woman is an idealization of what he wanted his first wife to be. Rena let him down, so he made alternate Rena's in ... big-eyed waifs with limitless reserves of toughness. Borzage never got over the charge of this contrast, and he never got over Rena ["Flesh and Desire"].

Read in comparison to the true story that inspired Hemingway's novel, Borzage's revisionist adaptation of *A Farewell to Arms* can be interpreted as a parallel to the Hemingway ouroboros. The love story in Hemingway's original novel is based on the author's unrequited love for Agnes von Kurowsky, the English Red Cross nurse who cared for his war wounds in Milan. Whether their affair was ever consummated remains a point of contention, but Kurowsky's letter to Hemingway on March 7, 1919, announcing her marriage to another man, depicts her view of their relationship as very similar to that of a typical Borzage romance. Agnes writes:

> Now, after a couple of months away from you, I know that I am still very fond of you, but it is more as a mother than as a sweetheart. It's all right to say I'm a Kid, but I'm not, and I'm getting less and less so every day. So, Kid (still Kid to me, and always will be) can you forgive me someday for unwittingly deceiving you? You know I'm not really bad, and I don't mean to do wrong, and now I realize it was my fault in the beginning that you cared for me, and regret it from the bottom of my heart. But, I am now and always will be too old, and that's the truth, and I can't get away from the fact that you're just a boy—a kid. I somehow feel that someday I'll have reason to be proud of you, but dear boy, I can't wait for that day, and it is wrong to hurry a career [qtd. in Villard and Nagel 163].

The similarities between Kurowsky's letter and the typical "Borzage woman" character type are striking. Both Kurowsky and Borzage's idealized Rena, reimagined in *A Farewell to Arms* as Catherine Barkley, are strong, independent women who become involved with men who return their love with dependent, childlike devotion hidden behind masks of bravado. However, the ouroboros breaks circle at the point of marriage as the goal of romance. For Borzage, who was married in real life to the object of his idolatry, the logical choice was to incorporate ceremonial marriage and its attendant Christian ideology into the story of Frederic and Catherine's romance. In contrast, Hemingway, whose love for Kurowsky was defeated by her marriage to another man, did not see marriage or Christian ceremony as necessary validations of the relationship between his autobiographical characters. For Hemingway, love's existence, once professed, was self-validating and assumed the place of religion.

Hemingway's description of the sexual relationship between Frederic and Catherine, as well as the theme of sexuality in general, are also downplayed in the Borzage film. For example, although Hemingway's original novel contains numerous references to the soldiers frequenting prostitutes and Rinaldi's fear that he had contracted syphilis, these references are wholly omitted from Borzage's film. Also, the trysts that Frederic and Catherine share both in his hospital bed and in Switzerland in Hemingway's novel are missing from Borzage's film. The absence of these references to sexuality is due, at least in part, to Hays Code restrictions of the era. However, they may also be the result of the personal preferences of Helen Hayes, who was known for choosing roles that showcased a wholesome, unworldly image both on screen and off (Pace). In all likelihood, Hayes's association with *A Farewell to Arms* encouraged Borzage, already a conservative director in many ways, to channel Hayes's demure personality through Catherine's, diffusing sexual tension present in the novel.

Additionally, Hemingway's references to possible acts of government and military subversion after the Italian army's demoralizing defeat and retreat in the novel are almost wholly missing in the film adaptation. Adolphe Menjou and Gary Cooper were both widely known in Hollywood, both before and after *A Farewell to Arms*, for their conservative stances on what material was suitable for motion pictures. In the years following the film, both men went on to testify for the House Un-American Activities Committee, and to become founding members of the Motion Picture Alliance for American Ideals, which claimed in its "Statement of Principles":

> In our special field of motion pictures, we resent the growing impression that this industry is made of, and dominated by, Communists, radicals, and crackpots. We believe that we represent the vast majority of the people who serve this great medium of expression. But unfortunately it has been an unorganized majority. This has been almost inevitable. The very love of freedom, of the rights of the individual, make this great majority reluctant to organize [Society of Independent Motion Picture Producers].

Once one considers that Cooper and Menjou were both moral conservatives and staunch pro-military supporters, many of the differences in theme and tone between Borzage's film version and Hemingway's original novel begin to make sense, even as they detract from efforts at a consistent artistic vision in the adaptation.

One thematic nuance in Hemingway's original that is lost in the film adaptation is that the two characters' distrust of political and military action also seems to be linked psychologically to sexual overindulgence and venereal disease. One might read this odd juxtaposition of concepts as Hemingway's exploration into what the author perceived as a warped sense of values that led to World War I. In the Italy of Hemingway's novel, the purest masculine motivation for action, risking one's life in war on the nation's behalf, is perverted by incompetent and uncaring military leadership. Also, Hemingway's original seems to suggest that the purest masculine motivation for sexuality, the true love of one man for one woman, is perverted by war, which forces couples into rushed, random encounters borne of an immediate need to gratify sexual appetites, instead of entering long-term relationships grounded in strong emotional bonds.

Based on this premise, Hemingway's connection between diseases of state and sexuality may be read similarly to William Shakespeare's play *Hamlet*. In *Hamlet*, the state of Denmark is made "rotten" because of Claudius's murder of his brother, King Hamlet, based upon the dual sinister motivations of political usurpation and sexual conquest of his sister-in-law, Queen Gertrude (1.4.90). In comparison, Hemingway's overarching political and psychological theme in *A Farewell to Arms* seems to be that if the Italian state is metaphorically sick with the disease of unjustifiable war and governmental corruption, then individual sexual relationships between men and women subjected to that war will manifest actual symptoms of venereal illness that testify to the rottenness of the society in which they live. In short, both *Hamlet* and *A Farewell to Arms* demonstrate that unjust war corrupts not only the state as a whole, but also the physical bodies and romantic relationships of men and women forced to take part in that war.

This theme is missing from Borzage's adaptation. No mention is made in the film of Rinaldi's syphilis, or the disillusionment he feels toward the war because of it. Early in both the film and the novel, Rinaldi displays a playful, carefree attitude toward sexuality. During this time, Rinaldi frequently teases the priest about women he will never have and engages in playful banter with Henry about his relationship with Catherine, asking him, "Is she good to you?" multiple times, hopefully to invite juicy discussions of their sex life (*Farewell* 169). Henry seems to take Rinaldi's jaunty nature in stride, saying, "He had spent two years teasing me and I had always liked it. We understood each other very well" (*Farewell* 169). Yet after Rinaldi contracts syphilis, he loses his sense of humor about both sexuality and the war. Complaining that the Italian military hospital is trying to force him to take a leave of absence because he has syphilis, Rinaldi says to the priest and Henry:

> To hell with you and the whole damn business.... They try to get rid of me. Every night they try to get rid of me. I fight them off. What if I have it. Everybody has it. The whole world's got it.... You'll never get it. Baby will get it. It's an industrial accident. It's a simple industrial accident [*Farewell* 175].

In this passage, Rinaldi's paranoia about his disease is intertwined with his growing sense of disillusionment with Italy's role in World War I. As an army surgeon, Rinaldi is engaged in the industry of war. In turn, Rinaldi seems to view his reliance on prostitutes for sexual gratification as one of the pitfalls of his job. Therefore when Rinaldi says "to hell" with the "business" of war, and characterizes his syphilis as an "accident" of the industry, in reality he is questioning the value of war in general as a cold enterprise that creates too many incidental casualties. Although such a viewpoint would garner a great deal of sympathy with 21st-century audiences, who are accustomed to seeing the post–Vietnam entertainment industry constantly question governmental motivations for war, it would have been unacceptable in 1932, under the Hays Code, when Borzage produced the adaptation. Also, it is highly unlikely that Adolphe Menjou, an actor widely known for his conservative political and moral stances, would have played Rinaldi's role with the level of governmental contempt that Hemingway intended. As a result, the complex Rinaldi of

Hemingway's original is reduced to a light romantic foil for Henry, stripped of all possibility for political or social commentary.

Further, Hemingway's most meaningful recurring natural symbol from the novel, rain, is presented in such a distorted manner in Borzage's adaptation that it actually reverses its original meaning. As Gene Phillips has noted in his study of the adaptation:

> Hemingway was always depressed by rain and frequently complained about it in his letters home from the front. In the novel, he raised his natural dislike for rain to the symbolic level by making the deathly dark, relentless downpours that fall in several scenes, such as during the Caporetto retreat and Catherine's death struggle, signify the shadow of mortality that hovers over every human relationship [21–22].

In the novel, Catherine expresses her fear of rain, saying to Henry, "I'm afraid of the rain because sometimes I see me dead in it.... And sometimes, I see you dead in it" (*Farewell* 126). Although this statement is repeated verbatim in the adaptation, it loses its potential for symbolic significance twice in the latter part of the film, when the rain symbolism is misused or omitted.

First, although the retreat from Caporetto is depicted as occurring in the rain as in the novel, the potential is lost for rain to be seen as the natural environment's symbolic outcry against the horrendous treatment of soldiers and civilians by an army that has given up basic human decency along with its hope of winning. Further, by reducing the retreat to a soggy montage of troops slogging along in the rain, and attempting to overjustify Henry's choice to defect from the Italian army, Borzage's incorporation of Hemingway's rain symbolism is rendered almost meaningless in the film. Last, Borzage's choice to omit rain altogether from the closing image of the film completely alters Hemingway's original intent that Catherine's death should be read as a psychological defeat for Henry, who "[leaves] the hospital and [walks] back to the hotel in the rain" at the end of the novel (*Farewell* 332). Instead, Borzage ends his adaptation with an overdramatized scene of Henry holding Catherine's limp body in his arms while he repeats the word "peace" over and over, against a montage of Armistice notices, ringing bells, and doves wafting their way into the sky to suggest the flight of Catherine's spirit and a more hopeful outcome for Henry's life after the war. By omitting the rain symbolism from Hemingway's novel at the end of the film, Borzage completely dismisses the author's intended meaning behind Catherine's death: that even off the battlefield, war often causes senseless casualties that should force people to question whether armed conflict is worth the human cost.

Borzage's film ends as innocuously as possible, "by refashioning Hemingway's love story along the lines of popular screen romance" (Phillips 23).

Critics have noted that Borzage's adaptation "was tailored to avoid offending any segment of the mass audience" and that Borzage "felt that one of his duties as a director was to make his pictures financially successful, which is another way of saying he must please his audience" (Phillips 23). Although Borzage's adaptation succeeds in its short-term goal of catering to Hays Code–era sensibilities, becoming the highest earner of the year, even winning Oscars for cinematography and sound recording, it fails to hold up for today's audiences, who are more accustomed to Hemingway's original themes of questioning government's absolute power to conduct war and the necessity of social institutions such as marriage. As a result, even though Borzage's heavily revisionist adaptation attempts to incorporate the director's preferences with those of the original author and cast, his version of *A Farewell to Arms* fails to screen well in today's more skeptical social climate.

For Whom the Bell Tolls (1943)

After Frank Borzage's adaptation of *A Farewell to Arms* (1932), eleven years passed before another Hemingway work was made into a film. By 1943, Hemingway's level of celebrity influence had risen considerably, allowing him to use his notoriety to negotiate what was, at the time, a deal for the highest price ever paid by a motion picture company for a novel: $150,000 (Laurence 14). Reading the novel, it is impossible not to suppose that Hemingway was writing it with an eye toward film adaptation, especially since he sold the film rights to Paramount only three days after the novel was published (Phillips 41). Evidence of Hemingway's growing awareness of the allure of the movies crept into the subconscious of Robert Jordan, the author's semi-autobiographical alter ego in *For Whom the Bell Tolls*. As Jordan lies looking at his lover, Maria, he thinks that she is like "someone you have seen in the cinema who comes to your bed at night and is so kind and lovely. He'd slept with them all that way when he was asleep in bed. He could remember Garbo still, and Harlow. Yes, Harlow many times" (*Bell* 137). From this statement, by 1943, Hemingway was at least infatuated with the movies, if not in love with them.

Although the impossible love between Jordan and Maria is an important theme, Hemingway's chief motivation in writing the novel was the sense of disillusionment that the world faced as another world war seemed imminent. As Gene Phillips explains:

> By the time he began writing at the end of 1938, the Loyalist cause was clearly lost, and he had become progressively disillusioned with what he termed "the carnival of treachery and rottenness on both sides." That disillusionment would fall

like a shadow across the pages of his novel; but the book would also be a salute to the indomitability of the human spirit [37].

This pervading sense of post-war disillusionment is very similar to the one that fueled the development of the film noir genre. Most likely, Sam Wood, the director of the film adaptation of *Bell*, decided to use film noir staging in order to convey Hemingway's theme to audiences.

However, addition of film noir styling was not the only Hollywood technique incorporated into Wood's adaptation of *Bell*. Screenwriter Dudley Nichols, who penned the classic Western *Stagecoach* (1939), also used many characterizations common to the Western genre in his adaptation. Also, elements of 1940s "women's film" techniques can be seen in the portrayals of Pilar, the film's female guerrilla leader, and Maria, the wounded, but strong, love interest. All in all, the incorporation of these genre techniques, coupled with a strong sense of collaboration among the adaptation's original author, film director, screenwriter, and stars, serve to create one of the most cohesive cinematic works, which was well received by audiences.

The sense of collaboration begins with Sam Wood's choice as director to use the original epigraph from Hemingway's novel as the first shot in his film adaptation. The lines "No man is an island, entire of itself, every man is a piece of the Continent, a part of the main.... And therefore never send to know for whom the bell tolls, it tolls for thee" are some of John Donne's most famous, from his *Meditation XVII* (*Bell*). Hemingway found Donne's poem in *The Oxford Book of English Prose*, when he was looking for "a little parable about the interdependence of human beings ... the passage pointed up the theme of tragic loss and human solidarity with which he had been developing the story of Robert Jordan" (Baker 348–49). The epigraph serves as a touchstone for understanding both Hemingway's original novel and its film adaptation. As Phillips states, "Human loss anywhere harms mankind everywhere" (39).

Hemingway found inspiration to flesh out his characters among individuals whom he had met in real life. According to biographer Carlos Baker, Hemingway blended a nurse he had met in Mataro with his fair-haired then-wife Martha Gellhorn (348). Further, Robert Jordan's character was based in part on Robert Merriman, a California-native economics professor who served in the 15th International Brigade, but drew many character traits and personal details about his family from Hemingway's own life (Baker 348). Possibly because he incorporated his own life so heavily into the creation of his characters, Hemingway was obsessed with making the details of *Bell*'s film adaptation as realistic as possible. To support accurate articulation of his original artistic vision, Hemingway lobbied heavily for the casting of Ingrid Bergman as Maria and Gary Cooper as Jordan. Both Bergman and Cooper were close personal friends whom Hemingway felt he could trust to incorporate their own lifestyles into the characters (Laurence 224–225). However, Hemingway's quest for realism in the production was not without limits.

Hemingway realized that the action sequences in the film would be ramped up, saying to friends, "They'll have to do it Hollywood style, you'll see, the scriptwriters will blow the train right off, instead of opening quietly in the forest as I wrote it" (Laurence 119). Sure enough, Sam Wood's adaptation of *Bell* begins and ends with explosion sequences involving trains. Still, even though this Hollywood convention was most likely born of the necessity to attract maximum attention from general audiences, Wood's choice is artistically sound when viewed according to the principles of creating cohesive cinema. Hemingway's original novel begins and ends with bookended scenes of Robert Jordan lying "flat on the pine-needled floor of the forest," literally grounded in the same physical and psychological terrain as his comrades, in order to show the interconnectedness of Jordan's human sacrifice (*Bell* 1). By substituting endcapped explosion sequences, both set off by Jordan and a comrade, in place of Hemingway's quieter opening and closing, Sam Wood serves the audience's need for sensationalism while simultaneously preserving Hemingway's symmetry of form. The overall effect of this collaborative effort creates a cohesive artistic vision of human interconnection through tragedy.

Although the structural integrity of Hemingway's original novel was relatively easy for the production team to preserve, his politics proved much more difficult to bring to the screen. On a personal level, Hemingway was able to see the corruption on both sides of the Spanish Civil War; however, his experience as a journalist enabled Hemingway "to assess a political situation dispassionately, even while he was in the middle of it" (Phillips 38). As a result, Hemingway was able to depict both the code hero of the work, the older guerrilla fighter Anselmo, and his apprentice, the American outsider Robert Jordan, with equal amounts of respect for their different political viewpoints. Their sense of camaraderie borne of a feeling of obligation to perform penance for the acts of war they committed captured the spirit, if not the dogma, of Hays Code–era cinema, and most likely helped some of the film's more controversial scenes pass the censors.

However, the sensitivity of filming a book, at the height of World War II, about Spain, fascism, and communism caused a great deal of concern among the members of the production team. As Phillips claims, Sam Wood and the producers at Paramount worried about "having the film boycotted by the Spanish government or by Spanish groups in the United States—just as the same studio's officials had worried about offending Italians with the 1932 version of *A Farewell to Arms*" (43). Additionally, in 1943 director Sam Wood made himself infamous among the Hollywood community for testifying before the House Un-American Activities Committee. The result of Sam Wood's ultra-conservative politics combined with Hemingway's more liberal view of portraying all sides resulted in a compromise that can be seen during one of Jordan's monologues in the final film version, which was not part of Hemingway's original novel. In the monologue, "Jordan explains that he is in Spain because the Nazis and Fascists are testing their war machinery against democracy in order to get the jump on England, France, and America before they are ready to defend themselves" (Laurence 161). This statement helps to justify Jordan's involvement in the Spanish Civil War as an American, when to a Hays Code-era audience, he should not naturally have any political preference for either the Loyalist cause or for Franco's, because both were equally un-democratic and un–American. Interestingly, Hemingway, who found fault with many of the historically inaccurate details of the film adaptation, said relatively little about this alteration of the novel's original neutral political stance. In all likelihood, Hemingway had learned by 1943, after past confrontations with film censors, that such a compromise was acceptable as long as other aspects remained intact.

The addition of film noir elements to the film adaptation of Hemingway's novel may have served as another of Sam Wood's compromises, in an effort to preserve the psychological sense of distrust and disillusionment from the original in a manner that would be acceptable to censors. The screenplay was penned by Dudley Nichols, a Hollywood veteran who was experienced in writing *films noir* both before and after *For Whom the Bell Tolls*. Nichols's most notable film noir was *Scarlet Street* (1945), a classic of the genre featuring Joan Bennett as the prostitute Kitty March. By definition, a film noir is "decidedly pessimistic" in tone, and its action commonly takes place in "dark streets and dimly lit apartments of big cities" (Beaver 97). This sense of darkness is generally understood as reflective of the pervasive mood of paranoia and distrust in America and Europe during the World War II era. The film adaptation of Hemingway's novel certainly reflects stylistic influences of film noir, from the heavily shadowed meeting scene between General Golz and Jordan, during which Jordan receives his order to blow up the bridge, to Jordan's costuming throughout the film, which relies heavily on fedoras and trench coats until he reaches the guerrilla camp. Also, almost all of the scenes of the guerrilla camp that take place in their cave hideout are dimly lit in the classic film noir style, most likely to convey the mood of growing disillusionment among the rebels in Pablo's band as their leader falls further into alcoholism and insanity. The film noir style was also a sound stylistic choice to satisfy Hemingway's demand for realism. As Paul Schrader explains, during and after World War II, "the public's desire for a more honest and harsh view of America would not be satisfied by the same studio streets ... the realistic trend succeeded in breaking film noir away from the domain of high-class melodrama, placing it where it more properly belonged, in the streets with everyday people" (583). This stylistic approach was perfect for adapting a novel about the gritty realities of life as part of a guerrilla warfare group, since to film such a story as a classic Hollywood romance-at-war tale would have proven almost laughable. Last, the film noir genre's "almost Freudian attachment to water," which seems to "increase in direct proportion to the drama," is a perfect way to heighten the dramatic tension in the guerrilla camp, as the fighters wait for the treacherous Pablo to return in the snow, where his tracks will most certainly give away their secret location. In short, the addition of film noir genre elements by Nichols and Wood to Hemingway's original were a wise choice that made the novel translate more easily to film.

Also present in the film adaptation of *For Whom the Bell Tolls* are significant doses of 1940s pro-feminist women's film. This stylistic addition was a natural fit for the adaptation, considering that Hemingway's original novel contains characters, Pilar and Maria, who may be read to represent the two women's film archetypes: the superwoman and the superfemale. Molly Haskell defines a "superwoman" as someone with "a high degree of intelligence or imagination ... who adopts male characteristics in order to enjoy male prerogatives or merely to survive" (505). In contrast, the "superfemale" is "a woman who—while exceedingly feminine and flirtatious, is too ambitious and intelligent for the docile role society has decreed she play," so as a result she exerts her creative energies in efforts to control those around her (Haskell 505). Pilar, portrayed in the film by the excellent Greek classical actress Katina Paxinou, may be classified as a "superwoman," in both the novel and the film, because she has taken over her common-law husband Pablo's role as the leader of the guerrilla band, after the atrocities of war cause his courage to fail him. Paxinou, who won the Academy Award for Best Supporting Actress in the role, contributes her biographical history of being a third-generation descendant of Greek guerrilla fighters to create a sense of strong, yet wounded, dignity that is perfectly suited to her role as Pilar (Wood, "Additional Materials"). In her first line of the film, Pilar enters asserting her authority among the men she leads, yelling at Rafael. "You lazy unspeakable son of an unmentionable Gypsy" (Wood). Pilar's opening line is the only one of many lines in the film adaptation that retains Hemingway's original, creative way of cursing. Hemingway's technique not only bypasses censorship restrictions, but also shows that Pilar has adapted men's ways in order to function as their leader. Sadly, however, Pilar must assert her authority as a female in charge of men by denouncing her own heritage, because as audiences learn moments after her admonishment of Rafael, Pilar is also a Gypsy. Perhaps out of this dual sense of being a woman and also a member of a repressed social class, Pilar learns that she is doubly oppressed and must over-assert her opinions to be heard.

Still, Pilar seems to have enjoyed a colorful past as the girlfriend of many handsome bullfighters, despite her claim that she "was born ugly" (Wood). In a lengthy and touching scene, Pilar asks the young and attractive Maria, "Do you know how it feels to be ugly all your life, but to feel in here [she touches her heart] that you are beautiful?" (Wood). Although she quickly recovers by taking the man's route of bragging about her sexual conquests with bullfighters in her youth, even this recuperative bravado is tinged with sadness, as Pilar tells Maria of her two greatest fears, of "being old and ugly" and "to see the panic in the face of a boy when I say I might kiss him" (Wood). This scene, wonderfully acted by Paxinou, demonstrates the paradox of being a superwoman in 1940's women's cinema. Although a woman may be physically strong enough to operate machine guns and emotionally strong enough to command her husband's band of guerrilla fighters, she is still hampered by the chief self esteem-weakening fear that women of any age are susceptible to: the fact that much of her power over men comes from sexual energy, and, once that is lost, she will be rendered helpless in situations where she used to be powerful.

In contrast, Ingrid Bergman's Maria is a "superfemale" because she chooses to control her vulnerable situation as the rescued ward of a band of rebel fighters by withholding her sexuality until she finds a man, Robert Jordan, whom she deems worthy to be her protector. As Maria quickly tells Jordan upon first meeting him, "I am the woman of no one" (Wood). Yet, even though Maria presents herself as very strong, viewers learn over the course of the film and novel that she has been the victim of a brutal gang rape by Fascist troops who have murdered her mother and father in front of her. Although she tells the story bravely, claiming that she would have yelled, "Long live the Republic!" just as her father had done before he was shot, Maria is never given the chance to assert her political position. Instead, Maria is treated only as a sexual object. After she is raped by the soldiers, Maria feels that she will never be respected by most men for her intelligence, only exploited for her beauty. As a result, she craftily uses her beauty to gain the trust and admiration of Jordan, after she learns that he is an educated man who is likely to fall in love with her not only for her body, but for her mind. The innocent, clean-scrubbed beauty that Bergman brings to the role of Maria, when coupled with the actress's customary steel will, helps to express on film the fact that the Maria of Hemingway's novel is much more than she appears to be.

The overall effect achieved by Bergman and Paxinou's excellent portrayals of their characters is that audiences are able to see a more feminist side of Hemingway's original tale than they may have been able to grasp in the novel. Also, the women's film stylings present in the adaptation may be due in part to director Sam Wood, who had experience in directing women's films before and after *For Whom the Bell Tolls*, including movies such as *Kitty Foyle* (1940), starring Ginger Rogers, and *The Devil and Miss Jones* (1941) with Jean Arthur. Perhaps one of the most easily discernable visual manifestations that a film is feminist oriented is the presence of the "female gaze" as described by Eva-Marie Jacobssen in her response to Laura Mulvey's well-publicized writing on the "male gaze." Jacobssen, like most critics, stops short of Bracha Ettinger's assertion that women can return or even initiate a gaze toward a male object of interest. However, her statement that Hollywood movies are often "a conscious and unconscious effort to preserve the patriarchal order" and that "to preserve the male gaze is to preserve a patriarchal order of society" is useful here to examine how differently the film version of *For Whom the Bell Tolls* presents the "female gaze."

Pilar frequently gazes disparagingly at Pablo and the other men from higher positions that suggest her authority. Yet, when she gazes at the young bullfighter-turned-soldier Joaquin, who rejects her sexual innuendos, Wood places Pilar in a lower position, forcing her to gaze up at the male object of her affections, suggesting a lack of control. Further, in almost every scene in which Maria and Jordan express their emotions for one another, from the infamous sleeping bag scene to Jordan's final good-bye, the camera lingers on Bergman's reaction from a higher position, suggesting that her character, Maria, maintains a sense of control over her emotions and the relationship. These staging choices indicate a wide spectrum of emotions that may be evoked from well-written female characters, which demonstrate that the female gaze is just as powerful and complex as the male gaze.

Further, Wood's adaptation causes those familiar with the Hemingway canon to recall other strong female characters present in his fiction that helped shape the idea of what the 20th-century New Woman could be. Pilar's character might be viewed as a much older and more mature version of Brett Ashley from Hemingway's first novel, *The Sun Also Rises*. Both women had an exciting youth, pursuing and being pursued by many lovers, including bullfighters, who represented an ultimate sense of masculinity in the Hemingway oeuvre. By the time Hemingway reached his early forties, his sympathies for the plight of women seemed to become more mature, allowing his writing to appreciate Pilar not only for the physical magnetism retained from her youth, but also for the emotional strength and resilience that she earned through experience in war and with men. Also, Maria might be viewed as character similar to Liz from Hemingway's early short story "Up in Michigan," albeit one produced by a much more mature writer who has a clearer understanding of and sympathy for a young woman who has been the victim of rape. Through giving both Pilar and Maria more time on his pages, compared with earlier female characters, to speak their minds and express their feelings about their respective lives, Hemingway demonstrated that his concern for women and their status in society actually increased in intensity and depth of perception as his writing matured. Sam Wood's choice to include lengthy sequences in the film of Pilar recounting the violent acts of war that she engaged in and of Maria relating the circumstances of her rape to Robert Jordan serve to empower both women by giving them a substantial voice that cannot be overlooked by audiences. The final product is a film that does something the best film adaptations should always aspire to do: deepen the audience's total understanding of not only the author's original work, but also the society in which they live.

The Western is the last and most subtle genre whose conventions seem to have influenced Sam Wood's adaptation of *For Whom the Bell Tolls*. As mentioned earlier, Dudley Nichols, the screenwriter of *Bell*, also penned *Stagecoach*, arguably the most definitive Western of the old Hollywood era. Through careful reading of Bell through the lens of genre, viewers can pick out the various Western archetypes and stylistic elements present in *For Whom the Bell Tolls*, all of which are detailed in John Cawelti's seminal text on Westerns, *The Six-Gun Mystique*. Robert Jordan is the "mysterious outsider," who comes onto the scene to restore order. Pilar, as a common-law wife and a woman with an extensive sexual past, represents the "saloon girl." Maria, of course, embodies the opposing good-girl or "schoolmarm" archetype, who is the natural object of the stranger's affections due to her innocence and need for rescue. Anselmo is the wise sidekick, or "professional," whose handicap is age but isn't prevented from assisting Jordan on his quest with his special knowledge of the territory. Pablo is a typically complex Western town villain, one who has some sympathetic tendencies, but who somewhere made a wrong moral turn to the dark side and must be removed by the outsider because he poses a threat to the stability of the community. Plus, the austere setting of rural Spain mimics the desert Southwest, with the Spanish-speaking guerrilla fighters standing in for the Spanish-speaking Mexicans, present in many American Westerns. Last, For *Whom the Bell Tolls* was filmed in California's Sierra Nevada mountains, not in Spain, with a final gunfight scene staged similarly to those of countless American Westerns filmed in that area (Phillips 41). All of these similarities to Western genre films prompted director Jerry Wald to become interested in remaking *For Whom the Bell Tolls* as a Western during the 1970s (Laurence 174).

One has to wonder, based on Wald's intriguing revisionist interest in the novel, what themes might be brought out in a new adaptation of *For Whom the Bell Tolls*? Could the already-present elements of women's film and Western be combined to create two completely new, empowering female archetypes: the superwoman/schoolmarm and the saloon girl/superfemale? Would this give rise to an exciting new genre, the Women's Western? A film produced in this manner of adaptation would certainly give viewers and readers of the Hemingway canon a completely new way to view the author's work, and might prompt interest in the possibility of viewing Hemingway as a feminist author. Again, the possibilities for this novel in future adaptations are endless, but point to the best function that a film adaptation can perform in relation to the original work on which it is based: to reinterpret and revive interest for a new generation.

As it stands, Sam Wood's adaptation of *For Whom the Bell Tolls* remains one of the best visual interpretations of a Hemingway novel. Even Hemingway, who famously derided most film versions of his work, was happy with Gary Cooper and Ingrid Bergman's performances in their roles (Phillips 47). Further, the production team on the film appears to have been so synchronized that director Sam Wood could even intuit Hemingway's original ending. According to Carlos Baker, Hemingway "professed to be reluctant to kill his hero after having lived steadily in his company for seventeen months" (349). As a result, in the original manuscript, Hemingway composed an epilogue for the novel, in which General Golz and Karkov meet together in Madrid, "discussing Jordan's blowing of the bridge and his subsequent disappearance" but not his death or the recovery of his body (Baker 350). Although he had no access to this epilogue, because it was edited out before printing, Dudley Nichols nevertheless wrote an ending to the film that closes in from the injured Jordan to the point in which the audience looks directly down the barrel of his machine gun, including the audience of the tolling of the bell that Hemingway intended for every man to hear in the deaths of others. This ambiguous ending comes just after Jordan's final monologue, the only lengthy one in the film presented in its entirety in full Hemingwayesque clipped style, lifted directly from the last pages of the novel. Jordan's exit line before the shot pulls out to the end of the machine gun barrel, "She's going home with me," referring, of course, to Maria, captures perfectly the intertwined desperation and disillusionment of Hemingway's original character (Wood).

By the end of the film's production, Hemingway had learned his lesson about being a fiction writer in Hollywood. Filmmaking is a collaborative effort. If he wanted to see the fullest extent possible of his original vision, Hemingway would have to maintain an active presence in the filmmaking process, insisting on cast members and fighting for historical accuracy, even after his film rights were sold. For the remainder of his life, Hemingway continued to use his celebrity clout to have his say in the production of films based on his works, and the quality of those films improved dramatically because of his influence. Despite the standard Hollywood treatment given to it, Sam Wood's adaptation of *For Whom the Bell Tolls* succeeds in retaining the structural and thematic integrity of the original, creating a cohesive work of cinema that pulls its entire production team, for the first time, inside the circle of the Hemingway ouroboros.

To Have and Have Not (1944)

Although Ernest Hemingway considered *To Have and Have Not* to be "his worst novel" because "he had written it for money," the book has been adapted for film three times (Phillips 50). This situation raises two inevitable questions. First, what keeps bringing filmmakers back to the work? And second, why has each adaptation been so well received by audiences?

The novel certainly did not start out as a top-rate cinematic property. Hemingway sold the initial film rights to Howard Hughes in 1941, for the low price of $10,000 (Laurence 85). Unable to put together a production team, producer Hughes then sold the rights several years later to Jack Warner of Warner Bros. for $92,000 (Phillips 51). The reason for the increase in price was simple. During the interim, Paramount's adaptation of Hemingway's *For Whom the Bell Tolls* had been a runaway success, both with audiences and at the Academy Awards. Also, Hemingway's increased media presence during World War II as a journalist and über-masculine lifestyle brand made any project carrying his name a profitable commodity. Given the increase in Hemingway's value as a celebrity, no one in Hollywood was surprised when director Howard Hawks was able to generate a tenfold return on Warner's investment with his adaptation of *To Have and Have Not*, especially with a big-name star like Humphrey Bogart in the leading role of Harry Morgan, and his much younger girlfriend, Lauren Bacall, playing Harry's love interest, Marie. The only person unhappy with the adaptation's success was Hemingway himself, who, after Hawks told him what he made off the picture, "did not speak to me for three months" (Phillips 51).

Although Hemingway did not consider the novel to be among his best, *To Have and Have Not* still contains four of the author's most prevalent themes: male individualism, the value of comradeship, reciprocal relationships between the sexes, and psychological alienation. Hawks's adaptation of the novel is certainly revisionist; however, most of his points of revision are based in sound historical, socio-cultural, political, and psychological manners of adaptation relevant to the time period of the film, as well as the tastes of audiences and censorship concerns of studio executives at Warner Bros. Further, the changes to the text made by screenwriters Jules Furthman and William Faulkner added both visual symbolism and stylistic consistency that were missing from the original. Last, the inclusion of tough-guy star Humphrey Bogart and Hawksian heroine Lauren Bacall expanded awareness and comprehension of Hemingway's standard code hero and New Woman archetypes and caused audiences to blend the public persona of Hemingway the author with his semi-autobiographical characters, making the Hemingway cinematic ouroboros readily apparent.

Frank Laurence has written extensively on how Warner Bros.' trademark "gangster film" genre style was a perfect fit to articulate visually the "tough guy" persona that Hemingway and his characters had acquired by 1944 (82). Typical characteristics of gangster film heroes include "the desire for recognition and success, a tough, crude façade, hints of gentleness and sensitivity beneath the toughness, and an intimation that the gangsters are victims of circumstance" (Beaver 112). Certainly, Hemingway's original Harry Morgan bears all of these qualities. Morgan is highly motivated to succeed in his smuggling business so he can provide for his wife and three daughters. Yet, he shows his sensitive side through intimacy with his wife, Marie, and his kindness to Eddy, his perpetually drunken friend. Last, Harry clearly articulates in the novel that his turn to a life of crime is because he is one of the "have not's" of society, when he says, directly to the reader in first person, "I don't want to fool with it, but what choice have I got ... I didn't ask for any of this and if you've got to do it, you've got to do it" (*Have Not* 105).

In terms of film history, the production of *To Have and Have Not* at Warner Bros. under the direction of Howard Hawks was a great combination. Warner Bros. had built a studio chiefly on gritty crime dramas, including Hawks's *Scarface* (1932), a classic of the genre. In all likelihood, Hemingway had seen at least a few of these pictures, since their impact on the original novel seems apparent, given the close association of Harry Morgan with the gangster archetype. Also, one might speculate that Hemingway, with his avid interest in the local history of Cuba, considered his rumrunner, Harry Morgan, a latter-day analog of the 17th-century English pirate Harry Morgan, one of the most infamous privateers ever to have sailed the Caribbean. Given Hemingway's exploits during World War II as captain of his own boat, *Pilar*, patrolling the Caribbean for possible Nazi ships while the film of *To Have and Have Not* was in production, audiences received plenty of information to connect the Captain Morgan's of both the pirate era and the popular novel with the seafaring author, creating a perfect storm of publicity.

Additionally, Hemingway and Hawks shared an interest in making drastic changes to the plot and characters in order to make the project as film-friendly as possible. According to Hawks, "We decided that the best way to tell the story was not to show the hero growing old, but to show how he had met the girl and, in short, show everything that happened before the beginning of the novel" (qtd. in Phillips 85). In truth, this agreement is not as far from the scope of the novel as it may seem. During the final pages of Hemingway's novel, Marie copes with Harry's death by remembering how wonderful their relationship was when they first met. Particularly, Marie recalls how Harry made her feel beautiful with her new hair.

> I walked down the Prado to the café where Harry was waiting and I was so excited feeling all funny inside, sort of faint like, and he stood up when he saw me coming and he couldn't take his eyes off me and his voice was thick and funny when he said, "Jesus, Marie, you're beautiful."
> And I said, "You like me blonde?"
> "Don't talk about it," he said. "Let's go to the hotel."
> And I said, "O.K., then. Let's go." I was twenty-six then.
> And that's how he always was with me and that's the way I always was about him. He said he never had anything like me and I know there wasn't any men like him. I know it too damned well and now he's dead [*Have Not* 259–60].

Marie's memories of her courtship with Harry show the couple as a typical Hollywood romance, in which two people have an instant attraction that somehow magically defies all odds and lasts for decades, even after both are no longer young or attractive. For Hawks, as a filmmaker looking to appeal to a wide age demographic of audience members, the choice to set the romantic dimension of the film earlier in the characters' lives was sound. Younger audience members would find it easier to identify with the attractive heroine, played by Lauren Bacall, while older audience members, who were more likely to have read the original novel and known Harry and Marie as a more mature couple, would find the sense of nostalgia for their earlier romantic lives appealing, and would relate to Bogart's character.

Still, one cannot ignore that, in the original novel, Hemingway demonstrates far more sympathy for the emotional life of a middle-aged housewife than does the standard Hollywood movie mogul. Hemingway's novel is filled with passages that capture not only Marie's feelings, but also Harry's lasting affection for his wife, who is clearly past her physical prime, but who nevertheless retains a strong sense of attractiveness for him. Hemingway further demonstrates his sympathy for Marie by causing the novel's unappealing, philandering writer character, Richard Gordon, to sneer at Marie and negatively speculate about her love life, saying:

> Look at that big ox.... What do you suppose a woman like that thinks about? What do you suppose she does in bed? How does her husband feel about her when she gets that size? Who do you suppose he runs around with in this town? Wasn't she an appalling looking woman? Like a battleship. Terrific [*Have Not* 176].

The overall effect of this passage is to hint to the reader that what the "have not's" of society, such as Harry and Marie, actually have are more meaningful emotional bonds that cause a romantic relationship to endure after physical attraction wanes. In contrast, Richard, as a "have" of society, possesses no true sense of love or fidelity for either his wife or his mistress. Unfortunately, this part of Hemingway's social commentary about relationships between the sexes had to be omitted because of the choice to cast a much younger actress for Marie in Hawks's adaptation. As such, its absence remains one of the more significant thematic flaws in the film, and possibly shows that Hemingway, although many have tried to prove otherwise, was much less chauvinistic than the tastes of Hollywood dictated during his lifetime.

Instead of using the novel's middle-aged Marie as the basis for her screen counterpart, director Hawks looked much closer to home to find her visual inspiration. At the time he made *To Have and Have Not*, Hawks was married to Lady Nancy "Slim" Keith, a socialite well known for being the original California Golden Girl. As Keith summarized her life story:

> I had been married to the film director Howard Hawks; I had been married to the great literary agent and impresario Leland Hayward; I was now, thanks to my marriage to Sir Kenneth Keith, bearing a title, the Lady Keith. Along the way, I had discovered Lauren Bacall, and Howard Hawks had used my image to create hers in *To Have and Have Not*. I had made the best-dressed list innumerable times, I had shot with Hemingway, traveled with Capote, and been wooed by Gable [qtd. in Jefferson].

As the model for Marie in the film, Slim's image set the standard for what would come to be called the "Hawksian woman," a character type who frequently appeared in her husband's films, and who bore a striking resemblance to Hemingway's New Woman archetype, set by Brett Ashley in *The Sun Also Rises*, who was in turn inspired by Hemingway's real-life acquaintance, Lady Duff Twysden. In *Sun*, Hemingway described Twysden's fictional alter ego by saying, "Brett was damn good looking. She wore a slipover jersey sweater and a tweed skirt, and her hair was brushed back like a boy's She started all that. She was built with curves like the hull of a racing yacht, and you missed none of that with that wool jersey" (*Sun* 29–30). Like her real-life counterparts, the fictional Lady Brett shared with Lady Twysden and Lady Keith the tendencies to collect rich husbands like jewelry, set fashion trends, and inspire writers and filmmakers. As a result, Lauren Bacall's Marie in Hawks's adaptation of *To Have and Have Not* should be read as an incorporated adaptation of both Hemingway's other New Woman characters and also the live-action love interests of the film's director and original author, representing a complete circle of Hemingway's celebrity author ouroboros.

The next question to answer, after one understands why the Harry and Marie characters were altered in adaptation, is to determine how such incorporation alters Hemingway's original theme from the novel that marriage works best as a reciprocal relationship which provides positive emotional reinforcement for both partners. Many Hemingway scholars, such as Thomas Hemmeter and Kevin Sweeney, disagree with this reading, claiming that "rather than challenging Harry's feelings of isolation, Marie, by her own dependence, actually reinforces Harry's alienation" (66). This reading is erroneous, because it wrongly supposes that Hemingway wrote Marie to be a typical subservient housewife of the Depression era. In actuality, Hemingway shows Marie not as a woman totally dependent on her husband for a sense of identity, but instead as a woman who, although she loves her husband deeply, is able to act independently and on self-preservative instinct. Rather than going to Harry's funeral at the end of the novel, and accepting her socially-acceptable role as a mourning widow, Marie stays home to sort out a new life direction, saying:

> I couldn't go to the funeral. But people don't understand that. They don't know how you feel. Because good men are scarce. They just don't have them. Nobody knows the way you feel because they don't know what it's all about that way.... Nobody's going to tell me that and there ain't nothing now but to take it every day as it comes and just get started doing something right away. That's what I got to do" [*Have Not* 261].

Contrary to Hemmeter and Sweeney's reading of Marie as a drain on Harry's emotional resources, Hemingway's novel depicts a resilient Marie, who is determined to rebuild her life without her soulmate. Read in this way, Hemingway's original Marie is a complex woman, who is strong enough to justify the reader's sympathy while she endures the worst tragedy of her life.

In his film adaptation of the novel, Hawks obviously chooses this more positive reading of Marie's character through the way in which he directs Lauren Bacall in the role. The film contains a lengthy sequence in which Marie and Harry pass a bottle of wine back and forth between their rooms as they exchange witty barbs charged with sexual innuendo. Ultimately, Marie wins the debate by figuring out that Harry is reluctant to become emotionally involved with a woman because he fears emotional vulnerability. Once she gains this admission, and she is sure of her upper hand in the situation, Marie takes the wine bottle back for the final time, saying, "This belongs to me and so do my lips" (Hawks). Only after she uses her intellect to solicit the desired response from Harry does Marie engage him sexually. Finally comfortable that Harry has exposed his emotional vulnerability, Marie at last trusts him enough to allow him to assume the traditionally dominant male role in their relationship. As a signal of her agreement to engage in a reciprocal relationship, Marie utters one of the most famous lines in film history, "You know how to whistle, don't you? You just put your lips together and blow" (Hawks). Harry immediately picks up on Marie's hint that a woman is not to be whistled at like a dog to be summoned, but instead as an awesome presence to be admired and respected. Hawks ends the scene with a shot of Harry whistling in approval at Marie, whom he has found to be his intellectual and emotional equal, in addition to being sexually attractive. This ending articulates Hemingway's original theme of the benefits of reciprocal marriage well, by showing the audience that Marie is Harry's equal by choice, not out of necessity.

Although Hemingway's ideas on marriage were easy to fit into the gangster film genre to produce a film marketable to a World War II–era audience, his politics proved much more problematic. By its title, *To Have and Have Not* is intended as a novel of social commentary about the cultural differences between the affluent classes and the working classes. The struggle between Harry and Johnson, the wealthy businessman who charters Harry's boat for a fishing expedition, is the most obvious example in Hemingway's original novel of this conflict. While on the trip, Johnson hooks a large black marlin, which he loses, along with Harry's expensive fishing rod, after ignoring Harry's directions on the most correct and sportsmanlike way to reel it in. As Gene Phillips states, "Johnson's behavior bears out Hemingway's conviction that when a man cheats at sports as Johnson did in the way he handled the big fish, he is unlikely to live up to his obligations in other areas of his life" (55). Even though Hemingway's theme is morally sound within the context of his canon of code hero behavior, it was not timely for World War II audiences. As Frank Laurence explains, *To Have and Have Not*'s political undertones "showed little promise as movie material since it was too much a proletarian novel of the thirties ... now there was a war going on, and no one was interested in seeing a movie about the class struggle between the 'haves' and the 'have not's,' let alone about a minor revolution in Cuba" (87). As a result, Hawks's production team had to find a more relevant political theme for the times.

Perhaps this was another reason that Hawks relied so heavily on gangster film staging in his adaptation of the novel. Gangster films, with their mentality that society could take anything a man had earned away from him at any time, without just cause, provided a substantially similar outlet for Hemingway's original concern regarding differences between the idle rich and the working class. Describing the enduring appeal of gangster characters in American cinema, Robert Warshow explains:

> Thrown into the crowd without background or advantages ... the gangster is required to make his way, to make his life and impose it on others. Usually, when we come upon him, he has already made his choice or the choice has already been made for him, it doesn't matter which: we are not permitted to ask whether at some point he could have chosen to be something else than what he is [578].

As a man who pilots a charter fishing boat, Harry is in a social situation similar to that of many gangsters in the early scenes of their films. The nature of Harry's work puts him in constant contact with spoiled rich people who are not as skilled as he, and who are constantly dependent on his expertise in order to enjoy as recreation that which Harry relies upon to earn a living. This puts Harry in a natural situation of opposition against men like Johnson, and the expected hostility and resentment result.

Further, Warshow states, "We are always conscious that the whole meaning of his career is a drive for success: the typical gangster film presents a steady upward progress followed by a very precipitate fall. Thus brutality itself becomes at once a means to success and the content of success ... the unlimited possibility of aggression" (579). Warshow's explanation for a film gangster's violent behavior also helps justify the reasons behind Harry's violent outbursts, which are toned down from the novel, but still present in the film. Throughout the novel, Harry frequently claims that the only thing a man like him has to make his way in the world is his *cojones*, meaning that only by violent demonstrations of his physical power can he show his true power against a world of richer men who seek to emasculate him. In short, just like the protagonists of most gangster films, the only way that Harry can prove his worth in the world is though acts of physical aggression intended to intimidate those who are financially superior.

Employment of this underlying gangster film psychology also relates to the historical undercurrent of pirate lore that runs through the novel and its adaptation. As said previously, Hemingway's original Harry Morgan was named after the legendary 17th-century Caribbean pirate Henry Morgan. In many ways, Harry can be viewed not only as a gangster, but also as a latter-day pirate, considering the fact that he operates under his own code of ethics while engaging in rum-running and other illegal activities on the high seas that put him at odds with the government. Like gangsters, movie audiences often sympathize with pirates because of their rebellious lifestyle, which is usually depicted as appealingly risky and glamorous on film. Given that he was prone to prowling the Caribbean on his own heavily armed vessel during World War II, it is not too far of a stretch to suppose that even Hemingway fancied himself one of these dangerous rogues, and subconsciously imitated the lifestyle of a film pirate, Hollywood's gangster of the high seas.

Certainly, Howard Hawks sought to model his adaptation of *To Have and Have Not* in the style of another film that combined these elements of genre. From the beginning, Hawks sought to make his film a vehicle for Humphrey Bogart, who after the release of *Casablanca* (1942) was the biggest star at Warner Bros. According to Laurence, because of Hawks's intention to re-create the earlier film's success, "*To Have and Have Not* seems at least as much an adaptation of *Casablanca* as of the Hemingway novel" (89). In truth, the two films share many similar elements. In addition to Bogart as star, both films share similar elements of romantic intrigue, exotic locales, daring criminals, anti–Nazi paranoia, political subterfuge, a lust for money, and female love interests with shady pasts in their plotlines. Today, *Casablanca* could almost be considered a subgenre itself, with its first spinoff as this Hemingway adaptation.

Regardless, Hawks's choice of exotic locale was not solely to clone *Casablanca*. The change of setting for his adaptation, from Hemingway's original Cuba to Martinique, was purely due to fear of political repercussions against Warner Bros., because "Hawks was told the only place in the Caribbean he could locate the story was the island of Martinique, since that was French territory and out of the jurisdiction of the Office of Inter-American Affairs" (Laurence 88). As a result, Hawks, together with screenwriters Furthman and Faulkner, rewrote the story as set in Martinique, with the chief political conflict being between the pro–Nazi Vichy French and the Free French deGaullists. Although the alteration may seem far-fetched at first, it is not too much of a stretch when one considers that, in Casablanca, Rick, Humphrey Bogart's character, occupies a precarious political situation of neutrality between the Vichy and Free French factions that is exactly replicated in the actor's portrayal of Harry Morgan in *To Have and Have Not*. In sum, Hawks's team overcame a potential production obstacle the right way: by incorporating logical elements from a thematically similar film that would resonate with audiences who recognized Bogart from his earlier role.

William Faulkner deserves primary credit for this coup, since he was the one who initially suggested the Vichy plotline (Phillips 52). Considering that he was working against time to complete each day's shooting script only hours before it was put before the cameras, Faulkner's work on the film is very impressive. Even more impressive was the Pulitzer prize winner's willingness to cooperate with the actors in the film, who often chose to improvise over his carefully-crafted lines. As Phillips notes, "Faulkner seems to have enjoyed these give-and-take sessions very much, for he later said that 'the moving picture work which seemed best to me was done by the actors and the writer throwing the script away and inventing the scene in actual rehearsal before the cameras turned'" (53). Humphrey Bogart seems to have equally felt that Faulkner was open to his suggestions on the script, because once, when he was presented with a scene in which he felt that Faulkner had written too much dialogue, he presented the writer and Hawks with the overwritten, six-page scene inquiring, "I'm supposed to say all that?" (qtd. in Phillips 54). Bogart's ability to be open with his director and screenwriter on the film shows through in the quality of emotion that he is able to bring to his role of Harry, creating one of the actor's best dramatic performances.

Perhaps also, Bogart was able to create one of his most genuine screen characters because of the presence of Lauren Bacall as his love interest. The May–December romance of Bogart and Bacall is one of Hollywood's greatest love stories, and the Warner Bros. publicity team took full advantage of this first occasion to show the two stars in love in posters advertising the film. Coincidentally, Hemingway was also engaged in a picturesque romance of his own during the original drafting of *To Have and Have Not*, as well as while Hawks was creating the adaptation. Journalist Martha Gellhorn was twenty-eight when she met the thirty-seven-year-old author, whom she married four years later. Gellhorn was clearly on Hemingway's mind as he wrote the novel, evidenced not only by his dedication of the book to her, but also through repeated references to the appeal of Jewish women (Martha was of ethnic Jewish descent) throughout the text. Based upon Hawks's close working relationship with Hemingway during filming, it is not extraordinary to suppose that the director made the connection between the author and his younger bride with the real-life romance of his leading actors, and incorporated both relationships into his portrayal of Harry and Marie onscreen.

This give-and-take sense of camaraderie amongst the cast and crew of the adaptation, combined with Hemingway's willingness to allow alterations to his original novel in the interests of communicating his major themes more effectively to audiences while remaining within the conventions of censorship and genre relevant to the era make *To Have and Have Not* an effective work of cohesive cinema. Nevertheless, Hollywood would go on to produce two additional remakes of the novel on film, *The Breaking Point* (1950) and *The Gun Runners* (1958). Each of these films would use additional changes to Hemingway's original novel along with further incorporations of new Hemingway lore to create adaptations that depicted the book in completely different ways, but that was each a commercial success in its own right. Perhaps

Hemingway was too quick to judge *To Have and Have Not* an inferior novel. Regardless, today Hawks's adaptation of *To Have and Have Not* represents a prime example of how the ouroboric cycle of literary celebrity can be mined to produce a cinematic classic.

The Killers (1946)

According to his last wife, Mary Welsh, "The only film made from his work of which Ernest entirely approved was *The Killers*" (qtd. in Phillips 73–73). The film, based on his early short story of the same name, appeared first in ephemeral form, and later in Hemingway's 1927 collection, *Men Without Women*. Perhaps at least on some level, Hemingway found the film most pleasing because of the $36,750 that he received for the film rights to the story—setting a record for the highest price ever paid by the film industry for a piece of short fiction (Server 114). On a higher level, Hemingway was likely pleased by the amount of consideration and artistic respect paid to him by the film's producer, Mark Hellinger. According to screenwriter Richard Brooks, "Hellinger worshipped writers ... at the end of the day you'd gather in his office for a drink. He liked nothing more than to sit with a writer and have a drink. Hellinger was a good man" (Server 115). Hellinger's willingness to involve fiction writers heavily in the creative process of adapting their works for film most likely began a solid, cooperative relationship with Hemingway that gained the writer's trust and confidence in the production. Further, Hellinger insisted on casting lesser-known actors in the starring role, as if to suggest that "he figured the star of the picture was Ernest Hemingway, and if there was another star it was going to be himself" (Server 120).

Nevertheless, the film made stars out of its two leads: Burt Lancaster and Ava Gardner. At the time *The Killers* was produced, Lancaster was best known as "part of the Armed Services Forces commission, entertaining the troops through the North Africa and Italian campaigns" (Server 120–21). Lancaster's attachment to military history, coupled with his former athlete's physique left over from his days as a circus gymnast, made the actor a perfect fit for the role of a tough, muscular Hemingway code hero. In contrast, for the role of femme fatale Kitty Collins, Hellinger wanted a woman who could believably coerce "a man to steal, go to prison, and die for her" (Server 120). By all accounts, everyone associated with the film adaptation of *The Killers* agreed that the young Ava Gardner was indeed that kind of woman.

The Killers is quite obviously a fine example of the late film noir genre prevalent in the half-decade following World War II. As Gene Phillips explains:

The dark, shadowy atmosphere of the film ... coupled with the equally somber, cynical vision of life reflected in its tale of betrayal, disillusionment, and death, mark the film as an example of late film noir. This trend in American cinema was in full flower when Siodmak's film was made, and the pessimistic view of life that characterized film noir—an outgrowth of the disillusionment spawned by World War II and its aftermath—is clearly in evidence in *The Killers*. In keeping with the conventions of the genre the film is characterized throughout by an air of grim, unvarnished realism [73].

This style of filmmaking was typical of *Killers* director Robert Siodmak, a Jewish immigrant from Germany who crafted films in the then-typical German style of stark sets and bleak countenance. Siodmak's opinion on film style and shot selection was rarely questioned by his studio executives at Universal, because at the time, Siodmak was "deemed the most talented specialist in suspense films since Hitchcock" (Server 119). A master in this post-noir style of "heavy shadows, controlled lighting, and striking camera angles" inspired by German Expressionism, Siodmak also typically featured both "a non-heroic hero" and "a Medea figure who can draw him by her witchlike powers into evil" (Kaminsky 127). As a result, Siodmak's films were often all about psychology, and a man's inner struggle to come to terms with the consequences of his actions. The story could be set in virtually any historical context, had no political agenda, and usually involved only one social class: the urban underworld. Therefore, any critical discussion of Siodmak's adaptation of *The Killers* should focus primarily on the psychological manner of film adaptation.

Behind the scenes, uncredited screenwriter John Huston also greatly influenced the adaptation of *The Killers*. Huston, director of the film noir classic *The Maltese Falcon*, was an ex-boxer, newsman, and war veteran who was largely considered in Hollywood circles at the time to be a "son of Hemingway" type (Server 115). Huston's pictures, such as the Hellinger-produced gangster film *High Sierra*, often depicted men dealing with moral crises. Together with Anthony Veiller, another army veteran turned screenwriter, Huston carefully crafted Hemingway's original story around a central thematic question: "What could bring a man so low that he would surrender himself to violent death?" (Server 117). This theme screens in Siodmak's adaptation of *The Killers* as a modern, film noir meditation on good and evil, centered around two paradoxes that are best worked out using the Socratic method to untangle Hemingway's meaning from the Hollywood ouroboros of cinematic celebrity culture.

According to Gene Phillips, this fundamental struggle between good and evil is present in all of Hemingway's Nick Adams stories, creating a moral dialectic between Young Nick Adams and Old Nick Adams. The code hero in Hemingway's print version of "The Killers" is Ole "Swede" Andreson, a washed-up boxer patiently awaiting his assassination after turning to a life of crime. From watching the two evil Chicago assassins who seek to murder Andreson, "Nick gradually grows in maturity from adolescence to young manhood, for it is by observing their behavior under stress that he learns how to face the harsher and more perplexing aspects of adult life" (Phillips 67). Hence, the Young Nick Adams can be thought of as a sort of universal innocent, unwise to the evil present in everyday life; whereas the Old Nick Adams represents the sum total of experiences witnessed by the average man on his course toward a jaded acceptance of immorality.

As a result, "Nick is exposed to life as in a Greek tragedy. The small town is not safe. No one is safe from fate and no one can do anything about it except face it with dignity, as Swede does" (Kaminsky 126). In this teacher/student relationship between Andreson and Adams, the Swede is clearly a victim of fate. Siodmak trusts that his audience will see, through the eyes of Nick Adams, how the Swede's guilty conscience erodes his morality and eventually his will to live. The real question presented by the adaptation, therefore, is what role, if any, a man has in controlling his own fate? Siodmak's film seems to trust the audience with the ability to determine the Swede's level of responsibility for his demise. Using a series of flashbacks to create a sense of Socratic method–styled inquiry, Siodmak leads his audience to the conclusion that Andreson is a victim of fate beyond his control because he was blinded by love for Kitty Collins. In contrast, Kitty Collins has a much higher level of culpable awareness regarding her self-serving schemes, and Siodmak's film trusts that his audiences will judge her more harshly.

Siodmak's sense of Socratic logic works well in conjunction with Hemingway's often-discussed Iceberg Theory of writing, in which the reader must intuit the internal conflicts of characters that lie beneath their superficially tough emotional facades. Much like the moral makeup of any average man or woman, in the Socratic method, there is most often not a clear-cut "right" answer to any moral question, but rather a series of if/then logical statements which lead to a number of plausible hypotheses and conclusions. This abyss of moral gray area creates what is commonly known as a Socratic paradox: an affirmative statement which can never be conclusively proven, but instead only rationalized through a series of judgment calls that must be made in order to lead one closer to the truth.

Siodmak's adaptation of *The Killers* presents two Socratic paradoxes: Ole Andreson's statement that "I did something wrong—once," and Kitty Collins's desperate plea, "Kitty is innocent!" Throughout the film, Siodmak uses a series of flashbacks to provide alternating solutions and hypotheses that test the validity of these statements through the corroborating testimony of other characters. With Andreson's statement, viewers are continually asked to question whether Andreson committed any wrong at all, and if so, how many different types of moral wrongs he has committed. The film offers many possible solutions, ranging from Andreson's only moral wrong being that he loved Kitty Collins, in Shakespeare's parlance, not wisely but too well, to a series of wrongs that included perjury, robbery, and betrayal of his friends. For Collins's exclamation, viewers are presented with the question of whether Kitty was innocent not only of causing the death of her husband, but also of the crimes of the heart leading up to his death that included the deception and betrayal of Ole Andreson.

Considering that Hemingway's most-often repeated quotation about morals is "Morality is what you feel good after and immorality is what you feel bad after," it is little wonder that the author was pleased with Siodmak's Socratic approach to filmmaking, which leaves the audience to ponder where to place blame with Andreson and Collins according to their own moral codes. Clearly, Andreson and Collins each "feel bad after" the lifetime of decisions that they have made, but at the end of the film the question still remains of whether justice was done to them regarding the means of their punishments. Ultimately, Andreson is executed for betraying his criminal cohorts, and Collins is sent to prison after her role in the robbery is revealed. Rearden, the insurance agent responsible for investigating Andreson's murder before paying off his life insurance policy, plays the role of Socrates or devil's advocate to an audience of Nick Adams–like students, as he slowly gathers evidence about Andreson's life in an effort to determine whether a life of crime has any real reward. Both Hemingway and Siodmak trust that, looking through this lens, their audiences will come to the correct conclusions.

To explore Andreson's Socratic paradox of "I did something wrong—once," further, one must consider each circumstance in which the fighter may have committed a moral wrong based upon choices he made in the film. Generally speaking, there are five possibilities for Andreson's moral errors presented through Siodmak's flashback sequences. First, Andreson could have committed a moral wrong in the boxing ring by taking a fall for money during one of his matches. Cheating at sports is commonly a sign of moral weakness in the Hemingway canon. However in the film, Andreson does not engage in such unsportsmanlike conduct. Instead, Andreson fights valiantly with a broken hand until he is so punch drunk he does not know that the bout is over. In contrast, the original real-life inspiration for Hemingway's short story, a boxer named Andre Andreson, would have failed by the same moral standard set in the film adaptation of Hemingway's retelling of his story. Andreson was murdered on April 1, 1926, in Chicago, after throwing a series of fights for money (Phillips

71). In consequence, Andreson can be judged morally correct on the issue of sportsmanship, because he exhibits the behavior typical of a Hemingway code hero by never giving up even though he knows he is beaten.

The second possibility is that the "something wrong" involved loving Kitty Collins and taking the fall for her theft of some jewelry early in the film. According to Stuart Kaminsky, heroes of films noir demonstrated "a romantic heroism, a streak of knightly valor stemming from the constant belief of U.S. popular culture that a good man can somehow hold the world together, right wrongs, and reaffirm existence" (128). The visual token of Andreson's knightly sense of valor is demonstrated in his keeping of Collins's green handkerchief. Often in courtly romances, a chivalrous lover will keep a token of love from his lady, such as a handkerchief or scarf, as a reminder of their bond. Inspector Rearden's revelation that Andreson wore Collins's scarf over his face while helping to rob the shoe factory is symbolic. Both literally and figuratively, Andreson used his love for Collins to cover up his moral failing of loving her too much and to hide from the realities of his conscience. Since Andreson displays awareness and shame for his shortcoming of allowing his love for Collins to cloud his judgment, this cannot be the fault for which he is punished either.

A more likely possibility for Andreson's punishment by death in the film is the third possibility: that the "something wrong" involved his turn toward a life of crime after his release from the prison term he served on Collins's behalf. Andreson's problem is that he needs money to attract and hold Collins's attention, away from Big Jim Colfax, the man that Collins found to support her while Andreson was in prison. However, as a washed-up boxer, he has no way of getting the money he needs to hold on to the girl he loves. Andreson's dilemma becomes an if/then statement: if he really needs money to get the girl, then he will sacrifice his moral code to make that happen. Andreson's decision here is the point of his corruption, of which the film audience is made abundantly aware. Sacrificing one's moral code for love by becoming a thief, rather than just taking the blame for one's beloved who is a thief, is morally reprehensible. For this, Andreson must be punished. Yet, as Siodmak said, "the ideal hero for a gangster picture is someone who has failed in life and has therefore committed a crime.... If you give such a person a good enough motive for the crime, the audience will be on his side" (qtd. in Phillips 72). As a result, even though Andreson is punished by death for his crimes, his death is made to seem like a noble act of coming to terms with his faults, making him a still-honorable code hero.

The fourth possible "something wrong" is a corollary to the third. Andreson's choice to double-cross his criminal cohorts, taking the heist money after a tip-off from Collins, may be analyzed similarly to his choice to steal in order to attract and hold Collins's attention. The typical Hemingway code hero places value on his relationships with male friends. In Hemingway's world, there is even honor among thieves, if the bonds of their friendship are genuine. Therefore, when Andreson double-crosses Colfax in order to steal his girl, Andreson allows his love for Collins to improperly supersede his natural instinct to protect his comrades. This choice ultimately leads to his death at the hands of Colfax's assassins, in a final settling of the moral score in a game that Andreson thought he had won long ago.

Last, Siodmak's adaptation forces audiences to consider whether Andreson's "wrong" involved his preoccupation with suicide. In the film, Inspector Rearden must unravel the mystery of why Andreson chooses to make his former landlady, Mary Ellen Queenie, the beneficiary of his life insurance policy. When Queenie reveals that she prevented Andreson from committing suicide one night after Collins left him, audiences are intended to believe that Andreson's choice to avoid self-destruction was a solid moral decision. As Phillips states:

> By electing to take his medicine for consorting with criminals in the first place and by facing death with dignity and courage, Ole Andreson, the once honest boxer, redeems his recent past. Ole is, therefore, as sympathetic a figure in the film as he is in the short story, and implicitly remains the fallen code hero who regains his status in death [72].

The final result of Andreson's actions is that by the end of the film, in a split decision, audiences should be able to find moral justification for the majority of his actions and to reach a final verdict that Andreson has completed his penance on Earth for his crimes. Still, the lesson remains that every man must ultimately pay the price for following an evil lover's siren song.

Of course, this conclusion brings into question the second Socratic paradox of Siodmak's adaptation. Was Kitty Collins an innocent person, and if so only in part, why were some of her wrongs justifiable? To begin this discussion, one must first determine what the term "innocence" means within the context of the Hemingway canon. Usually, whenever a Hemingway character does something purely for the selfless motivation of love, almost anything he or she does can be justified. Yet, based upon Collins's actions, it is hard to believe that she ever truly loved Andreson for any reason other than he was willing to act as her fall guy. In her initial meeting with Hellinger to discuss the role, the producer told Ava Gardner to think of Kitty Collins as "a nice girl who allowed herself to accept the easy way of life. She came from a good family but linked up with the wrong people who supply her with the wrong cues in life" (qtd. in Server 121). Further, Hellinger explained to Gardner that the romance between Collins and Andreson was doomed to frustration because both had met too late in life, after too many adverse circumstances had tainted both characters' views of what love could be. At that point in her life, Gardner had already failed in her first marriage to Mickey Rooney and her then-current marriage to bandleader Artie Shaw was crumbling. It was little wonder that Gardner found much to relate to in the role of Kitty Collins. As so many femme fatales cast in the Hemingway adaptation canon, Gardner became trapped in the artistic ouroboros of life imitating art imitating life. The actress would play Kitty Collins for the remainder of her life, through another failed marriage to Frank Sinatra and countless other romantic disappointments.

Regardless of any sympathy audiences then or now might have for Gardner, the fact remains that her character, Kitty Collins, only feigned affection for Andreson in order to serve her own selfish purposes. As a result, Collins cannot be considered innocent of any of the crimes that follow this action. Because she was guilty of stealing Andreson's heart for the wrong reason, it naturally follows that Collins must also be found guilty in the court of audience opinion for all of her other crimes in the film. From stealing the brooch that resulted in Andreson's jail time, to double-crossing her secret husband, Colfax, and finally in trying to get the dying Colfax to absolve her from her role in the cover-up surrounding the robbery, Collins is guilty of multiple crimes that cannot be justified under the catch-all cause of unselfish love. By the film's end, the only logical conclusion for audiences to derive is that Collins deserves to be punished with jail time for the worst crime of all: exploiting both men who truly loved her.

Kitty Collins's duplicitous nature is indicated by three visual symbols used throughout the film in association with her. The first of these symbols is the color green, which comprises the background of Collins's scarf that Andreson carries and is also present in the name of The Green Cat, a club where she meets Rearden to tell her side of the story. Green is a color of both positive and negative meaning, signifying both luck and greed. Also, green is the color of absinthe, a hallucinogenic liquor that can induce a range of emotions, from giddiness to sickness. Collins's character is all of these things at once, her love intoxicating men with the feeling of good fortune that she has chosen them, only to give way later on as they find they have been deceived by her intense self-preservative instincts.

The harp, seen in the film as the motif on the aforementioned green scarf, may be taken as a second visual symbol of Collins's dangerously deceptive nature. Circe, the Greek temptress with whom Collins is constantly compared in the movie, is closely associated with the harp to accompany her siren song. Also, "playing the harp" is a colloquialism used frequently in gangster pictures to indicate someone who has just been killed. Read together, Collins's association with harps in the film indicates that she is a temptress capable of luring men to their deaths. Last, Collins is often compared to cats in the movie, frequents The Green Cat nightclub, and is last seen escaping through a bathroom window like a cat after her meeting with Rearden goes awry. Throughout his fiction, Hemingway often used cats to indicate a sense of vulnerable, yet fiercely independent, femininity in works such as "Cat in the Rain" and *A Farewell to Arms*. Also, Gardner's biographer Lee Server has noted that Siodmak and other directors often sought to play up the actress's cat-like qualities, to create "a haunting erotic presence out of such things as the shift of her eyes and the feline sprawl of her exquisite body" (126). This combination of Gardner's natural appearance with one of Hemingway's most common symbols is a great example of how carefully screenwriters Veiller and Huston must have worked with director Siodmak and producer Hellinger to make a film adaptation that represented a strong balance of creative control to create a piece of cohesive cinema.

Siodmak's adaptation also uses visual symbols to relate common Hemingway themes with Ole Andreson's character. In an early scene, Nick Adams comes to warn the Swede that two assassins are on their way to kill him. Instead of looking at Adams, Andreson simply stares at the wall while he expresses his readiness to die. As Frank Laurence has mentioned, "in a simple way the wall is metaphoric. The Swede is a man up against the wall, or facing a future that is a blank wall ... he says there is no way to fix it because he got it all wrong" (187). In the Hemingway canon, a code hero often appears near the end of his life as a man with his back to the wall against the world. One example is *For Whom the Bell Tolls*, which ends with Robert Jordan sitting with a broken leg and his machine gun propped against a tree, waiting for the enemy army to find him. In many ways, these metaphorical walls are the realities that every man must face as he takes stock of his life and prepares to die. The lone man against this monolith of "otherness" can also be related to the other major visual symbol associated with Andreson in the film, which is the idea of Rearden as a doppelgänger. While Andreson spends most of the film gradually entangling himself further into a world of crime and romantic intrigue, Rearden stands on the other side, slowly unwinding Andreson's checkered past from its web of deceit. As a result, Rearden symbolizes a future of clear-cut answers and satisfying resolutions that audiences might choose for themselves, whereas Andreson remains trapped by his confusing criminal past.

Last, Siodmak's creative use of lighting and staging are also used in symbolic ways that make such stock film noir tropes resonate more meaningfully. Siodmak's employment of contrasts between light and dark to highlight Ava

Gardner's face greatly heightens the sense of duality in her character's personality between innocence and wickedness. Siodmak insisted that all of Gardner's close-ups were done without makeup, making her, according to the film's cinematographer, Elwood Bredell, "the first adult actress who had ever agreed to be filmed without makeup: All we did was rub a little Vaseline into her skin for a sheen effect" (qtd. in Server 123). A literally glowing temptation, Gardner's Kitty Collins is at once ghost and angel.

Siodmak's use of lighting, or rather, the absence of it, is also used to great effect during the nighttime scenes of the film. Hemingway's fiction often employs what has come to be called the Nada Concept. Most often, Hemingway uses a fear of the dark or nighttime to symbolize the restlessness of the dark nights of self-doubt within every man's soul. As Kaminsky has rightly pointed out, with Siodmak's lighting on the film, "there is no essential difference between the darkness of the outside and that of the inside" (131). Siodmak's staging choices on the film also support this reading. The sets of the film are constructed in such a way as to call attention to the unreality and artificiality of each scene, to make sure that the audience knows where reality ends and making pictures begins. Like the Gustav Dore engravings in Dante's *Divine Comedy*, Siodmak's stark black and white tableau-making serves once again to highlight the differences between right and wrong choices that determine people's lives. These staging and lighting choices cause *The Killers* to screen exactly as Hemingway must have intended his story to read, as a modern morality play brought to light out of the dark bowels of the criminal underground.

Apparently, cinema audiences in 1946 were receptive to this documentation of daily struggle between good and evil. The film was a great box office success and critical reviews were almost unanimously favorable, providing the foundation for the future success of stars Lancaster and Gardner. Particularly, critics praised Gardner's performance, hailing "her extreme beauty and for her effective embodiment of the femme fatale" (Server 129). However, the most uncanny thing about Gardner's performance in *The Killers* is that she seemed, both onscreen and off, to be the living embodiment of the New Woman Hemingway had spent his career writing about. Not surprisingly, the author and his favorite actress struck up a friendship that would last until the end of his life, in 1961, and also spawn two additional film collaborations of their work in *The Snows of Kilimanjaro* (1952) and *The Sun Also Rises* (1957). Watching Gardner star in films based on his writing brought Hemingway his greatest satisfaction with adaptations of his work. Hemingway introduced the ever-adventurous Gardner to his world of safaris, life on the Caribbean, and bullfighting, even introducing the actress to Luis Miguel Dominguin, the matador who would steal her away from the love of her life, Frank Sinatra (Server 291).

Too old to realistically pursue a romance with Gardner himself, Hemingway seemed content to re-enact their real-life relationship as if from the pages of *The Sun Also Rises*, playing Jake Barnes to Gardner's Brett Ashley, as once again the ouroboros of literary celebrity encircled the author together with the woman who became his final muse.

Under My Skin (1950)

In his essay "On Writing," Ernest Hemingway says that a fiction writer's job is neither to write biographies or to wholly invent characters, but instead "to digest life and create your own people" (qtd. in Phillips 98). Hemingway's statement certainly applies to his first published short story, "My Old Man" (1923), upon which Jean Negulesco based his film adaptation, *Under My Skin* (1950). Although critical accounts of both the film's creation and the story's genesis are surprisingly sparse, most agree that Hemingway used the history of turn-of-the-century racing celebrity Tod Sloan as the basis for Dan Butler, the tragic Hemingway code hero of the tale. Hemingway's use of actual people to inspire his fiction is not unusual, and is almost a trademark of the author's writing.

What makes "My Old Man" unique among Hemingway stories is that it has an almost prophetic quality. Although Hemingway had never seen a jockey killed during a race at the time he wrote the story, a week after the story's completion a jockey named George Parfrement was killed at the same jump as Hemingway's fictional character Dan Butler, causing the author to remark "that was just the way it looked" in his mind's eye while writing (qtd. in Phillips 98). Hemingway's actual inspiration for Dan Butler was a jockey named Tod Sloan, an equally tragic celebrity figure of early racing culture who also died young after his career was ruined by rumors that he conspired with underworld figures and bet on his own races. Further, John Garfield, the actor who played Butler in *Under My Skin*, also died a premature death by heart attack at age 39, only two years after completing the film. The similarity between the deaths of Garfield and his fictional counterpart, Butler, are uncanny. Most biographers of Garfield's life point to the actor's continuous struggles with the House Un-American Activities Committee (HUAC) as the cause of the stress-induced heart attack that ended his life. In a similar fashion, pressure from mobster Louis Bork to throw races is what ultimately kills Dan Butler in Negulesco's cinematic retelling. As a result of these coincidences linking the men whose stories together make up the character of Dan Butler, scholars should read *Under My Skin* as a film text with a high level of biographical incorporation, as well as strong historical and socio-political influences that expand the boundaries of the Hemingway ouroboric circle.

To begin at the beginning of Hemingway's story about failed jockey Dan Butler, one must start with the real-life biography of Tod Sloan. Although Sloan's racing career was rather short, lasting only from 1889 to 1901, he changed the sport dramatically during that time. Sloan is usually given credit for inventing the most popular riding style in racing used to this day. Called the "monkey crouch," this revolutionary style involves the rider leaning forward on the seat while keeping the legs bent and tucked forward. Largely because of this innovation, Sloan quickly became one of the most celebrated jockeys of his day, racing throughout England and America. According to Sloan's 1915 autobiography, *Tod Sloan by Himself*, Sloan's proudest accomplishments were winning the Ascot Gold Cup in 1900 while riding Merman, a horse owned by actress Lily Langtry, and being invited to race for the Prince of Wales's team in 1901.

Much of the rest of *Tod Sloan by Himself* is devoted to details about his life's rise from humble beginnings as the frail son of a Civil War soldier from Indiana, where his mother died when he was five and he was sent to live with relatives, to the racing world's first international celebrity. The volume generally reads as a cautionary tale of overnight success, and is filled with stories about Sloan's beautiful women, dangerous associations with mobsters such as Diamond Jim Brady, and a wardrobe that was lavish enough to require a full-time valet. Sloan's lowest career ebb came at the 1899 Epsom Derby, when his horse, Holocauste, stopped abruptly, broke a leg during the final stretch of the race and had to be euthanized. Speculation swirled around the incident, because though Holocauste had an early lead in the race, Sloan appeared to be holding the horse back for most of the final neck-to-neck stretch directly preceding the accident. Unfortunately, accusations about Sloan's mob connections and his willingness to bet on his own races continued to mount, and he was banned for life from racing late in 1901, without ever actually racing for the Prince of Wales's team.

Influences of Sloan's racing career can be seen in both Hemingway's original story and its film adaptation. In Hemingway's story, Butler is an aging American jockey in Paris, who lives at the Maisons-Lafitte. Sloan's tragic horse, Holocauste, "was the best of his generation at age two, winning the Criterium Maisons-Lafitte at a canter," and gained many other wins, before cracking his leg in a race at Chantilly, and breaking it completely in the ill-fated Epsom Derby, after which he was immediately euthanized (TBHeritage.com). Like his real-life inspiration, Gilford, Butler's death horse in the story, also suffered a fracture that left "his front hoof dangling" and was shot immediately afterward

("Old Man" 160). Holocauste's accident marked the beginning of the death of Sloan's career, whereas Gilford's accident actually caused Butler's death. In short, what Hemingway did in this early short story was substitute an actual death in fiction for a metaphorical one in the real world.

Unfortunately, Negulesco's adaptation completely misses this important historical metaphor that Hemingway must have drawn from Sloan's biography. Instead of either horse or jockey perishing after the fateful race, both live to the end of *Under My Skin*, providing a saccharine and unsatisfying Hollywood ending to the film. However, the film is not a total loss, and is in fact a fair example of the interpretation style of filmmaking. Negulesco sets the film in Paris, just after World War II, to take advantage of audiences' more likely familiarity with that war than World War I, which was the time period in which Hemingway's original was set. This intelligent choice to time-shift Hemingway's tale allowed Negulesco and screenwriter Casey Robinson to make many solid interpretive decisions that preserved other major themes present in the original story, and also from the biographies of Hemingway and Sloan.

For example, according to his autobiography, Sloan remained a public figure even after his forced retirement from racing. He performed in vaudeville theater and opened in Paris during 1911 what later became the famous Harry's New York Bar, between the Avenue de l'Opera and the Rue de la Paix. After overspending forced him home to the States in 1920, Sloan attempted a film acting career. Due to failing name recognition, Sloan was unsuccessful as an actor, and he died of cirrhosis of the liver in 1933 in Los Angeles, a monument to the boom and bust of the first decades of the twentieth century.

To compare, Dan Butler, the protagonist in both the short story and film, is a jockey definitely on the downside of his career. In the film, Butler has been forced reluctantly to maintain his connections with organized crime, represented by the ominous presence of Louis Bork and his constant demands for money. Although the film is clear that Butler took a bribe, but regretted it, and later chose to accept no more offers to rig his own races, in Hemingway's story, Butler's bribery is only hinted at on the final page. After Butler dies in the story, his bribery is alluded to in the whispers of men who knew him. One man says, "Well, Butler got his, all right," and another replies, "I don't give a good goddam if he did, the crook. He had it coming to him on the stuff he's pulled" ("Old Man" 160). Since the film detours away from the powerful emotional impact contained in Hemingway's original ending, the film audience is deprived of the author's intended resolution. Good men who make the bad decision to cheat have to pay for it in the end. Even if they later redeem themselves, the consequences of their shady dealings will always catch up with them, and most likely end up hurting those they love.

The ending of "My Old Man" is made tragic not necessarily by the death of Dan Butler alone, but instead by the reader's knowledge that Butler's son, Joe, has lost faith in his father's integrity. In the Hemingway canon, a man's integrity is inextricably intertwined with his manhood, which was to the author an important virtue. This sense of stand-up manliness seems, in the Hemingway oeuvre, to be the most important legacy a father can leave his son. Therefore, when young Joe learns at the end of the story that his father, whom he admired greatly, was corrupt, he says, "Seems like when they get started, they don't leave a guy nothing" ("Old Man" 160). This statement means that losing faith in his father's integrity as a man leaves Joe even more destitute than Dan Butler's actual death. Without belief in his Old Man, Joe is truly alone.

Interestingly, all three men involved in bringing Dan Butler to life, Hemingway, Sloan, and Garfield, shared Joe's position as a young man who wanted to believe in his father's manliness, but found themselves unable to do so for similar reasons. In his biography of Hemingway, Carlos Baker carefully chronicles the disgust the author had for his father, Dr. Clarence Hemingway's, failure to stand up to his dominating wife. Ultimately, Dr. Hemingway committed suicide, leaving Ernest to assume the role of head of household at twenty-nine, and also the struggle for dominance against his mother that went along with it. In contrast, both Sloan and Garfield grew up in single-father homes, where they lived in under-privileged circumstances before being sent to live with relatives. These similar situations put both Sloan, the man who inspired Dan Butler, and Garfield, then actor who would play the character onscreen, in the same situation as Joe Butler, connecting the inspiration for Hemingway's original story to its cinematic adaptation through shared personal experience. As a result, Joe Butler, on film as well as on the page, can be read as a proto–Nick Adams character, and one of the earliest evidences in the author's career of the Hemingway ouroboros.

Despite the lackluster conclusion of *Under My Skin*, the film team seems to have been well versed enough in Hemingway and Sloan lore to incorporate it into the film in other ways that did not concern the film's Hollywood ending. Hemingway was a frequent patron of Sloan's New York Bar, socializing among its crowd of regulars that included mostly former World War I soldiers and American ex-patriate writers. Also, in the original story, Butler and the other jockeys sit around at the Café de Paris all day, drinking and gossiping just like Hemingway's more literary crowd in bars on the same streets. As a result, the film as a whole stands as a somewhat consistent artistic vision of all collaborating creative parties.

However, in what screens today as an ironic twist of fate, Jean Negulesco's choice to cast tough-guy actor John Garfield as Butler in the adaptation almost makes up for his failed ending, when one considers the tragic ending of Garfield's life in comparison to Hemingway's original story. Like both Joe Butler, Hemingway's pre–Nick Adams era innocent, and real-life inspiration Tod Sloan, John Garfield grew up poor and shuffled off to the homes of relatives after suffering the death of his mother in early childhood. However, Garfield's rags-to-riches tale was set for the stage, rather than the racetrack. Watching Garfield in the role of Dan Butler, one cannot help but wonder what happened to his career after starring in two well-received Hemingway films, *Under My Skin* and *The Breaking Point* (1950). The reason why Garfield did not become another Humphrey Bogart is one of the saddest stories in Hollywood politics. As his daughter Julie said about her father's legacy, "It was almost as if Hollywood was so ashamed of what was done to him that they almost made him disappear" (Weintraub).

Today, Garfield's history in Hollywood is generally viewed in two ways. First, Garfield is a performer whose work broke new ground in the field of Method acting, paving the way for later stars from Marlon Brando to Robert DeNiro. Alternatively, Garfield is remembered as an actor whose career and life were destroyed by HUAC and the Hollywood Blacklist. Born Jacob Julius Garfinkel in 1913 on New York's Lower East Side, Garfield was

> one of the first dark-haired, working-class ethnic outsiders to turn into a Hollywood star, following the path of actors like James Cagney. Garfield's chip-on-the-shoulder style and his rugged looks often cast him as a social outsider on the screen: a boxer, a gangster, a soldier. The persona affected actors from the 1950's onward [Weintraub].

All of these physical characteristics and personality traits made Garfield a perfect candidate to become the screen articulation of a Hemingway code hero: strong, quiet, intense, and fortified with a self-created sense of honor. After working his way up through the New York scene in the famous Group Theater company, Garfield was offered a contract with Warner Bros., where he rose to fame in the 1940s playing a myriad of tough-guy characters including a sexy drifter in *The Postman Always Rings Twice* (1946), a morally-compromised boxer in *Body and Soul* (1947), and lawyers of shady character in *Gentlemen's Agreement* (1947) and *Force of Evil* (1948). However, Garfield's success in these roles pigeonholed him as an actor. According to Robert Nott, author of his biography, *He Ran All the Way*, Garfield was frustrated with Hollywood:

> John Garfield faced the same challenge every film actor faced during the heyday of the studio-system style of filmmaking. He was under contract to a studio that had the right to cast him in any movie it saw fit.... The forces that prevented him from getting high quality roles were really the result of the combined willpower

of Warner Brothers, the studio system in general, and the general public, which also had its own perception of how Garfield, or Cagney or Bogart should appear on screen [qtd. in Gould].

As a result of this sort of monetarily-motivated typecasting, John Garfield developed a particular on-screen persona as a "sensitive tough guy, an urban sharpie who has doggedly pulled himself up from poverty while somehow retaining a tarnished soulfulness" (Gould). However, although Garfield's morally-questionable screen self made his career, it is difficult to wonder in hindsight whether it did not also make him a very visible target for the HUAC witch-hunts.

In 1950, Garfield was accused of being a Communist and called before the HUAC committee to testify. Although he was offered complete immunity if he would name names of others in Hollywood he suspected of being Communists, Garfield failed to do so. Never one to carry strong political affiliations, in all likelihood Garfield was targeted because of his Jewish ancestry and because he demanded that his friend, African American actor Canada Lee, receive equal treatment on projects in which both of them were cast. The HUAC committee also held against Garfield the fact that his wife, Roberta, was a registered member of the Communist party. Refusing to testify against his wife or colleagues, Garfield said in his official statement before the HUAC committee, "I have nothing to hide and nothing to be ashamed of. My life is an open book. I am no Red. I am no Pink. I am no fellow traveler. I am a Democrat by politics, a liberal by inclination, and a loyal citizen of this country by every act of my life." Still, Garfield's protestations were of little avail. HUAC officials were looking for a high-profile, visible name to add to their growing blacklist of writers and directors, and thereby increase public suspicion of a Communist presence in Hollywood.

As a result, John Garfield lived the last two years of his life like the film noir characters he often portrayed, as a wrongly accused man on the run. As his daughter Julie recalls:

> He didn't know what happened to him in the end. He didn't understand why they were hounding him. He was scared. It killed him, it really killed him. He was under unbelievable stress. Phones were being tapped. He was being followed by the FBI. He hadn't worked in eighteen months. He was finally supposed to do *Golden Boy* on CBS with Kim Stanley. They did one scene. And then CBS cancelled it. He died a day or two later [qtd. in Gould].

From Julie Garfield's account of her father's struggles, it is easy to find the actor's inspiration to portray Hemingway character Dan Butler. Although he claimed no affiliation with the Communist party and that he engaged in no Communist-sponsored activities or fund-raising efforts, Garfield had once, on behalf of his wife, signed a roster in support of a Communist-affiliated event in which Roberta participated. This mistake came up in HUAC hearings, and continued to haunt Garfield during his final two years of life.

The circumstances leading to the demise of his fictional counterpart, Dan Butler, are surprisingly similar in the film *Under My Skin*. Butler makes an agreement with mobster Louis Bork to lose a race he is expected to win, so that Bork and he can win money betting against the odds. However, Butler, partly out of conscience and partly out of circumstances, fails to throw the race as scheduled, and Bork loses the high-stakes bets he made. As a result, Butler spends the remainder of the film on the run from Bork, who demands that he repay the money by throwing more races. Butler's refusal to do so regains his integrity, but almost costs him his life. In contrast, John Garfield's choice to sign the pro–Communist petition on behalf of his wife could be viewed in the same light as Butler's small moral compromise. Both men did something that they knew could have detrimental consequences in the future without thinking much about it. However, in Garfield's case, even though he regained a firm sense of moral integrity by not lying about his friends to HUAC in an effort to save himself, the stress of dealing with the mafia-like governmental entity ultimately proved to be the death of him. This common background makes Garfield's life story akin both to Hemingway's story and the life of jockey Tod Sloan that inspired it. The final meaning that might be derived by comparing these tales is that even though Hollywood creates new tragedies on-screen every day, it is ill-equipped to handle the tragedies that inspire such fictions in everyday life.

Regardless, it is easy to see how the production team of *Under My Skin* may have drawn on the real life of John Garfield in order to emotionally flesh out their adaptation of "My Old Man." Early in the film, Garfield's character, Butler, is constantly peering out windows and looking over his shoulder, anxiously awaiting the arrival of Bork and his henchmen. Butler's attitude of paranoia in this sequence seems to imitate the sense of paranoia that Garfield must have felt during the Red Scare as he was harassed by HUAC. Further, immediately before the first confrontation scene with Bork, Butler has a conversation with his son Joe, saying that he can't go back to America because it "is on the fritz!" (Negulesco). For the remainder of the film, every time that young Joe tries to talk up the possibility of returning to America, Butler exhibits nervous behavior, which in turn only causes the boy to defend his homeland even further, insisting fervently that "America's the best country in the world!" (Negulesco). What seems to be happening in this ongoing exchange between father and son about America is that Butler seems painfully aware that America is unsafe for him, and possibly others, at the time. In contrast, his son, because of his naiveté and blissful acceptance of patriotic rhetoric, is perfectly willing to accept that nothing is amiss in America during the early 1950s. In short, the discussions between Joe and Dan Butler about America most likely reflect the HUAC-era paranoia of the cast and crew during that historical period, and, as such, are appropriate thematic additions to flesh out the sparse character details of Hemingway's original story.

Last, the addition of French actress Micheline Prelle as nightclub owner Paule to the film adaptation of Hemingway's story can be read as much more than a simple inclusion of a stock femme fatale character. Trained as a stage actress, the Paris-born Prelle began her film career in the early 1940s, playing typical romantic-comedy ingénue parts. However, during the post-war years of her mid-twenties, Prelle starred in a number of literary adaptations for the French market in "more weighty parts, now as the mature, and often sophisticated, woman of the world" (Cousins). After marrying American actor William Marshall, Prelle made her American debut in *Under My Skin*. Prelle's character, Paule, adds further socio-cultural and historical depth to the production mostly because of her scenes with Butler, in which she compares the emotional heartbreak of hearing young Joe talk about his mother's death to the gruesome scenes that she witnessed during the German occupation of Paris.

When Butler suggests wrongly that she has had an easy life, which has made her overly sympathetic to Joe's situation, Paule replies, "What do you think it is like to see a kid with his heart showing?" (Negulesco). This statement should be read with double meaning. Viewing her as a substitute mother figure, Joe opens himself up emotionally to Paule, allowing his metaphorical heart to show. In contrast, Paule compares this response to the young soldiers whom she knew during the war, who had physically been ripped open, leaving their hearts to show. The overall message behind this comparison is that, according to Negulesco's adaptation of Hemingway's story, the young fighting men of the world wars were like innocent children. They believed in fighting for their countries with all of their hearts, only to have their physical bodies destroyed many times because of their patriotism. This theme is possibly why Negulesco changed the name of his adaptation of "My Old Man" to *Under My Skin*—because under the skin of every soldier and person back home supporting him or her is a heart prepared to break. This reading seems logical in the context of Hemingway's work, in which the author continually calls into question the worthiness of war in light of its great human cost.

The ultimate result of Negulesco's choice to blend biographical elements with undercurrents of socio-political and historical commentary on the post–World War era is a film that remains mostly thematically consistent with

Hemingway's original text. In many ways, *Under My Skin* is very much a film of the early 1950s, because it perfectly captures the post-noir air of paranoia that permeated America during the Red Scare. Yet, the film also retains Hemingway's original theme of how innocent young men can be miseducated in the ways of the world when those in whom they trust are proven to be corrupt. The film's only major flaw is its too-upbeat Hollywood ending, which loses the sense of desolate resonance and resignation to fate that makes Hemingway's works so clearly modernist. Still, the parallels between Tod Sloan's autobiography and John Garfield's struggles with HUAC behind the scenes of the film stand as strong reminders that Hemingway code heroes exist in everyday life, even though most fade so quickly into the shadows of celebrity that audiences don't even notice they have gone.

The Breaking Point (1950)

Michael Curtiz's film *The Breaking Point* (1950) is the second adaptation of Ernest Hemingway's novel *To Have and Have Not*. At first, studio executives were skeptical as to whether another adaptation was warranted so soon after *To Have and Have Not* (1944), with Humphrey Bogart and Lauren Bacall's iconic roles in the piece so fresh in the public memory. However, screenwriter Ranald MacDougall "convinced Warner executives that a screenplay that was more faithful to the book and had less in common with *Casablanca* could be just as viable as the Hawks version had been" (Phillips 59). Ironically, *Casablanca*'s director, Michael Curtiz, was chosen to direct *The Breaking Point*. However, as Gene Phillips states, "this was all to the good since, having made *Casablanca* once, he was as interested as MacDougall in making a movie that stuck to Hemingway's story line and was not in any way similar to *Casablanca*" (59). Further, Curtiz's choice of John Garfield over Humphrey Bogart in the newer adaptation assured that this version would be different, and more personal.

Having lobbied hard for the part of Morgan, Garfield seemed determined to make this role, the second-to-last of his career, his best. At the time he made *The Breaking Point*, Garfield was being harassed by HUAC, making him a man who knew what it was like to be "a man alone" fighting against an insurmountable authoritarian enemy. Garfield's portrayal of Harry Morgan is more nuanced than Bogart's, a study in contradictions. A gentle family man at home, Garfield's Morgan is a veteran who suffers from post-traumatic stress disorder and depression, making him capable of moral compromises and violent acts throughout the film. MacDougall's script enhances these differences by incorporating parts of Hemingway lore, making Morgan not just a tastemaker or a tough guy, but instead a man trapped between external and internal conflicts. What results from the efforts of these three collaborators is a film that attempts a conversion of the latter half of Hemingway's original novel, but that ends up as an interpretive adaptation by incorporating parts of Hemingway and Garfield biography, along with elements of the gangster film and Western genres.

Almost all of *The Breaking Point*'s primary areas of focus are on the lesser-explored areas of Hemingway's original novel that were avoided in Bogart's *To Have and Have Not*. First and foremost, the film emphasizes the importance of Harry's relationship with his wife and family. Garfield's Morgan is a devoted family man, whose best character seems brought out when he is around his two young daughters. In one early scene, Morgan and his wife, Lucy, are arguing about their ongoing money struggles. Suddenly, their girls pop into the kitchen asking for money to go to the movies. Although Lucy tells them no, Morgan gives them the money, providing them with a distraction to get out of the house so that they will not have to listen to their parents argue. This scene is one of many in the film in which Morgan demonstrates that he will do anything to provide for his family and their happiness, even if it means compromising his own morals. In later scenes, the film shows how much Harry and Lucy are willing to do to earn money honestly. As Gene Phillips points out:

> To avoid a loss of audience sympathy for Harry, the movie goes to a great deal of trouble to demonstrate that he is driven to act as an accessory to a robbery solely for the sake of bailing his family out of debt. This is established in a montage sequence in which Harry reduces the daily rate for renting his charter boat from $40 to $25, and his wife is shown working far into the night earning money by mending sails while Harry guiltily lies awake nearby [60].

This choice by MacDougall and Curtiz, to focus on the mundane struggles of a working-class family, is directly in keeping with Hemingway's original novel. However, it represents a strong contrast from the earlier Bogart adaptation of the novel, which is far more stylish, witty, and sophisticated. By putting Harry Morgan in a situation in which he is forced to swallow his pride and work for a lower wage, and also watch his wife labor long hours for unfair wages, the film sets up a contrast between the haves and have not's of society that is both Marxist and very much part of the Hemingway oeuvre.

In their essay on "Marriage as a Moral Community" in *To Have and Have Not*, Thomas Hemmeter and Kevin Sweeney point out that in Hemingway's original novel, "although Harry generally values his marriage, the relationship fails to overcome his moral alienation. Rather than challenging Harry's feelings of isolation, Marie, by her own dependence, actually reinforces Harry's alienation" (66). Even though in the film Morgan experiences the same sense of alienation, one must notice the important difference between the novel's Marie and *The Breaking Point*'s Lucy. Lucy is proactive in her efforts to help her husband. Rather than just talking to him about their financial troubles, she offers a possible solution: to sell the boat and go to work on her father's lettuce farm. When Morgan refuses this option, Lucy chooses to go out and take in work. However, by doing this, Lucy causes more separation in the marriage by assuming the masculine role of provider, thereby emasculating Morgan, who seems to feel usurped by Lucy's take-charge attitude. Morgan stated that watching his wife work longer hours than he did at work she hated, "broke my back" (Curtiz). Therefore, *The Breaking Point* should be read as pushing Hemingway's common theme of masculine alienation, even when in a marriage, further than the author does. By showing Morgan as a man unable to accept help from the most likely candidate, his wife, without serious damage to his ego, Curtiz's adaptation explores the psychological dimension of gender interaction in his film more than Hemingway does in his original novel. The outcome of this exploration is that, oftentimes, a man feels completely alone because his pride, not just his circumstances in the world, prevents him from accepting help from those most ready and able to offer it.

Still, audiences of the film should not ignore Curtiz's decidedly pro-worker stance either. In *The Breaking Point*, Hemignway's original location is moved from Cuba to the fishing village of Newport, California. Although the reasons for moving the location of the film likely included budgetary concerns, given that the film was shot in black-and-white, an ancillary reason was probably that filming a working-class tale in Cuba in 1950 would have been a politically risky venture. During the era of HUAC-era paranoia, a film that pointed out the struggles of the proletariat and offered a solution of going back to a more hands-on, agricultural-based means of subsistence as a way of regaining a sense of individual worth and manhood would have been viewed as suspect, and possibly pro–Communist.

Further, Curtiz's choice to cast John Garfield, then embroiled in serious legal troubles with HUAC, as the lead actor to articulate these struggles would have cast even more negative light on the production. At the time, Garfield was considered somewhat of a maverick in his field. According to Bernard Weintraub, "Garfield was one of the first actors to set up his own production company, which made some of his most significant films, including *Body and Soul*, in which he insisted that Canada Lee, the black actor, appear with him. For John Garfield to advocate Canada Lee was an enormous step." Garfield's interest in casting Lee in the production was both professional and personal.

Lee and Garfield had become friends while working together in productions at the Pine Brook Country Club, the summer home of the Group Theatre of New York. Additionally, Garfield worked diligently in all of his later productions to advocate for the casting of African American actors, including Juano Hernandez as his on-screen best friend, Wesley Park, in *The Breaking Point*.

Hernandez's performance in the role of Morgan's first mate Park, who symbolizes the better parts of Morgan's conscience in the film, was extremely well received by critics. Bosley Crowther of *The New York Times* called Hernandez's performance "quietly magnificent," and said further, "As a matter of fact, the suggestion of comradeship and trust that is achieved through the character played by Mr. Hernandez, and the pathos created by his death, is not only a fine evidence of racial feeling, but it is one of the most moving factors in the film." However, this feeling of "comradeship" between a black man and a white man on film in 1950 carried with it dangerous political implications for the actors involved. In one early scene which today comes across as endearing, Morgan encourages his two young Caucasian daughters to walk to school with Park's African American son. As both fathers encourage the children not to be shy, the girls join hands with Wesley Jr. while they wait for the bus to school. Although in hindsight, the friendship between the two families is rightly viewed as positively promoting racial equality, during the HUAC era it was most likely read as yet another of Garfield's choices to officially push the social envelope toward a Communist agenda.

Later in the film, Morgan is forced to watch as the gangsters, whom he is supposed to assist in a robbery, shoot Park in front of him. While he can do nothing at the time, Garfield's facial expression of pent-up anger, stress, and lost at being trapped in a social situation in which he can do nothing to help his friend speaks volumes. In *The Breaking Point*, Harry Morgan is not only "a man alone," who "stands no chance" in his own world, but he is also a man who is aware that his life would be infinitely more difficult if he were African American under similar circumstances. This unarticulated theme is furthered by other scenes in the film that nonverbally communicate the symbolic death of Park as Morgan's social conscience. In the final scene, after a presumably dying Morgan is carried away surrounded by white friends and family, young Wesley Jr. is left completely alone to wander the pier looking for his father, whom the audience knows to be murdered and floating somewhere in the bay. Wesley Jr. becomes the film's symbol of what is left behind if a man gives up his moral values and social conscience, allowing his true friends to die under meaningless circumstances. Without a strong sense of social responsibility regarding both financial status and race, men are left to wander as vulnerable as lost children, and just as apt to fall prey to involvement in amoral or illegal activities because of this absence.

The Breaking Point makes it easy to trace actual events of Harry Morgan's moral decline; however, it is much more difficult to pinpoint exactly how Morgan came to be put in this position of childlike vulnerability in the first place. One possible explanation that has been little explored by critics is that both the original novel of *To Have and Have Not* and its subsequent film adaptation suggest that Morgan suffers from post-traumatic stress disorder, caused by his service in World War II. In *The Breaking Point*, Morgan argues with Lucy over whether he should go through with the robbery as planned or give up, sell his boat, and go to work on her father's lettuce farm. The argument concludes with Morgan storming out and saying, "This is my business. It's a job like any other job. I did worse in the Philippines, and I got a medal for it" (Curtiz). These lines demonstrate that Morgan, a veteran, has done many things in war that he regrets. Still, cracks appear in his weathered-veteran veneer, beginning after he kills the villainous Mr. Sing in self-defense and also after Wesley Park is murdered. What seems to be going on is that Morgan uses his military service to give him courage and justification for violent acts that he feels he must commit and witness in order to survive; however, internally he remains hurt and shocked at the atrocities of which he is capable.

This masking behavior is a classic demonstration of post-traumatic stress disorder (PTSD), frequently exhibited by veterans. According to the National Institute of Mental Health:

> PTSD is an anxiety disorder that some people get after seeing or living through a dangerous event. When in danger, it's natural to feel afraid. This fear triggers many split-second changes in the body to prepare to defend against the danger or to avoid it. This fight-or-flight response is a healthy reaction meant to protect a person from harm. But in PTSD, this reaction is changed or damaged. People who have PTSD may feel stressed or frightened even when they are no longer in danger [nimh.nih.gov].

Morgan shows symptoms of PTSD many times over the course of the film. In a scene with the shady lawyer, Duncan, Morgan completely overacts when he feels that Duncan is going to cheat him out of some money. He shoves Duncan against the wall and accuses him of secretly plotting to double-cross and kill him. Many times in the film, Morgan is shown sweating profusely over small conflicts with other characters, including the harbor police and coast guard officials. Last, Morgan hides guns all over his boat while preparing for the gangsters to arrive, because he suspects that they might murder him if the plan goes awry. Although the people with whom Morgan is dealing are of character questionable enough to cause a person to always be on guard, Morgan's chief reactions to his circumstances, obsessive worrying usually followed by sudden and intensely violent reactions, show that his time in the military has left him a physically tough but emotionally damaged man, who possibly suffers from PTSD.

Also, Morgan's choice to keep putting himself in potentially perilous situations shows that he has come to thrive on dangerous circumstances and needs the adrenaline rush that they provide in order to feel alive and effectual. These choices are also likely to be results of his military service, during which period he came to feel that being under intense stress and fearing for his life were normal in order to survive. Many of Hemingway's characters in other novels, such as *The Sun Also Rises*, *A Farewell to Arms*, and *For Whom the Bell Tolls*, share Morgan's eager engagement in potentially life threatening activities, almost as if they are trying to re-create the intense feeling of liveliness that they felt in the military, when their lives were truly threatened.

This sense of reckless urgency is frequently described by psychologists today as "adrenaline addiction." As counselor Patrick Lencioni explains the addiction, "Always overwhelmed, adrenaline junkies seem to have a constant need for urgency, even panic, to get them through the day" (3). Lencioni also points out that adrenaline addiction is particularly insidious because "unlike other addicts, whose behaviors are socially frowned-upon, adrenaline addicts are often praised for their frantic activity … and so they often wear their problem like a badge of honor, failing to see all the pain it causes" (3). Perhaps the original source of adrenaline addiction for so many Hemingway characters is their author himself. A veteran of World War I, during which he was blown up and almost killed, Hemingway seemed to spend the remainder of his life actively seeking out other circumstances in which he could cheat death. From acting as a war correspondent who took an active role in combat, to engaging in amateur bullfighting, and even in his often hectic personal life, Hemingway seemed to strive on the sort of high-stress level that today can be interpreted as adrenaline addiction. Curtiz's production team seems to have incorporated Hemingway's behavioral tendency into the film, by greatly expanding the action sequences and exploring the emotional conflicts even further than the author's original novel. In short, the final product is a film that moves faster and is much more emotionally intense than the novel that inspired it, largely due to incorporation of Hemingway mythology.

Stylistically, the film incorporates not only additional biographical lore about Hemingway, but also many of the common tropes of gangster films, which were still widely popular in 1950. The main plot of *The Breaking Point* ultimately leads Morgan to participate in a genuine gangster robbery, in which his boat is supposed to be used as the getaway vehicle. Along the way, he meets many of the standard gangster film characters: Leona, a femme fatale, Duncan, a duplicitous attorney, and a mob boss accompanied by heavies. Morgan, in this scenario, is the gangster-in-training, or anti-hero, whom the audience gets to see make the mistakes that will lead him down the road to ruin. The most important part of Morgan's personality in this role is his paradoxical awareness and fear of being "a man alone." As Robert Warshow has noted, "No convention of the gangster film is more strongly established than this: it is dangerous to be alone. And yet the very conditions of success make it impossible not to be alone, for success is always the establishment of an individual preeminence that must be imposed on others, in whom it automatically arouses hatred: the successful man is an outlaw" (580). Morgan fits this description perfectly: he is a man who, because of his intense drive to succeed, alienates himself from the very people he wants to benefit.

Morgan's alienation as a gangster anti-hero becomes complete when his wife, Lucy, utters the most frightening words any married man can hear, "I'm sorry I ever married you" (Curtiz). These words, which come at the end of an argument between the pair in which Morgan attempts to justify his choice to engage in criminal activity to help pay the family's overdue bills, effectively shut him off from his family. When Lucy tells him further that, even if he comes back alive from his dangerous mission, she and the girls will be gone, Morgan knows that he has lost every reason he previously held for going into a life of crime. Oddly enough, this situation only insures that he will go through with his plans, because now he has become a man with nothing to lose, who is completely alone.

The importance of female characters in gangster films cannot be ignored. Most often, they come in two forms: the damsel in distress and the femme fatale. In *The Breaking Point*, MacDougall's script splits Marie, Morgan's wife from Hemingway's original novel, into two women who each embody one of these archetypes. Lucy, as the woman who faces financial ruin, is the damsel in distress. Even though she is already married to Morgan, their relationship is tenuous because she constantly challenges her husband's bad judgments. In contrast, Leona is the femme fatale. Leona sees Morgan as a symbol of the sort of man she gave up to live a life in the fast lane, only to later understand that such a life brings little lasting satisfaction. As is typical in most gangster films, the gangster-in-training remains alone, despite receiving plenty of attention from both women. As Hemmeter and Sweeney have stated:

> Harry sees Lucy and Leona only as projections of a private *mise en scene*, allowing him to distance himself from the moral dialog these two women initiate. He ignores his wife's sexual identity, driving her to dye her hair blond to attract him. He also keeps his distance from Leona and cannot respond to her need to be loved as a real person" [71].

By maintaining emotional distance from both women, Morgan effectively creates a situation in which he can only be a "man alone." There are many possible reasons why he does this, but most likely Morgan is afraid that both women are his moral superiors, and would frown upon his choice to engage in truly criminal activity. As a result, when he is finally scheduled to meet up with the gangsters, he does not want either of the women in his life, or even his male friend Park, to witness his moral downfall. In short, if Morgan wishes to justify his bad choices, he also wants to be sure he is the only person who must suffer their moral consequences, so he chooses to act completely alone.

Of course, the concept of a man acting alone against sinister forces is common to another genre of films, the Western, which also seems to have influenced construction of *The Breaking Point*. However, most of the characters commonly found in this California sea-coast Western in some way reverse what is expected from their archetypes. First, Morgan, the hero of the piece, dresses all in black, whereas the various enemies he faces, from coast guard officials to underworld figures, dress in white or at least light-colored clothing. This choice to put Morgan in black possibly signifies that he is an anti-hero, not a pure hero. In contrast, pitting Morgan against the white-clothed coast guard official could show that, at least in part, some of Morgan's actions are not morally justifiable, and his character in fact has a dark side. The gangsters, clad in various shades of light gray, represent the various personal and ethical compromises they made to reach their current stations of moral corruption.

Clothing color is also important in regards to Duncan, the corrupt attorney who lures Morgan into a life of crime with the promise of easy money. Duncan, who always dresses in white, is a typical Western genre "drunken professional" character. As John Cawelti explains, "The drunken professional is a doctor or lawyer who, we are given to understand, had a promising eastern career that went sour" (50). From descriptions of Duncan's history and law practice in the film, audiences are given to understand that he is exactly this type of person, who has decided that easier money can be made in assisting criminals than in pursuing justice.

Also, there seems to be a reversal of symbolic color scheme concerning the two women in the film, who take up the traditionally opposing roles of dance-hall girl and schoolmarm, other characters common to Westerns. As Cawelti explains, in the dichotomy of most Westerns, "the blonde ... represents genteel, pure femininity, while the brunette ... symbolizes a more full-blooded, passionate and spontaneous nature, often slightly tainted by a dubious past" (48). However, in *The Breaking Point*, Lucy, Morgan's demure wife, begins the film as a brunette, while Leona, the other woman who attempts to seduce Morgan, is a blonde. What the reversal in hair color versus character here appears to symbolize is that no one is always what she appears to be. Although she looks innocent, Leona has actually suffered romantic disappointments in her past that have left her somewhat predatory in her instincts toward men, until she meets Harry Morgan. Morgan, because of his apparent strong moral focus at the beginning of the film, attracts Leona's more domesticated brunette roots, and causes her to reexamine why she chose adventure over love. In fact, brown hair seems to symbolize a natural, down-to-earth quality in *The Breaking Point* that is indicative of unadorned, inner beauty that even the Other Woman must appreciate. This idealization of the natural is possibly why Lucy begins the film as a brunette. Still, when she sees that the blond Leona turns her husband's head, she decides to win his heart back by bleaching her hair blond, in an attempt to capture the false sense of innocent appeal that Lucy thinks Leona embodies. The result is not what she hopes to achieve, since Morgan, although he attempts to save her feelings, expresses a preference for Lucy's naturally brown hair color. The overall message of this reversal of Western hair color symbolism is not truthfulness is the greatest virtue a woman can possess to attract a man, and gain his respect as a moral guide.

This theory seems to hold when one considers the fact that Morgan's best friend in the adaptation, Wesley Park, is a darker-skinned African American. Normally in Westerns, when the sidekick of the hero is of an ethnic minority, that character is present to provide mere comic relief. However, Park serves as the only completely stable moral conscience of the film, suggesting the sort of father and provider Morgan could aspire to be if he were completely morally upright. Of course, as the only truly honest character in the film Park must die in order to capture the sense of moral bleakness present in Hemingway's original novel: no truly good man can survive in a corrupt world.

What results from this displacement of Morgan's better moral side into a supporting character is the same split of personality that is achieved my making Hemingway's original Marie into two female characters. After Park is murdered, Morgan's darkest tendencies are unleashed, and he lashes out violently, killing all of the gangsters aboard his boat. The fact that Morgan is shot in the stomach and left arm can be read as symbolically significant of his moral retransformation back into a whole person after his external moral conscience, Park, is killed. A stomach wound usually produces a slow death. Therefore, Morgan's stomach wound can be read as the slow bleeding out of his value system, as the harsh realities of poverty sap his willpower to earn an honest living. However, because he is at heart a good man, Morgan must eventually part with the eviler side of his personality, symbolized in the film by amputation of the arm on his left, sinister side. Tragically, Morgan must also lose the most honest and innocent parts of his character, signified by the death of his best friend, Park, along the road to his transformation.

Perhaps this is why Curtiz leaves the ending of *The Breaking Point* open. In Hemingway's original novel, *To Have and Have Not*, Morgan unquestionably dies of his wounds in the end, showing that he has finally paid the consequences for his moral misdeeds. However, in *The Breaking Point*'s ending, audiences are left to wonder whether or not the critically wounded Morgan lives or dies. Although this ending has been often criticized, it is actually consistent within the context of the film, and also with Hemingway's original work. After he is shot, Morgan repeats several times the mantra of both works, that "a man alone has no chance, no chance at all" (Curtiz). Yet, the Harry Morgan of *The Breaking Point* is a man who only perceives himself to be alone, when in fact, he has the support of family and friends, who surround him as he lies in his sickbed during the film's last scene. What results is a film with a final message that suggests a man is alone with no chance only if he chooses to ignore the support of those who seek to help and warn him that he is following the wrong path in life, just as Morgan does in Hemingway's original novel, *To Have and Have Not*. The takeaway is the cohesive bond that holds *The Breaking Point* much more thematically closer to the novel than its previous Bogart and Bacall adaptation, even though the earlier film has endured longer in America's collective cinematic conscience.

The Snows of Kilimanjaro (1952)

Henry King's *The Snows of Kilimanjaro* (1952) is the most highly incorporated adaptation of Ernest Hemingway's work. Upon first seeing the film, Hemingway was not pleased and remarked, "I sold Fox a single story, not my complete works" (qtd. in Phillips 14). Hemingway's ire was somewhat justified from a copyright standpoint. Producer Darryl Zanuck purchased the film rights to the single "Snows" story for $75,000, and assigned the screenwriting responsibilities for the project to Casey Robinson (Phillips 14). Robinson, who had previously scripted *Under My Skin*, an adaptation of Hemingway's short story "My Old Man," was considered at the time to be a master of literary adaptation and somewhat of a Hemingway aficionado. The resulting product was an adaptation of "Snows" that included significant plot, character, and thematic elements from the author's life story as well as from five other Hemingway works: "The End of Something," *The Sun Also Rises*, *A Farewell to Arms*, *For Whom the Bell Tolls*, and "The Short Happy Life of Francis Macomber." Fortunately, these inclusions for Hemingway's canon are carefully selected and thematically consistent enough to create an adaptation in the interpretive style that represents a mostly consistent artistic vision.

Hemingway's original short story, "The Snows of Kilimanjaro," first appeared in *Esquire* magazine in August 1936. The story, which chronicles the regrets and death of a failed Hemingway-esque writer named Harry, was originally intended by the author as a sort of cautionary tale to himself. After reading his friend Scott Fitzgerald's series of *Crack-Up* essays in the February, March, and April 1936 issues of *Esquire*, Hemingway could not help but include a reference to what he felt was Fitzgerald's distasteful display of self-pity and fawning over the rich in his next published story, "Snows." In the original version of "Snows," Hemingway refers to Fitzgerald as his friend Julian in a derogatory way, saying:

> He remembered poor Julian and his romantic awe of them and how he had started a story once that began, "The rich are very different from you and me." And how someone had said to Julian, "Yes, they have more money." But that was not humorous to Julian. He thought they were a special glamorous race and when he found out they weren't it wrecked him just as much as any other thing had wrecked him ["Snows" 53].

Justifiably, Fitzgerald was troubled by Hemingway's slight, and wrote to his friend. "Please lay off me in print. If I choose to write *de profundis* sometimes, it doesn't mean I want friends praying aloud over my corpse" (qtd. in Baker 290). Hemingway's choice to upbraid his friend for showing too much self-pity in print is ironic when one considers "The Snows of Kilimanjaro" is very much the same sort of confessional writing as the *Crack-Up* series, only Hemingway chose as usual to conceal his autobiography behind a thin veil of fiction. Also, the two friends, though they shared similar insecurities about their failings in life and career, articulated them differently. Fitzgerald told their editor, Max Perkins, that Hemingway's self-doubt was similar to his own. "Ernest is every bit as nervously broken down as I am," Fitzgerald added. However, "his inclination is toward megalomania, and mine toward melancholy" (qtd. in Baker 290–91). As a result, the original short story of "Snows" is best read in the same confessional, autobiographical style as Fitzgerald's *Crack-Up* essays, albeit with Hemingway's expected level of exaggeration.

The film adaptation of *The Snows of Kilimanjaro* certainly seems to take this approach to interpreting the story. The film debuted in August 1952, only a few months after Hemingway won the Pulitzer for his then most recent novel, *The Old Man and the Sea*. Many critics then and now considered Hemingway's win to be a sort of lifetime achievement award, a sentiment which primed audiences to receive an adaptation of "Snows" that served as a sort of tribute to the author's life and canon of works. With *Snows*, director Henry

King made his first foray into the Lost Generation oeuvre, but it would not be his last. Apparently fascinated with the era and its writers, King would go on to direct the next Hemingway adaptation, *The Sun Also Rises* (1957), as well as two Fitzgerald-centered features, *Beloved Infidel* (1959) and *Tender Is the Night* (1962). With each film, King seemed to become increasingly involved on a personal level with these projects, even ultimately choosing to cast his wife, Jennifer Jones, in *Tender*.

King drew upon his working relationship with actor Gregory Peck in his casting choices for *Snows*, putting Peck in the lead role of Harry Street. For the extremely versatile Peck, playing Harry Street was a chance to further expand his growing repertoire of characters beyond the love interests and tough-guy gunslingers he had played up to that point in his career. Although he had starred previously as white-hunter Robert Wilson in the Hemingway-based adaptation *The Macomber Affair* (1947), Peck's performance in *Snows* seems more truthful, perhaps because of the biographical connection added by the production team. Casey Robinson wrote in a second wife for the Harry Street character who was not included in Hemingway's original. Robinson's Scandinavian socialite Liz bears a strong physical resemblance to Peck's then-wife, Finnish-born real estate mogul Greta Kukkonen, and might be considered an inspiration for the character.

Although briefly alluded to in the italicized portions of Hemingway's original story, Harry Street's first wife in the adaptation, Cynthia, is largely invented by Robinson as well. Played by Hemingway's favorite actress, Ava Gardner, Cynthia screens today as a precursor to Gardner's later Brett Ashley role in *The Sun Also Rises* (1957). Wearing green emerald jewelry similar to that of her character Kitty Collins from *The Killers*, Gardner maintains a sense of character continuity from this earlier role as she allows Cynthia to become more secretive and duplicitous over the course of the film. Further, Robinson's choice to add an abortion plot to his screenplay of *Snows* might possibly reflect some difficult personal choices that Gardner was making in her real life. During the time of filming, Gardner was married to singer/actor Frank Sinatra, and the two quarreled often over the two abortions that resulted from their ongoing struggle for dominance as head artist of the household. Interestingly, Gardner's struggle to balance out the needs of a family and dual-career household with Sinatra seems to be mimicked in the relationship dynamic between Harry Street and his wife, Cynthia. Her portrayal of Cynthia represents yet another example of the ouroboric circle of art imitating life that can commonly be expected in the most truthful cinematic performances of works adapted from print.

Despite significant additions to the plot of *Snows*, King's adaptation maintains many of the essential themes of the original. The film opens with a voiceover reciting Hemingway's epigraph exactly as it appears in the story, while images of Mt. Kilimanjaro and scenes of the African countryside go by in the background. The epigraph also appears later in the film, when Harry's mentor, Uncle Bill, gives the passage to him as his deathbed legacy. In this second appearance, Harry is directed to read the epigraph as a riddle, which he recites in a Paris bar:

> Kilimanjaro is a snow-covered mountain 19,710 feet high, and it is said to be the highest mountain in Africa. Its western summit is called the Masai Ngaje Ngai, the House of God. Close to the western summit there is the dried and frozen carcass of a leopard. No one has explained what the leopard was seeking at that altitude [*Snows*].

After reading his legacy riddle, Harry seems puzzled as to what the solution might be. Although his friends in the bar offer cursory solutions, the real meaning for the audience is clear. The leopard is a stand-in for Harry, and in turn, every man. For Hemingway, a man's life is made worth living through a continual series of quests that give purpose to life. These quests might be to obtain the love of a woman, to find success in art or career, or simply to hunt and kill big game. Throughout the film Henry King uses visual and verbal metaphors involving hunting to evoke the sense that, in order to be satisfied in life, every man must stay hungry and keep hunting for the next adventure. The resonant theme in both Hemingway's original story is that a man's life will continue until he runs out of quests, and the only journey left is toward his own final rest, salvation, and possibly, if he is lucky and done enough to be remembered, immortality.

Henry King's adaptation of *Snows* employs many cinematic devices to support his articulation of Hemingway's main theme implied in the solution to the leopard riddle. Numerous flashback sequences are used to show all of Harry's former quests, usually performed in pursuit of a female. This metaphor of life-as-a-humble-quest is supported by King's choice of wardrobe for lead actor, Gregory Peck. In the film, Peck is perpetually seen wearing the same gray herringbone tweed suit. The suit becomes a sort of armor for Peck's character Harry Street, protecting him from the pretensions of the rich as he grows increasingly successful as a writer. In his later film *The Man in the Gray Flannel Suit* (1956), Peck would be given a similar wardrobe to evoke the sense of his character as a man part of the machinery of society who refuses to lose his soul within it.

Here in *Snows*, even Harry's second wife, Liz, notices and comments on the suit's significance. As Harry leaves their final cocktail party together after receiving a letter from his first love, Cynthia, Liz remarks, "You look like such a fool ... like a knight questing for the Holy Grail" (*Snows*). This statement can be linked to a another quip from Hemingway's original story, in which Harry blames his third wife, Helen, for providing him with a comfortable lifestyle that ruins his career, saying, "Your damned money was my armour" ("Snows"). The difference between these two statements about a man's personal armor that he uses as a defense mechanism against the world points toward the central thematic split between King's adaptation and Hemingway's story. In the story, Harry used money as his defense against the world, and when he reached a health crisis that cannot be remedied by money, he dies. However, in the film, Harry uses love as his armor, making his lifestyle choices based on the women he cares for, more so than for his own career or gain. As a result, the love of Helen, Harry's last wife, saves him from death. In short, the moral to be learned from comparing the story and its adaptation is that if one must choose between embarking on a quest for love or money, then love is the better choice.

Although Hollywood chose to allow Harry Street the redemption of having his quest for love rewarded in the end by allowing him to live, Hemingway's original story does not end as optimistically. In Hemingway's story, Harry dies knowing that the current relationship with his wife is a lie, when he says to Helen, "I love you really. You know I love you. I've never loved anyone else the way I love you.... He slipped into the familiar lie he made his bread and butter by" ("Snows"). This discrepancy has caused most critics to regard King's ending to *Snows* harshly. However, King's ending does represent a consistent artistic vision within the context of his adaptation. In King's *Snows*, Harry Street is a sentimental man, one who is often disappointed by love, but who is nevertheless capable of giving it one more try, especially after Helen proves her loyalty by saving his life with an emergency operation to let the swelling out of his infected leg. In contrast, Hemingway's Harry is completely jaded by the world, and incapable of having any genuine feelings toward Helen at all. Failing to find any saving grace in true love, Hemingway's Harry dies of the wound produced through his own self-neglect. Therefore, even though the ending of King's film is thematically inconsistent with Hemingway's original, it still should be read with an open mind toward the fact that it preserves thematic consistency within the context of Harry's character as envisioned by Hollywood.

One theme that does represent a complete cohesiveness among all collaborators on both the story and its adaptation is the idea that the Hemingway Hero represents vitality. As Hemingway describes Harry in the story, "He had sold vitality, in one form or another, all his life" ("Snows"). Hemingway might as well have been talking about his own image. By the 1950s, Hemingway had become a household name, not only for his writing, but also for his public image, perpetuated by the growing men's magazine industry. As David Earle has stated, "These magazines forwarded the idea of Hemingway as a world-wise traveler and gourmet, an expert on food and cocktails, on women and culture, even offering advice directly from the man himself. They sold the Hemingwayesque idea of masculinity, expertise, consumption, and travel" (103). This image of Hemingway as a cultural symbol of masculine vitality seems to have spilled over into the author's creation of Harry in "Snows," and in turn, King's film adaptation of the story. In both works, audiences see Harry engaging in typical Hemingway-esque activities, such as hunting, drinking, watching bullfights, writing, and enjoying the company of beautiful women. Therefore, even though Hemingway's original line about selling vitality does not appear in King's adaptation, it maintains a visual presence through every scene of Harry Street's story.

Another major theme from Hemingway's original text that King articulates particularly well through implementation of visual symbols is Harry's alternating emotions about death. Several times over the course of the film, hyenas are heard crying and seen skulking stealthily closer to what audiences suppose will be Harry's deathbed. Also, Harry sees buzzards circulating overhead and comments on them several times. Both of these natural harbingers of death appear in Hemingway's original story to suggest the imminent presence of death that is literally right next to Harry as he lies sweating on his field cot. Although it would have been easy to oversimplify these images and to merely show Harry's fear of death, such an approach would have been thematically inconsistent with Hemingway's original story. Instead, King's film shows Harry repeatedly growing bored with the prospect of death, even repeating the line from Hemingway's original story that Harry is "getting as bored with dying as with everything else" (*Snows*). For his part, Gregory Peck plays the complexity of Harry's emotional conflict about his impending death very well, using mostly non-verbal facial expressions and gestures to indicate Harry's dual sense of uneasiness and ennui. King's choice to show Harry as stoic about the idea of death resonates perfectly with Hemingway's common theme of silent, manly acceptance of one's fate, creating cohesiveness between the film adaptation and original story.

Hemingway's trademark stoicism is also illustrated in the flashback scenes of King's adaptation that appear to have been inspired by the author's early Nick Adams story "The End of Something." In this story, a young Nick Adams breaks up with his girlfriend Marjorie while on vacation at Horton's Bay. The circumstances of the break-up are non-dramatic, and conclude with Marjorie rowing silently away. To compare, in one of the flashback scenes early in *Snows of Kilimanjaro*, a young Harry Street breaks up with his girlfriend, who also rows away across the bay after a decidedly more heated argument. Still, the action that takes place after the conflict in both works is the same. Harry returns to the lodge and begins a discussion with his friend Bill. In the *Snows* film, Bill is Harry's uncle and mentor, and their conversation is much longer and more meaningful than in "The End of Something."

During their lengthy conversation in *Snows*, Uncle Bill tells Harry that the key to manhood is to "keep hunting," meaning that one should never rest on the laurels of accomplishment, but instead always be on the lookout for another adventure. After giving him this bit of advice, Uncle Bill gives Harry a Springfield rifle, which Harry then takes with him on safari in a later flashback sequence. The inclusion of the Springfield is, in all likelihood, intentional by screenwriter Casey Robinson. Hemingway favored the Springfield in his own African hunting, and specifically mentioned the brand in another short story, "The Short but Happy Life of Francis Macomber." In the story, Macomber uses a Springfield rifle to kill a water buffalo, a task that finally gives him the confidence in his own manhood to stand up to his dominating wife. The Springfield rifle, therefore, becomes in the film what it was in Hemingway's original stories, a symbol of man's quest for adventure in search of his identity.

However, symbolic use of firearms was not the only standard that Casey Robinson borrowed from the Hemingway canon to flesh out the script of *Snows* to feature-film length. Ava Gardner's character, Cynthia, seems to be an almost carbon copy of Lady Brett Ashley from Hemingway's first novel, *The Sun Also Rises*. An enigmatic figure, Brett was drawn from Hemingway's real-life acquaintance with Lady Duff Twysden, providing yet another example of life inspiring Hemingway's writing, only to return to life again when portrayed onscreen.

Like Brett, Cynthia was, in Hemingway's parlance "damn good looking," as she immediately caught Harry's attention in the Paris bar where they met (*Sun* 29). Cynthia shares also with Brett a certain amount of independence mixed oddly with a definite need to be loved and supported by the men she selects. The mention of Harry's first book, *The Red Hat*, is most likely an allusion to Brett's tendency, in *The Sun Also Rises*, to appear in flamboyant hats that were sure to get her noticed. Further, Cynthia's spur-of-the-moment decision in the film adaptation of *Snows* to leave Harry for a Spanish flamenco dancer in Madrid is similar to Brett's choice to engage in an affair with bullfighter Pedro Romero in *Sun*. Robinson's incorporation of all these details indicates that the screenwriter had a strong awareness and understanding of the New Woman and her place in the Hemingway canon, which is reflected in the final film adaptation of *Snows*.

Yet, Lady Brett Ashley was not the only Hemingway New Woman to appear in *Snows*. The maternity sequence of *Snows* is reminiscent in plot and tone to Catherine Barkley's ill-fated pregnancy in *A Farewell to Arms*. Despite the brave face that Catherine and Cynthia put on while pregnant during inopportune times, both women are rendered emotionally vulnerable during such times. On the surface, Catherine appears tougher than Cynthia, because she is able to face death during childbirth willingly, while Cynthia chooses to avoid the life-complicating dilemma of an unexpected pregnancy by having an abortion. However, Cynthia proves her bravery in another way, by joining the Red Cross as an ambulance driver in the Spanish Civil War.

Robinson's choice to transfer the act of Red Cross service from a male character, Frederick Henry, in *A Farewell to Arms*, to Cynthia, a female character, in his adaptation of *Snows*, can be read as feminist. By giving Cynthia an active, militaristic duty to perform, Robinson is effectively placing her in the position to be not only a New Woman, but also a Hemingway code hero. Given the fact that she gives her life for the cause, Cynthia may be read as having much more in common with code heroes such as Robert Jordan from Hemingway's *For Whom the Bell Tolls* than their far more passive romantic interests. After World War II, in which women were actively involved not only in overseas service with the Red Cross, but also in the military itself as WACs and WAVEs, the target audience for a new Hemingway film adaptation would have been much more receptive to a woman taking an active role in the war effort, instead of merely providing support from the home front. Read in this manner, Robinson's decision to make Cynthia the war hero who dies on the battlefield is an empowering plot move that serves to keep current the edgy spirit of Hemingway's typical New Woman characters.

Further, Robinson seems to have co-opted the entire Spanish Civil War plotline from *For Whom the Bell Tolls* and applied it to his adaptation of *Snows*. The general tone that wars are senseless and tend to be fought by people who will die for a cause remote to them is preserved in the interpretive transference from one Hemingway novel to another onscreen. In *Snows*, Harry Street's involvement in the Spanish Civil War seems to be mere happenstance—he joined the army in an attempt to find Cynthia. After Harry finds Cynthia trapped underneath an overturned ambulance on the battlefield, he arranges for her to be carried away on a stretcher. When he tries to follow her, Harry's Spanish commander shoots him in the back. This choice to show the heartlessness of Harry's commander to a man trying to accompany his fallen love off the battlefield is a convincing way to convey Hemingway's often-discussed disdain with government-sponsored military action that is expressed in *For Whom the Bell Tolls*. In Hemingway's hyper-masculine world, a man who shoots another in the back is no man at all.

Scenes of shooting as a visual symbol of masculinity abound in *Snows*, and several of them work together to re-create an entire sequence that seems to have been adapted from another Hemingway short story, "The Short Happy Life of Francis Macomber." However, significant alterations are made to Hemingway's original Macomber plotline in order to make it fit into the thematic arc of *Snows*. First, the Robert Wilson "white hunter" character from "Macomber" is interpreted as a helpful and non-threatening character when presented as Johnson in *Snows*. Whereas Robert Wilson has an affair with Margot Macomber, and attempts to undermine her relationship with Francis, Johnson offers both Cynthia and Helen helpful and friendly advice on how to maintain their relationships with Harry. This thematic variation is in keeping with the main story arc of *Snows* in adaptation—that Harry is supposed to have his masculinity reaffirmed, not destroyed, by his various brushes with death.

Also, it should be noted that Casey Robinson has deftly used the Springfield rifle as a connecting visual symbol of masculine vitality in the Macomber-esque sequence. The Springfield rifle that Harry is given by Uncle Bill, his masculine mentor, is the one with which he shoots the rhino as it charges toward Cynthia. This action makes the Springfield Harry's symbolic weapon of manhood in the film. An interesting corollary to the symbolism expressed by Harry's use of the Springfield rifle is that Cynthia is barely able to shoot her rifle at all, whereas her fictional inspiration, Margot Macomber, is good enough with her weapon at a significant distance to shoot her husband in the back of the head and make it look like an accident. The reversal of abilities from the "Macomber" story is yet another piece of evidence that King's adaptation of "Snows" intends to reaffirm Harry's choices in this circumstance because his masculine protective instinct is strong. By killing the rhino that could have killed his wife, Harry is facing fate head on and proving himself up to the challenges it presents. What results from this Macomber-reversal sequence in *Snows* is the sense that in Hemingway's world, part of being a man is being able to face fearlessly the physical and emotional challenges of the most dangerous hunt a man can engage in: the pursuit of a woman he loves.

Not surprisingly, Robinson's script of *Snows* also contains what appear to be numerous allusions to Hemingway's private life with his wives. The montage of shots that visually describe Harry's life in a small Paris apartment with his first wife, Cynthia, call to mind Hemingway's modest existence in that city with his first wife, Hadley Richardson. Many details in this sequence, including Harry's choice to leave the news service to write full-time, seem to be lifted directly from the pages of Hemingway's biography, which was just as well known through newspapers and magazines in the 1950s as it is today through more scholarly sources. Next, Hemingway's quarrel with his third wife, Martha Gellhorn, over his choice to cover World War II as a war correspondent is reflected in Harry's arguments with Cynthia over the same subject. Hemingway's personal relationship with his second, richer wife, Pauline Pfeiffer, appears to be implied by the inclusion of Harry's second marriage to Liz in the film adaptation of *Snows*. Last, the amicable, yet world-weary, dynamic between Hemingway and his fourth wife, Mary Welsh, is preserved in King's portrayal of Harry and Helen's relationship. Mary, who loved the outdoors and traveling as much as her husband did, was a fitting final spouse for Hemingway.

Apparently, director Henry King thought so too, since Susan Hayward, the actress he cast in the role of Helen, looked and spoke similarly to her real-life counterpart, Mary Hemingway. The overall effect of all of these references to Hemingway's actual spouses in *Snows* is to create a film that blurs the lines between where the author's life ends and his fictional characters' lives begin. This approach is fitting because in Hemingway's often highly autobiographical fiction, the line between reality and fantasy was never clearly drawn in the first place.

Perhaps this blurring between what actually happened in Hemingway's life and what the author thought should have happened, as expressed in his fiction, was the reason that King and Robinson felt justified in changing the ending of *Snows*. Rather than having Harry die full of "rot and poetry," the adaptation team of *Snows* allows Harry a second chance at life, facilitated by his quick-thinking wife, Helen ("Snows" 43). Hemingway's audiences and Hollywood were not ready to see their literary hero ascend the spiritual heights of Kilimanjaro, while despairing that his contributions to the world had not been significant enough. Instead, when Hemingway's Hollywood audience sensed their hero faltering in the text of the original "Snows," they preferred to uphold his image of stoic endurance. In the still-shaken, post–World War II America of the early 1950s, America still needed heroes, even after those heroes felt that they no longer wanted to play the roles that they had created. This is why the thematically inconsistent ending of *The Snows of Kilimanjaro*, while a great departure from the original story, is still consistent within the context of the film. By 1951, Hemingway may have been tired of being Hemingway, but he had already inspired a second generation of young men to buy into the lifestyle of vitality that he had sold all his life. As a result, no matter how weary he might be, the leopard had to keep searching, as the ouroboros of literary celebrity came full circle to include a new generation.

• FOUR •

Papa's Grace Under Genre Pressure, Part Two
Hollywood Adaptations of Hemingway, 1957–2013

The Sun Also Rises (1957)

The Sun Also Rises (1926) has what must be the longest connection to the film industry of any Ernest Hemingway novel. According to Gene Phillips, the director of *Sun*'s film adaptation, Henry King, met Hemingway in 1923, while he was still working on the novel. As King recalls, his first meeting with Hemingway was "in a honky-tonk on the Rue Fontaine which I discovered while I was researching a picture in Europe, in a tavern where Hemingway frequently used to go. The girl that was the source of Lady Brett in the novel was there with him at his table that night" (qtd. in Phillips 120). Perhaps because of this early acquaintance, King held Hemingway in high esteem for the rest of his career as a director. Disappointed that the author had disapproved of his adaptation of *The Snows of Kilimanjaro*, King was determined to produce a better film with his second Hemingway effort. To this end, King enlisted the help of the author himself, along with star Ava Gardner and screenwriter Peter Viertel, to re-create the best shooting script possible. However, the film's producer, Darryl Zanuck, hampered the production with poor casting choices and a cloying Hollywood ending that betrays the cynical heart of Hemingway's original. As a result, King's adaptation of *The Sun Also Rises* is a highly incorporated interpretive rendering of Hemingway's original novel that nevertheless suffers from inconsistencies in the artistic vision of film team collaborators due to an imbalance of creative command.

Hemingway's original novel, *The Sun Also Rises*, is one of those books that can truly be called the voice of a generation. Written to capture the general sentiments of disillusionment and hopelessness that pervaded the generation of young veterans after World War I, the novel has served as a touchstone for like-minded youth ever since. Often referred to as the Lost Generation, the original group that inspired Hemingway's novel was named by Gertrude Stein's mechanic, whom she overheard saying to an inept young employee, "All of you young people who served in the war, you are all a lost generation" (qtd. in Phillips 122). Even though he engaged in the same hedonistic behavior himself, Hemingway tended to regard his generation with disdain. He claimed to have chosen the quote from Ecclesiastes that opens the novel because he had "a great deal of fondness and admiration for the earth, and not a hell of a lot for my generation" (qtd. in Phillips 122). In this first novel, Hemingway established a pattern of idealizing men and cultures who exhibited a strong moral code.

In *Sun*, this moral code had a specific inspiration that forms the underlying theme of the novel, which Hemingway derived from observing patterns of masculine behavior in Spain. Explaining the concept years later in *Death in the Afternoon*, Hemingway said, "In Spain, honor is a very real thing. Called *pundonor*, it means honor, probity, courage, self-respect, and pride in one word" (91). Hemingway's interest in *pundonor* is displayed in *The Sun Also Rises*, which might be read as a meditation on what might happen to a man who loses his sense of personal honor and self-worth by allowing his emotions to get the better of him. This self-allowed violation of a man's honor by impulsive behavior, particularly when inspired by love or lust for a woman, forms the central theme of Hemingway's original novel.

Of course, the Circe at the center of *The Sun Also Rises* is Brett Ashley, portrayed in Henry King's film adaptation by Ava Gardner. As mentioned previously, the original Brett Ashley was inspired by Lady Duff Twysden, a then–32-year-old British semi-aristocrat with whom the younger Hemingway became fascinated during his twenties in Paris. Twysden's mysterious ability to attract and hold the attention of almost any man near her is the chief characteristic that links her with her Hollywood alter ego, Gardner. At the time she began filming *Sun*, Gardner was at the peak of her career and came highly recommended by infatuated screenwriter Peter Viertel for the part. As Gardner biographer Lee Server explains:

> Aside from the fact that she had not yet been widowed by an English lord, there was very little else about the actress that did not seem custom designed to embody Hemingway's creation, including but not limited to her physical allure, her capricious love life, her often desperate *joie de vivre*, and her intimate knowledge of bullfighters [342].

Apparently, Gardner herself agreed, and claimed that she "always felt close to Papa's women" (qtd. in Server 342). However, eager as she was to play Lady Brett because of the personal connection she felt to the part, after she viewed the script, "her enthusiasm turned to uncertainty" (Server 343). To her credit, Gardner made the best decision possible when she found the adaptation's script unacceptable: she took it to Ernest Hemingway hoping he could fix it.

Gardner gave Hemingway a copy of the script to redo, because "for your own pride you have to read it and change things. Everyone in the script runs around saying *c'est la guerre* and peachy things like that" (qtd. in Phillips 123). Hemingway read the script and agreed with his close friend Gardner. The author tried to meet with Viertel and Zanuck, claiming that he would sue if the film were made from such a bad script. Sensing a disaster, director Henry King also exercised astute artistic judgment and offered a compromise. King told Zanuck that he was not a Hemingway scholar, but that "I knew this book; and it seemed to me that neither of the writers who had worked on the script so far had read the book carefully. So I said that I was going to see that the next person who worked on the script was going to get inside the novel" (qtd. in Phillips 124). These moves toward compromise greatly improved the adaptation's script and represent the best sort of collaborative efforts by creative interests to produce a quality adaptation.

However, many Hemingway film scholars, such as Gene Phillips, blame the film's inability to capture the spirit of *Sun* on film on what they perceive to be poor casting decisions on the part of Darryl Zanuck, by choosing actors who were too old for their parts. True, Zanuck was most likely seeking marquee name recognition and what he felt would be certain box office success when he filled the male roles in the film with veteran actors, including Tyrone Power as Jake Barnes, Eddie Albert as Jake's buddy Bill Gorton, and Errol Flynn as Brett Ashley's fiancé Mike Campbell. Still, each of these actors arguably had enough personal connections to draw upon with the characters they played to give acceptable performances.

Tyrone Power, who portrayed the impotent soldier Jake Barnes, suffered the breakup of his first marriage, to French actress Annabella, reportedly because of the couple's inability to conceive a child together. Also, Power was a veteran, serving as a Marine pilot in World War II in the South Pacific, another situation which allegedly took its toll on his first marriage, largely because his wife felt that he returned from the war a much different man (IMDB.com). These life circumstances provide a background of melancholy disillusionment that show in Power's performance, which is given with a well-played sense of detachment that readers have come to expect from the Jake Barnes character.

Oddly enough, in his real life, the actor playing one of the most irresponsible characters in the film had the most in common with Hemingway's articulated goal of a strong moral code grounded in a connection to the earth. Eddie Albert, who portrayed Jake Barnes's easy-going fishing friend and former army buddy Bill Gorton, was also a veteran, serving in the navy in the South Pacific during World War II. Further, Albert has the most in common with Hemingway's love of the outdoors and its healing properties, which is articulated in the fishing sequences of both the novel and film. Albert was "a tireless conservationist, crusading for endangered species, healthful food, cleanup of Santa Monica Bay pollution and other causes," including speaking out in Congressional hearings against the use of pesticides near marine birds, leading to the banning of DDT ("Albert"). Watching the fishing sequences with this in mind, it is easy to understand why Albert's performance in the calm outdoor scenes of the film adaptation seem to come more naturally to him than to Power. The Minnesota-born Albert shared with fellow upper–Midwesterner Hemingway a sportsman/conservationist's love of the land and its ability to restore the men who seek its tranquility and who find in it a sense of permanence that fosters internal fortitude.

Perhaps the best casting decision made in the adaptation of *Sun* was the choice of Errol Flynn as Mike Campbell, Brett Ashley's drunken, bankrupt fiancé. In his early career, Flynn was defined by a suave, debonair, and devil-may-care attitude toward women and life that spilled over into his work. Flynn's public persona, both onscreen and off, was so identifiable that decades later scholar Benjamin S. Johnson would write a treatise, "An Errolesque Philosophy on Life," that turned the actor's name into an adjective to describe that type of lifestyle. However, by the time *Sun* premiered in 1957, Flynn was somewhat of a fallen idol, having allowed his career to dissolve into excessive drinking and drug use in the decades following his career-defining role as the title character in *The Adventures of Robin Hood* (1938). Still, Flynn's life-dissipation in the two decades following *Robin Hood* made him a perfect fit for Hemingway's Campbell character. Although Flynn was nominated for an Oscar in the part, many critics countered the assertion that Flynn's portrayal of Campbell was spectacular, and instead claimed that the actor was merely playing himself.

One might argue that, in a Hemingway film, such self-portrayal is permissible. Given the fact that Hemingway himself most often wrote only thinly veiled autobiography, it is easy to accept Flynn's work in the role as a natural extension of the Hemingway celebrity ouroboros. This is especially true if *Sun*'s director, Henry King, is to be believed when he describes how hard Flynn worked to achieve the correct emotional tone for his portrayal of Campbell.

Accepting Flynn's superficial veneer as a hard drinker and womanizer, King claimed:

> Underneath, he was a serious, hard-working actor. He showed in his soliloquy about temporarily losing Brett to Romero near the end of the picture the way a man really feels when his girl has left him. The scene was in the back of his mind from the first day of shooting. Acting did not come easily to him; he tended to rush through a long and difficult scene just to get the agony over with. But we would talk for hours about Mike's state of mind in that scene. I told him not to worry about projecting the emotions of the scene because once he had thought his interpretation through, the emotions would take care of themselves; and that is what happened [qtd. in Phillips 130].

Still, Hemingway was not impressed, and though he didn't see most of Flynn's performance, he is rumored to have smirked, "Any picture in which Errol Flynn is the best actor is its own worst enemy" (qtd. in Phillips 131). In his criticism of the film, Phillips is partially correct to argue that Hemingway was much too quick to dismiss films based on his work "with a derogatory quip—whether he had seen all of it or not—[and] causes one to suspect that he somehow felt required to knock almost any movie adaptation of his work in order to preserve his literary status" (131). However, Phillips ignores a possible ulterior motive that Hemingway may have possessed for deriding Flynn's performance. By that time in his career, Hemingway had well established that bad press generates more news than good press, and so by expressing displeasure in the films, he insured that people would see them, and thereby enhance his reputation by going out and reading the book to compare and see if he was wrong.

Whatever the case, both Phillips, in his professional criticism of the film, and Hemingway, in his personal critiques of it, were right about the incorrectness of Zanuck's decision to cast Robert Evans as Pedro Romero. For the role of Romero, director Henry King wanted to use a real bullfighter, Miguel Delgado, but "Zanuck said he looked more like a waiter than a bullfighter, and cast a young actor named Bob Evans instead" (qtd. in Phillips 132). The choice of Evans angered Hemingway not only because of the young actor's lack of authenticity in the role, but also because of the haphazard manner in which Zanuck selected him, without regard for any personal connections that Evans might have to the role. Instead of selecting a Spanish actor, which Hemingway would have preferred, Zanuck chose Evans simply because he looked right for the part, after meeting him in a nightclub. This arbitrary casting decision shows in the film, as Evans clearly struggles with a Spanish accent and also to find himself in the role.

Zanuck's impulsive casting also led to an unnatural extension of the role of Georgette, the prostitute Jake Barnes invites to accompany him during the novel's first nightclub scenes. According to screenwriter Peter Viertel in the commentary accompanying the DVD version of the film, Zanuck had read the novel, and had "some sort of visual hope for the thing," but "all that went out the window" after Julienne Greco was cast as Georgette. According to Viertel, Zanuck was introduced to Greco by Mel Ferrer, who portrayed Robert Cohn in the film. Zanuck liked her immediately and began an affair with her during filming, leading in turn to Zanuck's writing extra scenes for his new girlfriend, which "distorted the whole thing." Ironically, what seems to have happened with Greco's casting is that Zanuck inadvertently assumed the role of Robert Cohn, and compromised the overall artistic vision of his work in order to accommodate his desire for a woman. In short, he broke the very code of *pundonor* that Hemingway tried to express in his original novel, and the film adaptation of *Sun* suffers because of it.

Another problem with *Sun* is that the adaptation loses some of the spirit of Hemingway's original because it was produced in Mexico, not Spain. According to Phillips, Hemingway was "a stickler for realism" and "worried that audiences would notice that the film was shot in Mexico instead of Spain where the story was set" (118). The plot of *Sun* centers on the Festival of St. Fermin in Pamplona, which Hemingway and his friends attended in 1923, and he began writing about only two weeks later (Phillips 120). There are conflicting accounts regarding the choice to film in Mexico. In DVD commentary for *Sun*, Peter Viertel claimed that they were forced to make the movie in Mexico by the studio, "who thought that the production would get out of hand if allowed to go to Spain." It was impossible to reproduce the atmosphere of Pamplona in Mexico. In contrast, Phillips claims that Mexico was chosen because Pamplona, at the time the film scheduled for shooting, "was four feet deep in snow" (132). Regardless, the choice to use the city of Morelia, Mexico, with the bullring repainted to look like Pamplona, and intercut with actual scenes of Pamplona bullfights, does make the entire production appear more Central American than Spanish, and thus it loses a great deal of Hemingway's desired geographical significance.

Still, Henry King in the remainder of his interpretation of *Sun* manages to salvage the main underlying ideology of Hemingway's work, and translate it effectively from the Lost Generation of World War I to the similarly disaffected climate of post–World War II America. As Phillips notes, "The impotency of Jake comes across in the film, as it does in the novel, as symbolizing the incapacity of the disillusioned postwar generation to feel and love deeply; Jake's abiding respect for Romero also comes through in the film, as does his consequent recognition of the bullfighter as the norm of conduct against which he judges himself and his companions, Mike Campbell, Robert Cohn, and Bill Gorton" (125). Henry King's efforts to convey this code of conduct as a timeless essential to manliness is evident from the very first scene in the film. In the opening sequence, King's camera eye pans to the right, with the set decoration changing from Paris in the 1920s to the 1950s, while a voiceover intones, "Our story deals with another Paris ... in a bohemian world of poets and writers." This visual movement puts Hemingway's past into the then-present 1950s, and immediately afterward follows up with a scene in which the audience first learns about the causes and effects of Jake Barnes's impotency. The overall effect of this opening sequence effectively translates the problems of the Lost Generation, and the desires of its veterans to regain a sense of masculine identity after the trauma of war, into a context that 1950s audiences would have easily understood.

The matter of Hemingway's sense of natural versus organized religion was a bit more complicated to translate from page to screen. As Phillips states, "Hemingway's ethical code ... amounts to a kind of natural religion rooted in the pantheistic concept that the most intimate contact one can have with God on this earth is to be found wherever nature has remained uncontaminated by the encroachments of modern mechanized society. Such communion with nature purifies Hemingway's heroes" (125). This sensibility is shown in King's film through the fishing sequences with Jake Barnes and Bill Gorton, and also in the scenes in which Barnes goes away to swim and think alone after Brett leaves with Romero.

Still, even though Hemingway's sense of natural religion and its restorative properties is preserved among the male characters, Brett Ashley's similarly relaxed sense of natural morality is not conveyed as truthfully on film as in Hemingway's original novel. As Edward Murray notes, "Hemingway's Brett is depicted as a pagan goddess reigning over a wasteland, but in the movie, Brett prays devoutly at the altar for Romero" (qtd. in Phillips 126). Further, in the book, she continually renounces God, and although she says in the film there are things that they have "instead of God" she seems to seek divine approval anyway (King). The possible reason for this is that, in the 1950s, audiences and censors might have been prepared to accept male characters seeking spiritual solace in the outdoors, but they would have been less receptive to a female character carving out an individualized sense of morality based on sensual desires rather than organized religion and its dictates for passive femininity. As a result, in the adaptation of *Sun*, one finds that Hemingway's conception of acceptable standards of female behavior in the 1920s were much more feminist than Hollywood's of the 1950s, or any earlier era.

Finally, the most problematic thematic discrepancy between *Sun* as a novel versus the film is that the book ends in despair, whereas the adaptation ends with hope. The novel concludes with Barnes telling Ashley, "Wouldn't it be pretty to think so," regarding their possibility for happiness as a couple if he were still sexually whole (*Sun* 251). In contrast, the film ends with Ashley saying, "There must be some hope for us somewhere" (King). The difference between these two endings is that the novel ends in cynicism, dismissing the possibility of wholeness either in individual relationships or international security after a world war, whereas the film blithely dismisses these grave concerns in hopes of conveying a feel-good Hollywood ending. This choice by *Sun*'s production team loses the emotional resonance of Hemingway's original novel that makes it so indelible in the minds of his readers.

Without a penis, Jake Barnes is rendered physically unable to consummate his love for Brett Ashley. This physiological lacking is also responsible for Barnes's spiritual impotency as well, rendering him unable to find purpose in his life after the war, due to an overwhelming sense of self-doubt. This sense of complete despair, for Hemingway characters, is the only unpardonable sin, because it is the direct opposite of the self-confidence that comes with honor, or *pundonor*. By taking away this idea of ultimate defeat of a character that the author has caused his readers to feel such compassion for, the film adaptation of *Sun* loses the aura of epic tragedy that made the novel a generational touchstone. In short, the hopeful ending of King's film breaks the cycle of Hemingway's ouroboros, by robbing audiences of the story's natural conclusion.

In sum, Henry King's adaptation of *The Sun Also Rises* suffers from an imbalance of creative control toward Darryl Zanuck's arbitrary casting and Hollywood's perennial need for happy endings. Still, the film stands as a reminder of how effective cooperation among actors, writers, and original author can be in interpreting a novel on screen for a new generation.

A Farewell to Arms (1957)

David Selznick's production of *A Farewell to Arms* (1957) is a close, faithful conversion of Hemingway's original novel. It is much more reflective of Hemingway's themes than Frank Borzage's 1932 adaptation of the work. Still, Hemingway was suspicious of the second film production of his novel, mostly because of Selznick's involvement in the project. As Gene Phillips explains the situation:

> More than two decades later, just when Hemingway was beginning to feel that his novel's reputation had survived this initial attempt to bring it to the screen, he was chagrined to hear that producer David O. Selznick had purchased the screen rights from Warners and was bent on making his version of *A Farewell to*

Arms the epic picture of World War I, just as his production of *Gone with the Wind* was the great cinematic epic of the Civil War. To this end, Selznick hired Ben Hecht, one of the many uncredited scriptwriters who worked on *GWTW*, to do the screenplay [Phillips 26].

Hemingway's worst fear, that his novel would be turned into *GWTW* set in Europe, became reality. Today, the influence of Selznick's Southern epic is clearly evident both in the war sequences and personal scenes of character interaction throughout the film. Still, even though the conventional tropes of the historical epic genre are at work, and tilt the entire project toward the spectacular, Selznick's conversion of Hemingway's novel manages to retain a great deal more of the spirit of the author's work than the earlier Borzage version.

This result is ironic, considering Selznick's opinion on the role that an author and his work should play in directing the final film product. When asked about how much of Hemingway's actual words and dialogue he would preserve in his adaptation, Selznick replied that Hemingway's novel "was not Holy Writ, and he had no intention of becoming a slave to it" (Phillips 27). Further, Selznick made it clear from day one of production that there was to be no "Papa-worshipping groveling on this picture" (qtd. in Laurence 65). Instead, Selznick was the film's self-declared dictatorial creative force. And yet, the film remains the most faithful of adaptations to *A Farewell to Arms* currently available. Seen today, the film appears to be a battle of wills between Hemingway and Selznick that ultimately concluded in a laying down of arms on both sides, allowing a very well done adaptation to come into existence in the no man's land between where both creative geniuses were firmly entrenched.

Selznick's reluctance to allow Hemingway to become too involved in the project may have been justified based upon early interactions between the pair in the creative process. In the beginning, Selznick attempted to offer Hemingway $50,000 of the profits from the film, even though he was not legally bound to do so, because the author had previously sold his rights with the 1932 version. After seeing the casting decisions made for the film, Hemingway rudely dismissed Selznick's offer and gave the film a dim prognosis. Apparently, Hemingway thought that Rock Hudson was too young to play the war hero, Frederic Henry, and Jennifer Jones was too old to portray Henry's love interest, British Red Cross nurse Catherine Barkley. Hemingway's criticism of the casting of Jones must have particularly irked Selznick, because Jones was Selznick's wife, and he often risked his own career in order to secure her plum roles.

Further, Hemingway's poor opinion of the film was not improved after he saw the final product. The author reportedly walked out of a screening of *Farewell* after only a half hour, and said that if the film managed to turn a profit, Selznick should have the $50,000 changed into nickels and "shove them up his ass until they came out his ears" because watching a movie that bad was "like pissing in your father's beer" (qtd. in Phillips 32). Apparently Hemingway's prediction was correct. The film turned only a small profit and became Selznick's final picture. At last, the director's obsession with creating increasingly expensive star vehicles for his wife proved his downfall, and Selznick was never again able to secure funding for another project.

Yet, half a century later, after Selznick's overzealousness to make cinema audiences see his wife as the next Vivien Leigh has had some time to wear off, the film that he created screens as a much richer and more nuanced production than it was originally given credit for. Selznick's adaptation of *Farewell* is highly metaphorical. The producer's vision of the work centers on the idea of comparing and contrasting the actual, external war taking place in Italy during World War I, with the emotional, internal war that goes on inside a person as he or she is falling in love, but trying to resist that feeling. This take on how to translate Hemingway's work for the screen was completely at odds with the author's. Always a stickler for realism and accuracy, Hemingway was deeply troubled by Selznick's attempts to make the film's physical backdrops, whether in the Alps or in the Italian countryside, as dramatically picturesque as possible. Selznick recognized Hemingway's unproductive preference for exact realism early on during production: "If a character goes from Café A to Café B, instead of Café B to Café A, or if a boat heads north instead of south, Hemingway is upset" (qtd. in Laurence 63). As a result, Selznick simply chose to ignore the author's scathing commentary on his film process.

Perhaps the reason why Hemingway held such strong beliefs about the locational actualities of the production was because the novel, *A Farewell to Arms*, was so closely based on the author's own life. Hemingway's original tale was highly incorporated with details from his experiences in the Italian army and Red Cross during World War I, and also with the alleged love affair that he had with his nurse, Agnes von Kurowsky. In the novel, the real-life relationship between Hemingway and Kurowsky is transformed into the characters of Catherine Barkley and Frederic Henry. However, the fictional relationship stands as a sort of wish fulfillment, since Kurowsky claims that her relationship with Hemingway was never consummated.

To his credit, Selznick did seem to appreciate Hemingway's personal connection to the work, and even added additional details to the film's plot that make Frederic Henry even more like his real-life creator. In the film, Henry is a writer, whereas in the novel, he is an architect. This is a silent nod to the fact that Hemingway as a young writer fictionalized his own life in his account of Frederic Henry. Also, this choice uses the creative process of adapting a work for film to complete the Hemingway ouroboros, as the soldier whom the writer was re-forms back into the soldier who would become Hemingway.

The two chief themes of Hemingway's original novel are also preserved in Selznick's too often maligned film version. The first of these themes is how Hemingway calls into question the validity of war as a means of resolving conflict between nations. In the novel, Hemingway suggests repeatedly that war is more of a way for power-hungry leaders to assert their authority than for two opposing peoples to confront each other and settle their differences. Ultimately, Hemingway seems to say that the human cost of such action is too great, and oftentimes a nation's choice to engage in armed conflict is simply not justifiable, given the potential rewards.

Pursuant to this line of reasoning, Selznick was right to encourage his audience to draw a visual comparison between *A Farewell to Arms* and *Gone with the Wind*. In *Farewell*, Frederic Henry takes up the role of Rhett Butler in *GWTW*, as a man who claims to "have always had a soft spot in his heart for lost causes, once he knows they are really lost" (Fleming). Rhett Butler would have made a great Hemingway code hero. Clearly Frederic Henry, in both the novel and the film, behaves in this same way, taking up arms for the nation of Italy, even though it is already defeated before the war even begins. This sentiment lends a sense of quixotic absurdity to the idea of being a hero, since a traditional hero is supposed to win his conflict and vanquish his foe, whereas the typical Hemingway code hero, like the typical Confederate soldier, enters into a conflict based only on his own principles, even though he knows he will most likely fail. This idea of finding heroism in valiant failures has caused Gene Phillips to correctly note, "Hemingway demonstrated that heroism may be a condition of absurdity" (74). This theme is made readily apparent in every scene with the Frederic Henry character in Selznick's adaptation.

In the opening foreword of his 1957 film, Selznick begins his explanation of Hemingway's intention to question the validity of war in general, rather than to denounce the Italian effort during World War I in particular. The foreword on the first screen states:

> We tell a story out of one of the wildest theatres of World War I—the snow-capped Alpine peaks and muddy plains of northern Italy. Here between 1915 and 1918 the Italians stood against German and Austrian invaders. No people ever fought more valiantly, no nation ever rose more gallantly out of defeat to victory. But our story is not of war alone. It is a tale also of a love between an American boy and an English girl who bade their tragic farewell to arms while the cannon roared [Vidor].

This foreword was probably included to assuage patriotic audiences and critics, and also to preserve the general pro–Italian sentiment that nevertheless runs through Hemingway's original novel, even as he criticizes the nation's political officials for endorsing such heinous acts as the executions on the retreat from Caporetto. This entire political dimension was glossed over in the 1932 version, most likely because it was too volatile to discuss at the time. By 1957, film audiences were more sophisticated, largely because of pictures like *GWTW*, to accept mixed messages from Hollywood about the validity of a government's involvement in war.

Marriage, the other universally revered social institution that Hemingway calls into question in his novel, is also treated more according to the author's original views in the 1957 adaptation. However, even in the 1950s, the choice of a couple to have a child together and remain unmarried was still too much for mainstream audiences to accept without significant qualification and explanation. As a result, Selznick had to partially compromise Hemingway's creative vision in order to salvage the overall collaborative effort of the film. Phillips explains:

> Selznick made some of the same kinds of commercial concessions to the public taste as Borzage had inserted. Selznick too inserted a spurious wedding scene ... Selznick has the lovers quietly exchange their vows in the most unlikely of settings: at the racetrack amid the noisy jubilation that accompanies the announcement over the track's public address system of another Italian victory" [Phillips 29].

However, it is arguable that Selznick's changes were not completely unwarranted, if one considers the producer's take on Hemingway's marriage views in a symbolic context. Marriage, it seems in the Hemingway world, is at best two people taking a chance against fate and the surrounding circumstances of the world, which seek to stifle their desire to express love on their own terms. Viewed in this light, a spurious wedding at a race track is not too far-fetched of a way to give visualization to the bond between Henry and Catherine on-screen.

Still, many critics balk at Selznick's attempts to make *A Farewell to Arms* into a super-spectacle on the scale of *Gone with the Wind*. True, the evacuation of Caporetto does looks almost identical to the evacuation of Atlanta sequence from *GWTW*. This coincidence caused critics like Gene Phillips to say that Selznick's creative vision "not only ran counter to that of the spare 1932 version of the book, which got its story told in a compact eighty minutes, but also to Hemingway's own concept of his novel, which emphasized the personal love story of his principals more than the wartime background against which that story was set" (26). Although this reading of the film attempts to prove that the lengthy and elaborate war scenes weigh down the production, a different perspective might suggest that they merely serve as a demonstration of Hemingway's famous iceberg principle.

Even though the actual number of pages in the novel during which Hemingway directly discusses the war is small, the background spectacle of the war is quiet large in its emotional capacity. The war story acts as a macrocosm of the inner turmoil that people who are in love often feel in microcosm when they are at war with themselves, fighting against the rising tide of emotions that threaten to overwhelm their reason. This concept seems most likely what is going on in the minds of the two principal characters, Catherine and Henry, who seem to be people in control of their emotions, but who nevertheless get overwhelmed by love. Catherine had been controlled in her love for the boy who died, claiming that she chose not to have a sexual affair with him or marry him before he left for war: "I thought it would be worse for him if we were lovers. Then of course, he was killed and that was the end of it" (Vidor). In contrast, Henry has had numerous sexual encounters with women for the short term, before he meets Catherine, but has withheld his true emotions from them. It would have been very difficult to show this internal emotional conflict on screen. Therefore, it makes sense that Selznick's production makes up the gap between what readers can learn from hearing the internal conflict within the characters' minds by showing the actual, physical conflict of war around them in great detail.

Selznick's intention was to make the film an epic, on both the personal and spectacular levels. He spent five million dollars to shoot in the Italian Alps and fill the film with lavish battle sequences including 11,000 extras (Laurence 65). Particularly, Selznick gave the retreat from Caporetto and the burning of the city "his most lavish worry," insisting on exact replication of the mix of people from that area of Italy, from pairs of infant twins to elderly blind people, and repeats the scene from *Gone with the Wind* about the dilemma of needing to move patients that is not in the book (Laurence 69). This emphasis on the human drama unfolding during times of war further proves that Selznick intended for the extravagant war scenes to be viewed as greater metaphors expressing the individual tragedies of war written large.

Historically speaking, the retreat from Caporetto was an excellent event to use to demonstrate both the futility of individual effort in modern warfare and the fact that governmental motivations for armed conflict were not always pure. Caporetto was one of the most devastating events of World War I. The Italian losses, 11,000 killed, 20,000 wounded, and 265,000 taken prisoner, were enormous and the ludicrously harsh disciplinary regime of Italian Commander Luigi Cardona crushed the morale of the Italian troops, many of whom deserted immediately afterward (Simpkins 352). According to historians, the Battle of Caporetto became a synonym in Italian culture for a terrible defeat, and this failure of the Italian government to protect its people was used by anti-government propagandists and is still used today in arguments against the credibility of the Italian state (Townley 16). The historical significance of Caporetto as a metaphorical context for human defeat at all levels due to governmental inadequacy justifies the manner of adaptation used by Selznick in creating his artistic vision for *Farewell* on film.

Still, it would be incorrect to say that Selznick's vision was solely responsible for creating all the visual metaphors used in the film. Screenwriter Ben Hecht and director Charles Vidor continually employed visual symbolism to convey psychological meaning throughout their work on bringing *Farewell* from page to screen. In particular, five uses of props and scenery stand out from the film as examples of effective visual metaphor.

First, unsheathed swords are often employed to suggest to the audience that sexual intercourse has occurred in the film. The closeup of Henry's sword on the floor in the greenhouse as he initially makes love to Catherine implies that theirs is a holy union, despite its unconventionality. The sword has found the chalice which will become the vessel that carries his child. Similarly, the two rowing sequences in the film seem to act as opposite but mirroring bookends. The initial sequence, with Henry rowing calmly as Catherine swims along beside, denotes the peaceful tranquility with which they began their journey on love's waters, while the frantic rowboat flight to Switzerland near the end of the film foreshadows the tragic death of mother and child that concludes the film. Taken together, the two sequences can be read to suggest that a flood of romantic emotion, left unchecked, can prove dangerous and even fatal.

Another excellent use of mirrored symbol to denote change of emotional environment in the film occurs with the two hemorrhage sequences. Early in the film, Henry lies in the lower bunk of an ambulance while a man hemorrhages to death in the bed above him. Later, in the movie's ending sequence, Catherine dies of a hemorrhage following an unsuccessful Caesarean operation. In the first instance, another man's blood is literally falling on Henry, metaphorically showing the lieutenant's moral responsibility to his fellow soldiers. In contrast, Catherine's death by hemorrhage is indirectly a result of her affair with Henry that produced a child under dangerous circumstances. Read side by side, the inference here is that Barkley's death is also Henry's moral cross to bear, implying that he should have been more responsible in keeping his sexual desires in check, at least enough to prevent an unexpected pregnancy.

Two of Hemingway's favorite visual symbols, rain and cats, are also translated in successful ways to convey meaning in this adaptation of *Farewell*. Rain falls on the windows as Henry and Catherine make love for the first time, offering the audience a sense of foreboding because it gives Jones the opportunity to express Catherine's fear of the rain because she "sees herself dead in it" (Vidor). Later, as Henry walks away from the hospital where Catherine has just died, his tears mingle with the rain falling on his face, as if the whole of the sky is joining in his personal grief and making it universal. Last, cats, although they do not appear in Hemingway's original novel, are seen scurrying away in the rain as Catherine walks Henry to the train station, heading off to battle. Hemingway often used cats in his fiction to symbolize the contradiction between female physical independence and emotional vulnerability. The most clear use of this kind is Hemingway's famous short story "Cat in the Rain." Here, in Vidor's visualization of Catherine's attempt to keep a brave face even though she feels emotionally bereft at Henry's departure, it makes perfect metaphorical sense to have Hemingway's often-used cats hurry across the wet street into the darkness.

For her part, Jennifer Jones uses facial expressions and vocal tone to convey Catherine's inner turmoil throughout the film. Her performance is particularly good in her meeting scene with Henry, and later in the mirrored bedroom scene, where she fears that she has become a whore, even though her motivations for beginning the affair were based on true love. Vidor's direction and Hecht's script of *Farewell* is much more explicit about the nature and details of the affair between Catherine and Henry than the 1932 adaptation of the novel. However, their heightened allegiance to emotional honesty may have cost the film some degree of mainstream acceptance in the still morally rigid socio-cultural climate of the 1950s. Even though both Catherine and her baby die, and Henry is clearly left devastated at the end of the film because of their affair, the Catholic Legion of Decency "designated the movie 'morally objectionable in part for all audiences'" (Phillips 31). In the legion's view, the film lacked a sufficiently clear moral compensation for what it termed "the picture's unrelieved emphasis on illicit love" (Phillips 31). The legion's displeasure with the film arguably may have cut down on the number of audience members willing to accept a storyline that encouraged them to sympathize with a couple coping with the aftereffects of an extramarital affair. Still, the choices of Vidor and Hecht to preserve Hemingway's original intent, that the couple's choice to define love on their own terms warrants social acceptance, stands today as a perfectly reasonable adaptation decision.

Similarly, Rock Hudson's portrayal of Frederic Henry is also well done, and the actor accurately conveys Henry's internal struggle through facial expression and vocal delivery. Hudson's performance in the more emotionally intense scenes of the film go a long way in conveying the spirit of Hemingway's character without resorting to recitations of actual dialogue or thought processes from the novel. However, some critics still deride the over-dramatization of some of these scenes, particularly the one of Henry's desertion from the Italian army following the execution of his friend Rinaldi.

Frank Laurence claims, "The execution of Rinaldi is theatrics, even to the blindfold bit. It is sensationalism, too, in that the movie seems excited for the chance to show an execution that Hemingway left off scene" (Laurence 74). This reading is unnecessarily harsh. By showing the execution and making it especially horrific, Selznick's team is more clearly able to justify Henry's choice to desert the Italian Army, by showing that it was not only a morally noble act, but one of self-preservation. Other critics say that Hudson's overall performance of the character is too much. Phillips states that "Frederic's ruminations about death and defeat in the final hospital scene seems to be a cry of genuine anguish in the book, but appear self-conscious and overwrought in the movie" (Phillips 31). This interpretation is also arbitrarily dismissive, and represents a lack of acceptance for an actor's choice in personal style of delivery when in character. Hudson's gesture and pacing throughout this sequence create an even more intense sense of foreboding that culminates in a satisfying climax with Catherine's deathbed scene, which leaves the audience with an adequate sense of closure.

Although the balance of creative command on the film was skewed by David Selznick's insistence on dominating the production, critics have generally been too harsh on his adaptation of *A Farewell to Arms*. Today, the film screens as one of the better examples of the conversion adaptation style. The film effectively translates many of Hemingway's historical, socio-cultural, and psychological themes from the original novel as a work of cohesive cinema.

The Gun Runners (1958)

From the very beginning of his work on *The Gun Runners* (1958), director Don Siegel was skeptical as to whether audiences wanted or needed a third film adaptation of Hemingway's novel *To Have and Have Not*. Considering that two well-received cinematic versions of the book, *To Have and Have Not* (1944) with Humphrey Bogart and Lauren Bacall, and *The Breaking Point* (1950) starring James Garfield and Patricia Neal, had already been on the market within the preceding decade and a half, Siegel considered the market to be saturated. However, Siegel contracted to direct the film anyway, stating later:

> I realized how utterly ludicrous it was for me to remake *To Have and Have Not* and *The Breaking Point*, both of which had superior stories, both of which had

superior money, both of which had superior time. I thought it was absolutely stupid to remake *To Have and Have Not* and *The Breaking Point* ... I was very much against it, but I needed the money.... I'm sure the picture isn't any good [qtd. in Laurence 106–07].

The irony in Siegel's emphatic statement, that he knew it was wrong to take on the project but that he did it anyway because he needed the money, is that the director was in a similar position to the hero of his self-maligned film. Sam Martin, or Harry Morgan in the original novel, was a man who compromised his morality in an effort to remain financially solvent and independent. Don Siegel compromised his artistic integrity to make an adaptation that he knew would be subpar, in hopes of gaining enough money to finance future independent film projects. Nevertheless, the film that resulted from Siegel's efforts did not turn out as horribly as he feared, due to the efforts of Patricia Owens as Sam's wife, Lucy, and Eddie Albert as the villain Hanagan. Siegel's low-budget, interpretive adaptation screens today as a mostly cohesive work of collaborative cinema that, while not as strong as the two previous versions, still manages to capture the major themes from Hemingway's original novel, while also incorporating a few additions from the author's canon.

Given Siegel's reluctance to begin the project, one must wonder what external conditions made such an unappealing project appear financially lucrative. Glenn Erickson has explained the real reason for the production in his article for TCM.com:

> The answer lies in the way 1950s Hollywood was restructuring itself as the power of the studios waned. Former executives, agents and stars formed independent production companies, raising money on their own and contracting with studios mainly for distribution. Big stars like James Stewart and Bogart brokered sweetheart deals with the majors, but the equally marketable Burt Lancaster and John Wayne ran their own production companies. Because studios needed product to fill their distribution schedules, independent producers with the right connections were suddenly in demand: the industry now depended on the art of The Deal rather than a mogul's whim.

Founded by Ray Stark and Eliot Hyman, Seven Arts, the company that produced *The Gun Runners*, grew so rapidly in this freer filmmaking environment that it managed to buy out Warner Bros. after only ten years, creating the first independent studio/major distributor film company (Erickson). Seven Arts was helped by entrepreneurially minded directors like Don Siegel. After paying his dues for years making lower-budget films like *The Gun Runners*, Siegel was financially able to put together his own independent productions with stars he believed in, like Clint Eastwood, with whom Siegel produced many films. Given the rest of Siegel's early résumé, which is filled with similar tales of blue-collar toughs like Sam Martin, one might think of Hemingway's code hero as the literary grandfather of Eastwood's *Dirty Harry*.

In creating *The Gun Runners*, Siegel had to overcome other obstacles besides a small budget. With two previous adaptations of Hemingway's novel still relatively fresh in the audience's collective conscience, Siegel had to devise some sort of scheme to make his new version stand out. Apparently, Siegel decided to do so by using the old Hollywood trick of stirring up a bit of controversy surrounding the production. According to Frank Laurence, Siegel had his production team run several newspaper stories stating that Hemingway was lobbying against the film, "on the grounds that it implied his support of Castro's movement to overthrow the Batista regime and that he himself was involved with operations in contraband weapons" (106). After conjuring a little false political controversy, Siegel also issued some publicity statements intended to call attention to Gita Hall, a Swedish model who made her film debut in *The Gun Runners* as Hanagan's girlfriend, Eva. During the film's production, Siegel had Hall publicly announce that she was changing her name to Gita Hall Hemingway, "to indicate her lasting pride at being linked with a movie made from one of this great writer's books" (Phillips 63). This last ploy was too much for Hemingway, who had his attorneys threaten a lawsuit to stop Hall's proposed action, which in turn created even more of the controversial buzz that Siegel desired.

As it turned out, Siegel needed all the help from the popular press he could get for the film, which was almost unanimously panned by critics, who claimed that "*The Gun Runners* was little more than a crass exploitation of the Hemingway book, which did little credit to anyone associated with it" (Phillips 65). Stating that the film was simply an amalgam of the two previous adaptations of Hemingway's novel, critics also derided almost every new idea in the picture, from the casting of war hero Audie Murphy as Sam Martin to the upbeat ending that seemed completely out of sync with the bleak tone of Hemingway's original. The recognition of copying from previous versions was accurate, considering that Siegel and his main screenwriter, Daniel Mainwaring, admitted to studying MacDougall's script for *The Breaking Point* and borrowing from it as much as they could without fear of copyright infringement (Laurence 107). However, Siegel and Mainwaring's choice to move the setting of the film back to Hemingway's original choices of Key West and Havana, together with strengthening the female characters into more assertive foils for Sam, were choices that demonstrated an attention to incorporating details from the Hemingway canon that most critics overlooked.

In *The Gun Runners*, Lucy behaves much more like an early-career, Hemingway-style woman who is fiercely protective of her man, in the mold of *A Farewell to Arms*'s Catherine Barkley, instead of the passive wife depicted in earlier adaptations of *To Have and Have Not*. Further, although they repeated the character of Hanagan, who had been invented whole-cloth for *The Breaking Point*, Siegel and Mainwaring also made the villain's girlfriend, Eva, into a more outspoken, overtly sexual and self-preservative Hemingway woman, reminiscent of *The Sun Also Rises*'s Brett Ashley. These nods to earlier Hemingway texts create richer dialogue for the female actresses in the production to work with, resulting in much more nuanced characterizations than previous adaptations allowed.

Additionally, the choice to reset *The Gun Runners* in Key West and Havana allowed Siegel and Mainwaring to make their adaptation more topical and to interpret the border-crossing tension present in Hemingway's original novel within the context of a new generation's even more worrisome political climate. The choice to cast war hero Audie Murphy in a film set in revolution-era Communist Cuba during the 1950s can be read as "giving the film a pro–American, anti–Communist slant," even though the filmmakers "had no way of knowing how the struggle would turn out: their film was released exactly four months before Fidel Castro's victorious entry into Havana" (Erickson). Still, audiences watching the film today with the benefit of historical retrospect cannot help but wonder what interpretation Siegel and Mainwaring had in mind regarding Hemingway's reaction to the volatile politics in Cuba. The generally negative manner in which Siegel's film portrays Cuban government officials certainly invites further exploration into Hemingway's feelings on the subject.

On the surface, Hemingway was quite glib about Cuban politics. The author spent most of his time during the Cuban revolution away from the country, traveling to Idaho, Spain, and New York, while saying in letters home that he was having "a lot more fun than sitting on my ass in Cuba taking Cuban politics seriously" (Baker 546). Yet, there is reason to believe that Hemingway, who did not live to see the ultimate result of Castro's takeover, initially supported the dictator. Carlos Baker provides insight into Hemingway's hopes for the revolution:

> As an old student of revolutions, Ernest took the position that any change in Cuba was better than none. Batista's gang had looted the rich island naked, and Ernest estimated that he had made off with $600 to $800 million. If Castro could run a straight government, it would be great, but he was up against a hell of a lot of money. Some of the United States interests like United Fruit were well and responsibly administered; others had made "terrific deals" with Batista and were very "un–OK." "I wish Castro all luck," said Ernest. "The Cuban people now have a decent chance for the first time ever." His only regret was that he had not been on hand to see Batista pull out [543].

Statements like these, made by Hemingway during the Cuban Revolution, suggest that the author did in fact take Cuban politics more seriously than he boasted to casual acquaintances. During his travels in the military and for recreation, Hemingway had ample opportunity to see injustice among the social classes all over the world. The fact that Hemingway chose to set *To Have and Have Not*, a generally socialist novel about how a working-class man has little chance to get ahead in the world, in Cuba suggests that Cuba's class disparity was worse than in other cultures. To its credit, *The Gun Runners* is the only adaptation to date that even hints at the possibility of Hemingway's political hopes for the success of Castro's new regime that underlie the novel. Considering that the film was a product of McCarthy-era America, it is not surprising; however, that Siegel and Mainwaring chose to express mostly disfavor for the new Communist government. Regardless, *The Gun Runners* is notable for being the first Hemingway film adaptation to openly express political sentiment of any kind, thereby opening the doors for future discussion in less hostile times.

Instead of delving too deeply into precarious political waters, Siegel's film focuses on psychological conflict, chiefly within the character of Sam Martin, the renamed Hemingway hero known in the novel as Harry Morgan. Thomas Hemmeter and Kevin Sweeney have made the thought-provoking observation that *The Gun Runners* frames Sam's struggle with other life problems in terms of sexual conflict. In the film, Sam is provided with two blondes, Eva and the nameless floozy at Freddie's Bar, who attempt to win him away from his wife. Throughout the film Sam dismisses both of these women. According to Hemmeter and Sweeney, "his main concern is to keep his boat—a concern explicitly tied to his masculinity—his abrasive relationship with the blonds represents a parallel fight to keep possession of his wife. As in Hawks's film, to make the right choice in his dealings with women is to win the larger battle: Sam wins his boat as well as Lucy" (69). This observation demonstrates that Siegel's film is thematically consistent with a recurring theme in Hemingway's writing: that a man who allows a woman to make him compromise his morals is no man at all.

Viewed in this context, the seemingly incongruent happy ending of Siegel's adaptation makes more sense. In *The Gun Runners*, Sam Martin commits far fewer violations of his self-imposed moral code than Harry Morgan does in the original novel, *To Have and Have Not*. Sam Martin has no knowledge that he is smuggling guns until he is already in the act of assisting Hanagan load the boat, and he kills no one for personal gain, only as a last resort of self-protection. In contrast, Harry Morgan is completely aware that he is wrongfully smuggling illegal aliens and shoots them simply to avoid having witnesses

Four • Papa's Grace Under Genre Pressure, Part Two 183

when the plan goes awry. Therefore, it makes sense, within the Catholicized framework of Hemingway's system of punishment and reward, that Sam Martin would be wounded but allowed to return to his wife, whereas Harry Morgan must die and lose possession of his wife forever. By interpreting Siegel and Mainwaring's alterations in this way, *The Gun Runners* can still be viewed as thematically consistent within the Hemingway canon, although its plot departs from the original novel.

However, Siegel's adaptation wisely stops short of making Sam Martin an uncomplicated Hemingway code hero. Although Sam is less criminally involved than Harry Morgan, he still deludes himself into believing that he has no culpable mental state that would cause him to suffer the consequences of dealing with a shady man like Hanagan. Sam's guilty conscience is given voice through Hanagan's girlfriend, Eva, who tells him that he should have asked more questions before taking Hanagan's money, saying, "When they buy you for something, they buy you for everything" (Siegel). Eva's quip, which is repeated several times in *The Gun Runners*, might be read as key to the entire film. Whereas Hemingway's original novel and the two earlier adaptations center on the statement "A man alone has no chance," Siegel's catchphrase focuses instead on how interactions between men, no matter how small, can lead to extreme consequences that may alter the course of one's life. On the surface, this seems to be a shift of focus; however, it actually reinforces the desperation of the Sam Martin/Harry Morgan character's situation. Not only does a man have no chance when he is completely alone, but he also has no chance when he puts too much faith in others, who may prove untrustworthy. The only way for a man to survive with integrity is to take some sort of middle ground between total moral isolation and dangerous interdependence. In this no-man's-land between extremes is where the mettle of a Hemingway code hero is tested, and hopefully proven.

What is interesting about Siegel's film is that the catalyst who causes Sam to question where he stands on this moral battlefield is always a woman. Lucy makes Sam realize the possible consequences of assisting Hanagan in some sort of illegal operation by telling him that he could lose what he loves most, namely their relationship, by going through with it. Also, Eva causes Sam to question how little he has sold himself out for by telling him that she agreed to become Hanagan's co-conspirator under similar circumstances. By himself, Sam would most likely never have given a second thought to giving up his moral code, because he has already resigned himself to the belief that he can do no better. As Hemmeter and Sweeney sum up the issue, Siegel's adaptation "presents strong women's voices that defy this voice of alienated resignation and expose the moral dishonesty that lies behind it" (73). In short, the women in Siegel's adaptation perform like the women of Hemingway's early fiction, who often take up the role of code hero when the men in their lives falter.

This function of the women as catalysts for self-revelation is most obvious in the scenes of interaction between Sam and his wife, Lucy. A very attractive and sexually aggressive woman, Lucy is not afraid to tell Sam that she could walk away from the relationship if he becomes the sort of man whom she could no longer respect. Sam expresses his awareness of this situation when he says, just before he leaves to be interrogated by the police captain, "If it were real trouble, you'd walk out on me" (Siegel). However, Lucy also makes sure that Sam knows she wants to hold him to a high standard, because if he disappointed her, she would be lost too. Lucy replies, "If it were real trouble, I wouldn't know where to walk to" (Siegel). After his return from the police station, Lucy squeezes the truth out of Sam, mostly because he knows that it is futile to lie to her. The couple's ability to hold one another accountable, while still respecting the other's right to make judgment calls that each must live with, is seen in the dialogue that ends the sequence. Lucy says, "Now you know why I was out on the dock last night ... I can smell trouble. Don't press your luck, Sam, you're my world with a fence around it." (Siegel). Sam replies, "You think I want to sleep alone? That's what they make you do in jail" (Siegel). From this exchange, Sam learns that being married to Lucy is a privilege and a responsibility. This portrayal of marriage as a give-and-take interdependence replicates the dynamic of most of Hemingway's best-suited romantic couples, such as Catherine Barkley and Frederic Henry in *A Farewell to Arms*. Although Hemingway's writing in stories like "The Killers," and "Snows of Kilimanjaro" often warns against a man allowing a woman to make him compromise his ideals, the author presents in equal measure in his novels a contrasting relationship, in which an honest woman actually makes a man more steadfast. Siegel's choice to allow Lucy to set the boundaries for the relationship, and then hold Sam to those boundaries when he starts to waver, is thematically consistent within the context of the Hemingway oeuvre.

Although these scenes of interaction between Sam and Lucy are strong, the rest of Siegel's film is unfortunately uneven in its artistic merits and production values. In his defense, Siegel was not totally to blame for the fact that the film appears rushed, especially toward the end. Due to the low budget, the film was shot entirely in California, even though the story was set in Cuba. Also, Siegel had to hurry through a mere twenty days of shooting, filming each scene in chronological order directly from the script, because he had no time for retakes. This rushed atmosphere resulted in a shortened ending. Scott Hale, the film's dialogue director, noted that "since the picture was being shot in continuity, from beginning to end, Don in desperation simply had Audie kill everybody; and that was the end of the picture" (Phillips 64). Also, the director and screenwriter were working against a producer, Clarence Greene, who demanded final creative control over the project. Not wanting to have the hero die in the end because he "preferred invincible heroes," Greene insisted that the script be changed, so that Sam was not mortally wounded, but instead had a chance to redeem himself morally (Laurence 108). These arbitrary judgment calls, coupled with time and budget constraints, hampered Siegel's project and screen today as improper thematic inconsistencies resulting from latent creative conflicts during production.

However, Audie Murphy's performance in the film is too often unjustly maligned. Murphy, the most decorated soldier of World War II, had a great deal in common with both Hemingway and the hero of *To Have and Have Not*, Harry Morgan, upon whom Sam Martin was based. Like Hemingway, Murphy was determined to become a soldier. Rejected by both the Marines and navy on account of his height, Murphy was finally allowed to join the army infantry. Murphy's adventures in the army became the stuff of legend when he, again like Hemingway, became the cover subject of a special edition of *Life* magazine in 1945. Seeing the cover, James Cagney encouraged Murphy to get started as an actor, despite the war hero's protests that he had "no talent" (Arlingtoncemetery.mil). Still, Murphy's popular appeal made him a huge box-office draw, and films like *To Hell and Back*, based on Murphy's own autobiography, allowed the soldier-turned-actor to become a star simply by playing himself, in a manner very similar to the way that Hemingway constructed his own public persona. Unfortunately, also like Hemingway, Murphy suffered from post-traumatic stress due to his wartime experiences and "said that he could only sleep with a loaded pistol under his pillow" (Arlingtoncemetery.mil). In addition to sharing life circumstances strangely similar to Hemingway's, Murphy would have found a lot in his own Texas sharecropper upbringing to relate to the blue-collar struggles of the character Sam Martin that he portrayed in *The Gun Runners*. What Murphy represented in the role was exactly the sort of realism that Hemingway had requested in previous casting decisions, but had never been able to convince the studio executives was correct.

Murphy's choice to portray Sam Martin as a straight-faced, stoical man of few words seems perfectly in alignment with Hemingway's vision of the character. Yet, critics like Gene Phillips have called Murphy's choice to under-emote in the role "uninspired," and that "one wonders if he could have played a character as complex as Hemingway's Harry" (65). What makes this observation inaccurate is that the role of a stone-faced ex-veteran from a poor background is virtually the only type of role that an untrained actor like Murphy could play, because essentially he was playing himself. If critics had sought the sort of complete authenticity that Hemingway intended for all of his films, Murphy's performance would have been found satisfactory, since any reactions he had to the part would have been genuine.

Further, Murphy's choice to portray Martin as an honest innocent, unwise to the machinations of more worldly men, is a perfect foil for Eddie Albert's smiling villain, Hanagan. Whereas Murphy's natural uneasiness at being in front of the camera translates into his awkwardness at the thought of engaging in criminal activity, Albert's grinning ease is perfectly suited to his role as the sort of man who was so comfortable with his shady lifestyle that he could have breakfast in bed while talking about killing men for money. A well-seasoned actor, Albert was also a World War II veteran; however, his military service consisted mostly of espionage missions, which involved, among other things, Albert's posing as a circus trapeze artist for a Mexican circus as part of the Navy's effort to uncover Nazi threats close to U.S. borders (USAToday.com). In their scenes together, the two actors give a sense of realism to their characters that far surpasses that of most other Hemingway adaptations, simply because of their naturally differing backgrounds.

In sum, although *The Gun Runners* was, as Gene Phillips states, "a curious amalgam of some of the elements of the novel mixed together with newly invented ingredients," the film is not the universal failure that many critics claim (63). Despite working with a small budget under short time constraints, Siegel was nevertheless able to create a mostly cohesive film that reflected the best efforts of creative collaboration that could be expected considering the circumstances. If not for the fact that two previous adaptations of the same Hemingway novel had been produced without these handicaps, critics might have been able to regard Siegel's film more favorably for the sense of realism and thematic consistency with the Hemingway canon that the production seeks to convey.

The Old Man and the Sea (1958)

From its collaborative beginning, one would suppose that John Sturges's adaptation of Ernest Hemingway's novel *The Old Man and the Sea* should have been the purest distillation of the author's original creative vision ever filmed, especially considering that Leland Heyward, Hemingway's agent, offered to produce the film adaptation of the novel himself, with Hemingway signed on as technical advisor (Phillips 138). However, after six years in production, the most costly adaptation of a Hemingway film to date still does not screen as the most articulate filmed version of a Hemingway text. Perhaps this discrepancy is due to the fact that although the press attempted to cast Hemingway as the production's prime moving force, in actuality the picture was nothing greater than any other standard Hollywood effort. More likely, Sturges's adaptation of *The Old Man and the Sea* (1958) stands as a persistent reminder of the fact that when the actual author of a text is too actively involved in the filming process, the result can ironically stray even farther from the intentions of the original than if he had been more removed from the enterprise, or at least more open to collaborative effort.

During the filming of *The Old Man and the Sea*, the Warner Bros. publicity department made every effort to suggest to the public that Ernest Hemingway was the primary creative force behind this adaptation of his Pulitzer prize-winning novel. According to Frank Laurence, publicity photos "showed Hemingway sighting through a movie camera, as if he had some actual charge over the camera operations" (11). Hemingway was also stated to have made his acting debut in the film, in the crowd backing the arm-wrestling match between Santiago and the unnamed black sailor. However, this publicity was greatly exaggerated. Although Hemingway's wife, Mary, appears in the crowd of a bar scene late in the film, Hemingway's image was left on the cutting room floor (Laurence 13). Even so, Hemingway's presence in the film was much more prevalent than in previous adaptations of his work. Hemingway was reported to have received $150,000 for the film rights, and an additional $75,000 to act as a technical advisor on the film's "combat shots" of fishing for Santiago's giant marlin (Laurence 15). For his part, Hemingway claimed that his involvement in the picture did not reflect an interest in Hollywood, but rather an interest in keeping his most-awarded work "honest and straight" for the screen (qtd. in Laurence 16). Yet, Hemingway's active involvement actually ended up slowing down the production, resulting in far less authenticity than if the rest of the production team had been allowed to construct these shots on their own.

In her excellent essay on the film, Linda Dittmar refers to Hemingway's obsession with maintaining absolute realism in the filming of *The Old Man and the Sea* as "larding the text" (54). What Dittmar means is that the author's involvement in the filming process caused an undue emphasis to be placed on supposedly realistic technical details that resulted in an under-treatment of the novel's most significant themes. Further, Dittmar makes the well-mentioned point that

> Hemingway's writing resists filming precisely because its minimalism is taut with repressed content that is not readily translatable into film. One way or another, the film's response to this problem involved a larding process whereby Hemingway's

original text—spare, withholding, and ultimately ineffable, became saturated with extraneous materials that end up depleting, not enriching, it [54].

Dittmar's statement begs the question of what the central themes of *The Old Man and the Sea* are, and how they might have been obscured by the production's over-attention to technicality. Those themes, which will be explained at length here, can be summed up as four R's: remembrance, resilience, religion, and realism.

As Dittmar states, *The Old Man and the Sea*

> depicts an existential struggle for self-definition. Santiago's tragic condition is that his heroic will to commitment faces inevitable defeat. Social concerns are marginal to the solitary man asserting his right to a place in creation, and human interest episodes would only deflect attention from the wonder Hemingway inspires toward the universe and its creatures [58].

Hemingway's emphasis on one man's struggle against both himself and the natural world necessitates that the film adaptation's focus be placed squarely on the actor who plays Santiago and also his chief antagonist, the giant marlin. As a result, much of the film's criticism has focused on the casting of Santiago, the depiction of the fish, and Hemingway's reaction to both.

Initially, Hemingway had wanted the Italian director Vittorio de Sica for the film, adaptation, because of de Sica's previous success in super-realist pieces such as *Bicycle Thieves* (1949). However, Warner Bros. was unwilling to comply with this request, and instead initially allowed Fred Zinneman to assume the director's role. Also, Spencer Tracy, then a major star for MGM, was loaned to Warner Bros. in an effort to secure a sure box-office performance. The choice of Tracy for the lead role of Santiago was made over Hemingway's objections. The author was happy with the choice of Tracy to perform Santiago's internal monologue, which appears in the film as voiceover, but Hemingway was skeptical of Tracy's ability to portray an accurate vision of the thin, poor Cuban fisherman on screen. Hemingway's reluctance to accept Tracy's casting began the first of several power struggles between the author and the rest of his production team, leading ultimately to many technical inconsistencies within the final film.

In constructing the original story about Santiago and his marlin, Hemingway claimed that his goal was "to write a story about a real old man, a real sea, and a real fish" (qtd. in Phillips 144). Instead, what resulted in Sturges's film adaptation was "an inauthentic Santiago, an artificial ocean, and a phony fish" (Phillips 144). Part of the blame for these discrepancies was the fact that, even though the finished film uses a high level of incorporation of details from Hemingway's life, very few of these technicalities add much to the audience's understanding of the novel's original themes.

For example, Sturges's film, perhaps more than any other Hemingway adaptation, uses a great deal of Hemingway's actual language as lifted directly from the text and translated into voiceover delivered by Tracy. Explaining his reasoning behind preserving so much of Hemingway's original language, Sturges claimed, "We put the words against a background that seemed commiserate with them. We used them simply to hear them: to let Spence say them. It seemed to me that what happened on the screen wasn't as powerful as what was said—literally the words" (qtd. in Phillips 146). Yet, as Gene Phillips points out, this reliance on dialogue often comes across as redundant, not to mention the fact that "the unlettered Santiago and Manolin could in any case hardly have been sufficiently articulate to give adequate expression to the nuances of their thoughts and feelings" (146–47). What Phillips means is that if the goal of Hemingway's production team was to produce as realistic a portrayal as possible, then one of the most inauthentic things that they could do was to put the author's highly-stylized words directly into the mouths of his illiterate characters. Although such material is necessary for a literary audience to hear, it comes across as completely false for viewers, who, if they had any familiarity with the real world that Hemingway and company were trying so desperately to portray, would know better than to believe that a fisherman and his apprentice spoke in high modernist verbiage.

Returning now to the major themes of the original text, Sturges's film does do an excellent job of incorporating Santiago's dreams of lions into audiences' then-current familiarity with Hemingway's life and reputation as an African big game hunter. The adaptation begins with Santiago dreaming of lions, as in Hemingway's novel. Both Tracy's voiceover and Sturges's montage of nature shots depict exactly the content of Santiago's dream:

> He dreamed of Africa when he was a boy and the long golden beaches and the white beaches, so white they hurt your eyes, and the high capes and the great brown mountains. He walked along that coast now every night and in his dreams he heard the surf roar and saw the native boats come riding through it.... He no longer dreamed of storms, nor of women, nor of great occurrences, nor of great fish, nor fights, nor contests of strength, nor of his wife. He only dreamed of places now and of the lions on the beach. They played like young cats in the dusk and he loved them as he had loved the boy. He never dreamed about the boy [*Old Man* 24–25].

This scene is one of many in *The Old Man and the Sea* in which Hemingway superimposes what are most likely his own remembrances upon the character of this aged Cuban fisherman. Although it is possible that Santiago, in his fictional youth, could have sailed to Africa, it is more likely that Hemingway is using the old man as an avatar for his own memories, especially considering that the subject matter about which Santiago no longer dreams comprises much of the content of Hemingway's biography. The playful lions and restful landscapes imply that both Santiago and his author are older men who have grown content with their individual histories, and, as a result, have made peace within their worlds. Sturges's choice to bookend his adaptation of Hemingway's novel just as the author did, with scenes of Santiago dreaming of lions, calls audience attention to autobiographical connections between author and character.

Although Sturges's adaptation eschews virtually any direct political commentary in its manner of adaptation, it preserves most of the religious symbolism present in Hemingway's original. Generally speaking, Hemingway was reluctant to reveal any intentional symbolic meaning placed within his characters, saying, "If I made them good and true enough, they would mean different things. The hardest thing is to make something that is really true and something truer than true. Then the parts become symbols" (qtd. in Dittmar 56). Yet, readers cannot ignore the obvious symbolic implications of *The Old Man and the Sea*. The old fisherman's name, Santiago, is Spanish for "saint" and the boy, Manolin, seems to have a name derived from Jesus's description as a man of linen, or one who sacrifices for others. However, Hemingway is not content to rest on the familiar associations of Holy Father and Son, but instead continually reverses and intermingles the roles of old man and boy to complicate this religious symbolism. Manolin is both an innocent whose constant faith restores his father-figure Santiago and who also behaves as a fatherly caretaker for the old man, bringing him food and monitoring his health. In contrast, the normally paternal Santiago also indulges in boyish daydreams about baseball and reckless, childlike behaviors, such as throwing his only knife and paddle away in frustration at an attacking shark. This role reversal is mirrored in the film by straightforward scenes of visual religious symbolism, such as Manolin carrying a lantern to light the old man's way to the harbor, and the weary Santiago stumbling under the weight of the cross-like mast from his ill-fated boat. Taken altogether, Sturges's film does a fine job of translating Hemingway's blending of Christian religious symbolism into visual metaphors that demonstrate how few differences there are between the younger and older parts of the Holy Trinity.

Ultimately, both Hemingway's novel and Sturges's film suggest that an individual's resilience, or his ability to overcome inevitable fate, is the true measure not only of what kind of man he is, but also how close he is to God. Dittmar explains Santiago's motivations simply:

> A man who wants to go on with the humble work he was born to do, a man who mostly dreams of graceful lions playing on a sandy beach, and whose one public

triumph occurred when he arm-wrestled against a worthy opponent—surely, readers come to feel, surely such a man has earned the right to catch his fish [57].

Hemingway's Santiago has a unique sense of pride in his life's work that is neither self-deprecating nor self-aggrandizing. Instead, he is simply a man who is truly self-aware. Under the normally accepted Christian order of things, Santiago should be awarded for his humility by being allowed to take home the marlin for which he has waited so long. However, even though Santiago by name is a walking Christian symbol, he is denied a Christian reward both in Hemingway's novel and in the film. Regardless, Santiago's stoic, one might even say saint-like, acceptance of nature's cruel denial of what should have been a just reward for his persistence proves the character as a Hemingway hero, his resilience making him above standard rewards.

Although the themes of remembrance, religion, and resilience are preserved in the transference from novel to screen, Hemingway's emphasis on realism in the original text suffers in Sturges's film adaptation. This problem is at least partially Hemingway's own fault, ironically because he insisted on trying to make the film too realistic. After being given partial control of the shooting script, Hemingway began making many demands about including scenes from the novel in the film that were simply unnecessary, such as watching Santiago get up to pee outside his shack every morning, merely for the sake of portraying the authentic everyday life of a fisherman (Laurence 28). The result of Hemingway's difficult demands was that Warner Bros.' studio team eventually lost patience with the author and took away much of the control over the production that Hemingway had in the beginning. As a result of his overemphasis on nonsensical details, Hemingway lost the ability to fight for realistic touches that actually could have added to the production, such as filming the boat scenes in Cuban waters rather than a studio tank (Laurence 35). Still, Sturges's efforts to preserve as many meaningful realistic nuances as possible resulted in some of the film's most visually intriguing scenes, particularly the sequence in which Santiago and the other fishermen depart each day by lamplight. These lights, which seem to symbolize the individual hopes of each man as he sets out on a merciless sea that could literally take him anywhere on his life's journey that day, were authentic details from Cuban fishing villages that took on additional symbolic meaning in Sturges's adaptation.

In the end, audiences are left today with an adaptation of *The Old Man and the Sea* that is not a poor motion picture *per se*, but one that certainly reflects its tumultuous production and leaves viewers wondering what might have been, if the production team had been more able to work together to produce a cohesive work of cinema. The first possible way that Sturges's production might have been a better representation of Hemingway's text is through the casting of a different lead actor in the role of Santiago. Hemingway's choice for the lead was to use "a real Cuban fisherman, someone like the Cojimar fisherman Anselmo Hernandez, who was a model for Santiago in some ways" (Laurence 20). However, Warner Bros. executives were not interested in creating an unsellable documentary about the life of a poor Cuban fisherman. Instead, they attempted to craft the film in such a way as to maximize the economic potential of making the book into a cinematic vehicle with a major star. Initially, Hemingway accepted the casting of Spencer Tracy, but after he refused to lose weight or learn a Cuban accent, Tracy lost Hemingway's approval (Phillips 143). Yet, Hemingway was not unhappy with Tracy in the role of Santiago simply because of the actor's lack of prep. According to Linda Dittmar:

> Hemingway saw Tracy's physique as an affront to his notions of manhood and heroism. Tracy's inability to diet, his rumored bouts with alcoholism, and his fear of flying embody weaknesses Hemingway could not abide—especially given his own aging. Tracy represented to him what he dreaded most: the decline of will and ability that he too was facing [55].

In creating Santiago, Hemingway had once again written an avatar to express his own feelings. However, Hemingway was not as emotionally secure as his fictional character. Seeing Tracy, who looked so much like his aging self, in the role must have been a shocking reminder to Hemingway that he, like everyone else, was mortal. Unwilling to cope with this visual manifestation of his impending old age, not as a lean code hero, but instead merely as a portly actor masquerading as such, Hemingway would likely have watched the dailies with a sense of devastation that his own public image had changed, no matter how hard he fought against it.

Whereas Hemingway's dissatisfaction with Tracy in the lead role was mostly a manifestation of the author's insecurity about aging, his rejection of Sturges's choice to use artificial fish in a movie about fishing was completely legitimate. Seeking to fill the film's second lead role with just the right giant fish, Hemingway requested funding from producer Leland Heyward to take an expedition and film crew down to Peru in an effort to land a marlin worthy of the novel's thousand-pound original. Unfortunately, according to Hemingway, "We fished every day for a month in those heavy seas with no luck" (Phillips 143). After losing thousands of dollars to Hemingway's effort to locate a prize-quality fish, and even more money in unsuccessful attempts to film some of the movie's other aquatic scenes, Heyward released Fred Zinneman, the adaptation's first director, and pulled Hemingway's second crew from Peru. Taking over the reins as director, Sturges moved production of the boat scenes to the tank on the Warner Bros.' studio lot, and sought out other sources for Santiago's giant marlin.

Eventually, Sturges bought documentary footage of a record marlin catch from professional Texas fisherman Alfred Glasell, which he "spliced awkwardly into the film, with the Tracy superimpositions visibly retouched into the Glasell backdrop" (Dittmar 55). Still needing better close-up footage of the marlin, Sturges commissioned a foam rubber model of a marlin to be made, which Hemingway detested, and reportedly remarked, "No picture with a fucking rubber fish ever made a dime" (qtd. in Phillips 148). Looking back on the film years later, even Sturges was disturbed with the distracting lack of realism that his phony fish scenes contained, causing the director to claim, "Technically, it was the sloppiest film I ever made" (Phillips 146). Sturges and Hemingway's disdain for the film's special effects is warranted. The foam fish and sloppy editing date the film, and take a great deal of attention away from Tracy's soliloquies, which are intercut with these unrealistic scenes.

The final film's general lack of technical realism is even more disappointing when one considers the effort that screenwriter Peter Viertel took to create an especially realistic script that was true to the spirit of Hemingway's original. Hemingway insisted that Viertel could not portray Santiago accurately until he experienced Santiago's life circumstances firsthand. According to Frank Laurence, Hemingway had Viertel spend the night in a mosquito-infested fisherman's cabin with no screens, and then abandoned him in an open boat for hours on the ocean, so that the screenwriter could experience the sensation of being lost at sea (27). Unfortunately, Hemingway's Method acting approach to screenwriting failed. Even though he "was being a good sport about suffering these various indignities," when Viertel became very seasick, Hemingway lost all faith in Viertel's ability to produce a script that would accurately reflect Santiago's experiences (Laurence 27). Although Viertel eventually produced one of the closest conversions of a Hemingway work to date, his efforts at producing a realistic chronicle of several days in the life of a Cuban fisherman seem overshadowed by technical difficulties.

Upon release, Hemingway's prediction about the film's low likelihood for success came true. The film was a financial disaster at the box office, hampered by ample bad press concerning the crew's inabilities to work together to produce a cohesive work of collaborative cinema. In an effort to promote interest among high school students studying the novel, Warner Bros. sent

> to teachers, librarians, and principals all over the country examination copies of a study guide they could buy for a few cents for their students to use. This pamphlet, in the series Photoplay Studies endorsed by the National Education

Association, described *The Old Man and the Sea* as "one of the finest motion pictures ever made" [Laurence 36].

This final effort to recoup the studio's losses on the most costly Hemingway flop ever produced serves today as a reminder that even when a production team seeks to involve a work's original author, over-attention to textual detail can actually harm a film's ability to convey realistic experiences and genuine emotions.

Adventures of a Young Man (1962)

A.E. Hotchner, the screenwriter for *Adventures of a Young Man* (1962), once said about his friend Ernest Hemingway, "Part of the mystique about Ernest stems from the manner in which he blurred the demarcation between fiction and fact. Fiction is a magnification of reality, he once observed, and when he told a story (and a splendid storyteller he was), it was hard to know whether it was fantasy laced with fact, fact seasoned with fiction, or fantasy" (Hotchner vii). By incorporating generous amounts of biographical detail about Hemingway's life into his adaptation of the author's Nick Adams stories, Hotchner creates what may be the most revelatory film about how the author's life influenced his fiction. Hotchner began his acquaintance with Hemingway in the spring of 1948, when the young journalist was sent to Cuba by *Cosmopolitan* with an unusual assignment: to ask Hemingway to write an article "The Future of Literature." Naturally, Hotchner was at first intimidated by the task. Explaining his trepidation regarding the task, Hotchner wrote in his biography of the event:

> From the time I read my first Hemingway work, *The Sun Also Rises*, as a student at Soldan High School in St. Louis, I was struck with the affliction common to my generation: Hemingway Awe. In my schoolboy fantasies I had identified with Nick Adams (he was approximately my age and was the protagonist of many Hemingway short stories) as he made his way through a murky world of punch-drunk fighters, killers, suiciding Indians, dope addicts and whores, and the rigors of war on the Italian front. During the Second World War, as an Air Force officer in France, I had been further awed by War Correspondent Hemingway's military exploits [Hotchner 3–4].

However, Hotchner's fear of meeting and working with his idol were unfounded. As he proceeds through his autobiography documenting his evolving friendship with Hemingway, Hotchner uncovers the most likely reason why generations of young writers have been drawn to the author. Through Hotchner's eyes, readers can see Hemingway in one of his more underappreciated roles, as a mentor to those who sought to emulate and expand upon the type of freewheeling writer's lifestyle that he had spent his career creating the mold for. In short, from reading Hotchner's autobiography together with his adaptation of *Adventures of a Young Man*, one can at last understand why so many writers remain eager to step inside Hemingway's ring of literary celebrity, and make their own fiction like his: truer than if it really happened in life.

In a move that seems quite out of character, given his general aversion to film adaptations of his works, Hemingway was initially eager to take an active role in translating the Nick Adams stories from page to screen. The first attempt at adapting the stories was for a sixteen-part CBS series in 1951. Hemingway spoke with his friend Hotchner about writing the adaptations, and seemed willing to participate in the process by providing opening voiceovers for each episode. Hemingway even went so far as to record three sample attempts for these introductions, but seemed unhappy with the results. Hemingway, who never enjoyed public speaking, wrote to Hotchner in a letter accompanying what the author considered to be the best of these demo reels, "I'm spooked about the whole thing, Hotch. If there was some way we could sell the stories without me talking or mugging, I would give anything" (qtd. in Hotchner 75). Although the television series was eventually produced to mixed reviews without Hemingway's voiceovers, Hotchner continued to seek out a better way to translate his friend's works for film.

Eventually, through ongoing negotiations with determined producer Jerry Wald, Hemingway signed an agreement with 20th Century–Fox for Hotchner to adapt ten of the Nick Adams stories as one continuous motion picture, which began production during the last year of Hemingway's life and was released in the year after his death. The adaptation produced is a fairly faithful conversion of Hemingway's original Nick Adams texts. Nevertheless, while Hotchner's work, brought to life by a star-studded Hollywood cast, is textually accurate for the most part, it fails to articulate clearly several common Hemingway themes. Although critics of the film tend to blame this failure on the unreadiness of Richard Beymer, who does seem a bit overwhelmed in the leading role of Nick Adams, the real culprit is Hollywood's general tendency to over-romanticize Hemingway's work, in favor of leaving his grittier material on the cutting room floor. In spite of these tendencies, the film can still be read to understand the interconnectedness of Hemingway's early life and work, both as the *kunstlerroman* of an artist coming into his voice and a *bildungsroman* of a young man growing to maturity.

The film begins with a facsimile of Hemingway's voice, as if the spirit of the recently deceased author continued to linger about to narrate the outdoor scenes of his fondest memories. The voiceover intones, in a meditative, Hemingwayesque baritone:

> In the place where you are born and where you grow up, you begin to learn the things that all men must know. Although they are the simplest things, it takes a man's whole life really to know them. And if you are to be a writer, the stories that you make up will be true in proportion to the amount of this knowledge of life that you have. So that when you make something up, it is as it would truly be, with the good and the bad, the ecstasy and the remorse, the people and places, and how the weather was [Ritt].

This passage creates the sense that the film is going to screen as a sort of collective memoir, not only of Nick Adams, but also of the author who created him, and the generation of writers that he inspired. As such, each vignette of Nick Adams's life serves as a lesson that all men must know in order to fully come into a psychologically satisfied state of self-awareness.

The first, and perhaps most emphatic, lesson that *Adventures of a Young Man* imparts from the Hemingway oeuvre is that a man must not allow himself to be dominated or intimidated by anyone. This theme is first articulated on screen through what appears to be an adaptation of the short story "The Doctor and the Doctor's Wife." In the sequence, Nick's father, Dr. Adams, played by Arthur Kennedy, allows himself to be bullied by a local Native American tough guy and then goes home to be intimidated yet again by his scolding wife, portrayed by Jessica Tandy. This unhealthy dynamic supposedly mirrored the tempestuous relationship between Hemingway's own parents, and between the author and his mother, Grace Hemingway, whom he greatly resented. According to Gene Phillips, "Hemingway said of this story that his own hatred for his mother was non-Freudian, and that she was an all-time bitch, and that the first psychic wound of his life had been occasioned by his discovery as a lad that his father was a coward" (82). The author's sentiment is echoed in Nick's exclamation to his father in the scene, "I wish you wouldn't let people take advantage of you all the time" (Ritt). However, Dr. Adams seems unfazed by Nick's attempt to make a man out of him. The older Adams finishes the scene by encouraging Nick to appease his mother by practicing his music before being allowed to go hunting.

Once again, this small detail is gleaned from Hemingway's own life. The author deeply resented the fact that his mother used the $50,000 inheritance left to him by his father's death to build a music room in her home. According to Hemingway's own admission, "Mother was a music nut, a frustrated singer, and she gave musicales every week in my fifty-thousand dollar music room. When I was in school she forced me to play the cello even though I had absolutely no talent and could not even carry a tune" (qtd. in Hotchner 116). Further, Grace Hemingway also used Ernest's lack of musical ability as a means to lord over the young man, and forced him to forgo activities that he enjoyed in order to indulge her fantasy of his becoming a competent musician. As Hemingway remembered, "She took me out of school one year so I could concentrate exclusively on the cello. I wanted to be playing football out in the fresh air and she had me chained to that knee-box" (qtd. in Hotchner 116). Considering Hemingway's emotional connection to the struggles he had with his own family, it make sense that Hotchner, in his adaptation, chose to place a scene based on "The Doctor and the Doctor's Wife" just before the sequence based on "The End of Something." Read together, this sequence shows the psychological connection in Hemingway's mind between his overbearing mother and his lifelong fear of being dominated by the women in his life.

In "The End of Something," a more world-wise, post-war Nick Adams breaks up with his girlfriend Marjorie. Nick fears commitment and also that if he does continue in the relationship, he is destined to a life of drudgery and compliance just like his father. When Marjorie confronts him as to why he is no longer interested in their relationship, Nick says, "It isn't fun anymore. Not any of it ... I feel as though everything has gone to hell inside of me. I don't know, Marge. I don't know what to say" ("End" 204). What Nick means in Hemingway's original story has more to do with his inability to reconnect with his old life after what he has experienced in war, with a fear of commitment only as a secondary concern. In contrast, in Hotchner's adaptation of the story, Nick breaks up with his girlfriend Caroline before going to war, but after witnessing his father lose face while trying to appease his mother.

This decision to place the breakup before his war experiences in the film demonstrates Hotchner's desire to revise a major theme in Hemingway's short story, using details from the author's personal life. Whereas the real-life Hemingway seems to have been motivated in many of his relationships with women based on negative reactions to his parents' marriage, the fictional Nick Adams makes his romantic decisions based upon his own experience, which makes him more mature than his friends. In short, whereas the author himself, and Hotchner's adaptive Nick, make choices based on fear, Hemingway's original character decides his fate based on rationality. Although not a flaw *per se*, this is a definite thematic difference between the story and film that demonstrates an inconsistency between collaborators on the film.

The next sequence in the film, based on the short story "Indian Camp," displays a similar sense of thematic inconsistency between Hemingway's original and Hotchner's adaptation. In Hemingway's original story, the father of an Indian mother kills himself in the bunk above where Dr. Adams performs an emergency Caesarean section on the woman using primitive implements and no anesthesia. However, in the film version, the Indian father is merely drunk and belligerent during the delivery. Hemingway's inclusion of the suicide provides an entry to an important discussion between Nick and Dr. Adams at the end of the story. The talk reads:

> "Why did he kill himself, Daddy?"
> "I don't know, Nick. He couldn't stand things, I guess."
> "Do many men kill themselves, Daddy?"
> "Not very many, Nick."
> "Do many women?"
> "Hardly ever" ["Indian" 20].

Read in the consideration of the fact that "Indian Camp" was published in 1923, five years before Hemingway's father would kill himself, and almost forty years before the author would take his own life, the exchange seems eerily prophetic. Given the fact that Hemingway committed suicide while the film was in production, Hotchner most likely chose to omit the passage out of deference to his friend.

Still, this omission stands today, in the context of reading *Adventures of a Young Man*, as a mistake, considering how much the inclusion of this moment between father and son could have informed the audience about Hemingway's thematic fear of death, and how that fear changed over time in relation to the author's realization of his own mortality. For Hemingway at the time he wrote "Indian Camp," suicide was the ultimate sign of cowardice, showing that a man had completely given up on his ability to control his life or the world around him. However, as Hemingway aged and began to see that he would never fully recover from his various long-term illnesses, suicide clearly became a possible source of relief that the author craved more than he feared death or damage to his reputation. One can only speculate as to how an older Hemingway might have revised the story for the screen, given his latter-life battles with depression. Yet, this type of speculation, which probes an author's motivations, is exactly the sort of place where a screenwriter can fill in the gaps of a story to best supplement the original author's themes in a new context for a new audience.

Hotchner could have used Hemingway's meditation on death as a defeat or an escape as an excellent transition into a later part of his adaptation, in which "The Battler" is translated for the screen. Apparently, "The Battler," a story in which Nick Adams encounters a mentally disturbed former boxing champion while hitchhiking, was a poignant story for Hemingway during his later years. Once, in a discussion with Hemingway, Hotchner recalls that he was working on a manuscript for *Adventures of a Young Man* when he inadvertently quoted a line from "The Battler" to the author. The line, "You've got a lot coming to you," comes from an exchange among Ad, the old boxer; Bugs, Ad's African American caretaker; and Nick. It reads:

"Where you say you're from?"
"Chicago," Nick said.
"That's a fine town," the Negro said. "I didn't catch your name."
"Adams. Nick Adams."
"He says he's never been crazy, Bugs," Ad said.
"He's got a lot coming to him," the Negro said ["Battler" 51–52].

Hemingway's hyperawareness of the context of hearing this line during his 1960 conversation with Hotchner is more than mere paranoia. When Hemingway wrote the line as a young man, he was predicting that Nick, like himself, would likely encounter many broken, or "crazy," men during his lifetime, and would hopefully learn to do better for himself from seeing their negative examples. However, the older Hemingway, who by 1960 had already undergone psychiatric treatment to try to reverse the negative psychological effects of head injuries sustained during multiple accidents, would have taken the line more personally. Perhaps, after a lifetime of living on the edge and seeking out his own pleasurable experiences at the expense of others, Hemingway felt somewhat guilty, almost as if his mental illness were a sign that he got what was coming to him for a lifetime of driving others insane. This speculative reading would have added much reflection and poignancy to the story, yet once again, Hotchner avoids it. Instead of meditating on Hemingway's self-reflective statement that "a champion can't retire like anyone else," Hotchner's adaptation of "The Battler" sequence in the film serves mainly as a showcase to display the immense acting range of Hotchner's friend Paul Newman, in his well-played role as the ruined fighter, Ad Francis (Hotchner 298). As a result, Hotchner's eagerness to protect his deceased friend's legacy actually creates thematic weaknesses in the film that prevent the audience from fully appreciating the prophetic quality that Hemingway's early works had in relation to the tragic end of the author's life.

To his credit, Hotchner's adaptation of the Nick Adams stories begins to become much more thematically consistent with Hemingway's original creative vision during the second half of the movie. Hotchner displays a firm grasp on the common Hemingway theme that "a man alone has no chance" (Ritt). This line, which Hotchner apparently lifted from another Hemingway work, *To Have and Have Not*, is voiced by Bugs in the transition between "The Battler" sequence and what appears to be a series of vignettes meant to explain Hemingway's entry into journalism by way of enlisting in the Italian army during World War One. In *To Have and Have Not*, Harry Morgan is a basically good man who succumbs, out of a desperate need to provide for his family, to a life of crime in hopes of earning easy money. The novel can be read as a consideration of a man's capabilities, if he allows his morality to slide down a slippery slope, of justifying his actions to fit his circumstances.

Hotchner picks up this theme, of how a man must learn to define his own sense of morality to protect his integrity from the influence of shady characters that he will encounter in life, during the burlesque sequence of his film adaptation. In those scenes, a young Nick Adams, who has been hitchhiking for quite some time, encounters Mr. Campbell, the drunken promoter of a burlesque show that is run by Mr. Turner. Campbell gives Nick the job of making sure he doesn't overdrink so much that he would be unable to meet Turner the next morning. Inevitably, Campbell does overdrink and oversleep, and when Turner arrives, he fires Campbell and hires Nick in his place, because Campbell is a man who "can't slide," or in other words, can't learn to bend his morality just enough to complete whatever his lifestyle requires (Ritt). Trying to teach Nick a lesson from the experience, Turner says, "You see to it that they call you Sliding Nick," meaning that Nick should learn to be the kind of man who knows just how much vice he can tolerate while still keeping his dignity and moral code intact (Ritt). This theme, of a man having to define his own morality based on the sum total of his experiences, is classic Hemingway, and Hotchner does well in preserving it throughout the film.

Further, Hotchner captures the manner in which the real-life Hemingway happened into the newspaper business in a unique way, by blending the author's personal history with his own in the film. Both Hemingway and Hotchner held ties to St. Louis, Missouri. Hemingway's first three wives were from the city, while Hotchner grew up there, before moving to New York to work as a journalist after World War II. Perhaps Hotchner's experiences as a young man from St. Louis who moved to New York as an aspiring journalist inspired him to incorporate his own biography into Hemingway's already semiautobiographical Nick Adams character. After being turned down by a prominent New York publisher, Nick decides to join the Italian army in order to gain enough life experience to be a good writer. Nick's trajectory in this film adaptation represents a blending of biographical detail far more than in Hemingway's original stories and can be viewed as the most complete example in the Hemingway film canon of full incorporation of the lives of both the author and the screenwriter responsible for adapting him.

Hotchner also incorporates a great deal of detail from Hemingway's novel *A Farewell to Arms* into *Adventures of a Young Man*. This choice is solid, because Hemingway's Nick Adams character in many ways can be seen as a younger prototype for the author's later protagonists, including Frederic Henry from *Farewell*. However, Hotchner does not merely add details from *Farewell*, but instead traces Hemingway's epic of war and first love back to its earliest origins. In a Nick Adams tale called "A Very Short Story," Nick falls in love with a nurse while he is recuperating in a military hospital, providing the genesis of what Hemingway would later retell as the romance between Frederic Henry and Catherine Barkley in *Farewell*. Of course, both stories have even deeper biographical roots, in Hemingway's own relationship with Agnes von Kurowsky, the Red Cross nurse who took care of him after he was injured in Italy during World War I. This careful attention to biographical detail helps Hotchner capture one of Hemingway's most prevalent themes from his early work. As Gene Phillips explains the significance of Hemingway's most popular plotline, "the hero loses the first person to whom he has been able to commit himself in a lasting love relationship and is left desolate and sobered by his experiences of love and war" (84). This sentiment is perhaps best summarized by Hemingway's maxim, "Man can be destroyed, but not defeated" (qtd. in Hotchner 304). In the context of Hotchner's adaptation, Hemingway's statement can be taken to mean that even though a man may experience many personal tragedies, over time those struggles only make him stronger, and help to galvanize his character so that he will be able to face future misfortunes more stoically.

The closing scenes of Hotchner's adaptation of the Nick Adams saga blends elements of Hemingway's short stories "Soldier's Home" and "Big Two Hearted River." In these stories, a young veteran must try to overcome what would be described today as post-traumatic stress. In the final scenes of *Adventures of a Young Man*, Nick returns home to find that his father has killed himself, but that his mother has carefully avoided telling him this truth. Nick takes Mrs. Adams's choice to withhold this information as a personal affront, an affirmation that once again, his mother is trying to deny him full access to his manhood. When Nick goes to the cabin by the lake where his father shot himself, he finds a letter that his father wrote to him just before he died. However, upon inspection, Nick becomes furious when he determines that his mother has opened and read it, out of a jealousy that Dr. Adams cared more to write to Nick than to her.

This drama of the letter has a close parallel to Hemingway's own life, which he related to Hotchner over the course of their friendship. As the author explained to his friend, "The thing that bothered me the most was that I had written him a letter that was on his desk the day he shot himself, and I think if he had opened that letter and read it, he wouldn't have pulled the trigger" (qtd. in Hotchner 115). Although the contents of the letter are not known, it is highly possible to infer from it that the younger Hemingway's correspondence was some sort of encouragement to his father, or perhaps even a plea or plan for Dr. Hemingway to finally be able to stand up to his dominating wife and overcome the financial problems that plagued him during the months leading up to his death. Regardless, Hotchner's inclusion of the letter drama in the film serves as a final incorporation of the author's actual life into this adaptation of his semi-autobiographical character Nick Adams. Its presence seems to suggest that both author and screenwriter believed in the power of words not only to convey information, but to heal psychological wounds and to even save lives.

The final images of *Adventures of a Young Man* capture Nick Adams as he returns to fish in the same river that he and his father enjoyed in the beginning of the film. This placement of fishing scenes as bookends for the tale of Nick's maturation promotes the audience to consider how much Nick has changed as a result of his experiences since the last time he was at the river. Once again in this closing sequence, Hotchner picks up on a common Hemingway theme that was best demonstrated in *For Whom the Bell Tolls*, which is that even though a man's life may change significantly in a mere matter of months, the natural world surrounding him remains constant, an eternal source of healing to which he can return when he needs strength. This sense of the restorative power of nature is one of Hemingway's most positive themes, and the ending of Hotchner's adaptation gives it equal weight to the author's more pessimistic viewpoints, most likely in an overall effort to offer catharsis to Hemingway fans still coming to terms with the author, who, to the outside world, had seemed invincible.

Hemingway himself best articulated what evidently became A.E. Hotchner's approach to adapting his friend's work: "Fiction is inventing out of what you have" (qtd. in Hotchner 199). In his adaptation of the Nick Adams stories, Hotchner reinvented the character using careful incorporation of historical and psychological details that revealed just as much about Hemingway and Hotchner as Nick Adams. Although the film suffers from some thematic inconsistencies, it stands today as one of the most deliberate efforts by a screenwriter to create a consistent, cohesive conversion of Hemingway's incorporated works for the screen.

The Killers (1964)

Ernest Hemingway is, more than anything else, a modernist writer. As a result, any film production team seeking to adapt a Hemingway text for the screen must stay within the modernist ethos in order to create a work of cohesive cinema that adequately represents a combined artistic vision. However, in his revisionist adaptation of Hemingway's short story, "The Killers," director

Don Siegel, using Gene Coon's screenplay, chooses to approach the author's heavily modernist subject matter from a clearly postmodern perspective. Unlike Robert Siodmak, who first adapted Hemingway's "Killers" for the screen in 1946, Siegel and Coon eschew almost any incorporation from the Hemingway biography or canon. Instead, they rely mostly upon postmodern methods of storytelling, which were becoming popular by the time of his adaptation in 1964, in an attempt to revise Hemingway's tale for a new generation. Unfortunately, the choice to remove the modernist ideological framework of the original and replace it with a more postmodern approach removes most of the symbolic significance present in Hemingway's story and leaves behind a film that is philosophically almost the exact opposite of its textual inspiration.

In order to understand why Siegel and Coon's adaptation of "The Killers" is so different from Hemingway's story, it is first necessary to point out some of the key differences in modernism and postmodernism. In his essay "Toward a Concept of Postmodernism," Ihab Hassan defines postmodernism as being the opposite of modernism by using a comparison chart. In this chart, Hassan claims that some of the key features of modernism include a sense of romanticism that nevertheless is symbolic and purposeful in working toward a certain goal (3). Modernists normally adhere to a master code of morality to achieve this goal, and if the order established by that morality is disturbed, they become paranoid, anticipating the negative intervention of fate by a wrathful God (Hassan 3). In contrast, Hassan claims that postmodernism's chief attributes are the exact opposite. For postmodernists, the world lacks a generalized sense of ordered morality, making attempts at forming a code of behavior futile (3). According to Hassan's reasoning, no definite sense of punishment or fate can be defined in a postmodern world, because the universe is perpetually in flux (3). What this dichotomy means in terms of the Hemingway canon is that the author's typical code hero behaves as a modernist. The Hemingway protagonist has a specific behavioral code to which he adheres, and this code usually causes his life to progress with a definite purpose toward some goal. However, if the Hemingway code hero allows himself to become distracted from his purpose in life, fate will somehow intervene to punish him. Eventually, his progress toward that goal will be derailed and he will perish.

In the original text of "The Killers," the Swede, Ole Andreson, has somehow lost his direction in life and is content to wait, even after Nick Adams warns him, for the gunmen to kill him as punishment. Robert Siodmak's film adaptation of the story offers an explanation for Andreson's choice to die. He has lost the love of his life, Kitty Collins, even after he compromised his moral code to keep her, by throwing a fight and taking blame for a theft she committed.

The overall message expressed by both versions is that if a man sacrifices his principles in order to fulfill short-term goals and romantic desires, eventually fate will catch up with him, and he must be ready to accept his inevitable punishment when it comes. Both of these chronicles of the Swede's demise are modernist in scope. However, as will be shown by comparison, Siegel and Coon's adaptation reverses this structured order of the Hemingway universe, to produce a film of "The Killers" in which random violence replaces the rightful justice of fate.

From the very beginning, director Don Siegel attempted to put distance between his and Coon's production and both Hemingway's story and its 1946 film noir adaptation. According to Stuart Kaminsky, Siegel wanted to reduce comparison of the two versions by calling his film *Johnny North*, but the studio, which owned the rights to the use of Hemingway's name, refused (131). The change of Hemingway's lead character's name from Ole "Swede" Andreson to Johnny North was only the first of many changes that distinguish between the two film adaptations. Siegel's film was originally intended to be the first television movie. However, the finished film was deemed by studio executives to be too violent, in light of then-recent circumstances and "because of President Kennedy's assassination, it was pulled from television showing" (Kaminsky 131). Kaminsky goes on to explain how the film was a sign of its time:

> By 1964, into the Cold War, after Kennedy's death, literature and film were dealing with men who had fallen back into corporate indemnification for protection against the confusion of the world. The films of the period increasingly dealt with the fight to salvage self-respect and identity, to find some meaningful antisocial values in the face of the corporate onslaught, the fear of the 1960s, of population fears, and of mass society [130].

Of course, Hemingway would have had no way to predict the Cold War or the schizophrenic atmosphere of fear that it inspired in the public that America's time might be running out. The influence of these events on the 1964 adaptation is therefore out of context with the original.

This generalized fear about the imminent demise of America is given voice through Lee Marvin's character, Charlie. As Charlie, one of the killers from the title, assassinates each victim, he refuses to hear their dying declarations, saying simply, "I haven't got the time" (Siegel). This refrain is completely different in many ways from the Swede's often repeated phrase in the first *Killers* adaptation, which is "I did something wrong, once" (Siodmak). First, by taking the film's catchphrase from the Swede and giving it to Charlie, Siegel is effectively shifting the focus of his film away from the Hemingway code hero and toward a villainous Other. Throughout Siegel's film, the audience hears much more about Charlie's thoughts than Johnny North's, who is the

Swede-replacement in the 1964 version. This alteration takes away the central focus of Hemingway's story and its original film adaptation, which is that a man resigns himself to a lifetime of guilt when he betrays his moral code. In contrast, the killer Charlie is a character who has no moral code, only a morbid curiosity about why his victim, Johnny North, was so ready to die. By replacing Hemingway's modernist master code with a postmodern chronicle of a hired assassin who lives in a perpetual state of randomly violent anarchy, the film ceases to be a cohesive effort of creative collaborators, and instead becomes Siegel's commentary on his era.

This absence of a fundamental struggle between good and evil, which is present in all the Nick Adams stories, is made even worse by poor casting and costuming choices for Siegel's film. To begin with, the boyish Nick Adams character from the story and original film is replaced by an old blind man at the school for the blind where Johnny North teaches auto mechanics. Although both characters perform the same plot function of warning the Swede/North about the assassins who are coming for him, the meaning conveyed by the presence of each messenger is completely different. In the 1946 film, Nick Adams remains the apprentice hero from Hemingway's story, who learns by Ole Andreson's negative example what can happen to a man who compromises his morality in an effort to win a woman. In contrast, the 1964 film's old blind man appears quite senile, unable to learn any sort of lesson, or act as an apprentice. Instead, the old blind man seems to be a literal signification of Siegel's interpretation of a world that has gone blind to the fact that codes of morality even exist. Perhaps this is why Johnny North teaches in a school for the blind, because he wants to blind himself to his troubled past. If this is the case, Siegel's take on the character is almost the exact opposite of Hemingway's original Swede, whose obsessive monomania would not let him forget a moment of the past.

Next, Gene Coon's choice to shift the script's chief point of view from Johnny North/Ole Andreson to Charlie Strom, the killer, seems to have more to do with the comparative star power of the actors playing the roles than any thematic significance. Although arguably a more capable actor in general, John Cassavetes, who portrays Johnny North, was not as big of a box office draw as Lee Marvin at the time *The Killers* was made. Clearly, the more subtle Cassavetes is overshadowed in his scenes with Marvin, who gives one of his better performances as Charlie, the clinical, business-suited killer. This upstaging of North's troubles by Charlie's morbid curiosity about why his target succumbed to death without so much as a whimper makes the film more of a playful, mysterious, postmodern mind game than a carefully paced chronology of modern moral decline.

Angie Dickinson's character, Sheila Farr, who replaces Ava Gardner's Kitty Collins from the 1946 adaptation, is unfortunately miscast, improperly played, and incorrectly costumed. Despite her appeal as a movie star during her 1960s heyday, Dickinson simply does not fit the mold of the typical Hemingway woman. Dickinson's on-screen personality and appearance in the film is of a straightforward Hollywood star: fair-haired and fun-loving, with a light, uncomplicated manner. Dickinson's ray-of-sunshine persona is accentuated by the fact that her character is perpetually costumed in bright shades of yellow throughout the film. The problem with these choices is that the average Hemingway female is more of a femme fatale, a good girl gone bad because of her desire to live the high life, but who still desires to be thought of as the innocent, vulnerable person, capable of falling in love at any moment, whom she is at heart. This feline duality of character is perfectly portrayed by Gardner in the original film, where she is costumed in sensual gowns that display her provocative dark side, and yet contrast sharply with her angelic face and girlish voice, which reveal Kitty's innocent heart within. Although Dickinson arguably could have given a similarly effective performance if directed differently, the far less complex gold-digger Shelia Farr whom she portrays on-screen is far from the type of woman a Hemingway hero would have been willing to die for.

Last, Ronald Reagan is completely miscast as villainous Jack Browning, the character who replaces Big Jim Colfax from the 1946 adaptation. To his credit, Reagan does the best he can with a role for which he is unsuited, choosing to play Browning with a calm, detached air. However, the soon-to-be political figure, here in his final film role, had never played a villain before. Reagan seems to strain when scenes require him to slap around his girlfriend, Shelia, or to take on the part of a criminal mastermind dominant over Charlie or Johnny. If he had been younger, Reagan might have been better cast as Johnny/Ole, given the actor's soft-spoken, somewhat resigned on-screen demeanor. However, his scenes playing against Lee Marvin's more formidable assassin, Charlie, stretch the boundaries of believability that this mild-mannered miscreant could organize any kind of crime.

Problematic casting aside, Siegel and Coon's *Killers* also suffers from a lack of subtle symbolism present in Siodmak's adaptation of the story. After the presence of a hero with a strong moral code, perhaps the second most dominant feature of any Hemingway work is the author's use of the iceberg theory. Generally speaking, Hemingway's lead characters have a tendency to erode gradually over time, as their conscience is steadily eaten away by small acts of immorality until their former self becomes unrecognizable. Yet, in the better film adaptations of Hemingway's works, the audience is usually provided with some sort of recurring visual symbol that stands as a static reminder of the man the fallen code hero used to be. In Siodmak's *Killers*, one of the most prominent symbols is Kitty Collins's handkerchief, on which is stitched a harp. The handkerchief gains meaning as a symbol of the tragic romance between the Swede and Kitty. Since medieval times, the gift of a lady's handkerchief has signified the bond of courtship between the damsel in distress and her protective champion. In the 1946 *Killers*, these roles are fulfilled by Kitty, who continuously puts herself in perilous circumstances through her own greed and selfishness, and Ole, who must continuously rescue her from them. The harp stitched on the handkerchief carries additional meaning, that despite her claims of innocence, Kitty is actually a Circe figure, whose siren song will inevitably lead her lover Ole to ruin.

Since Siegel and Coon's revisionist adaptation emphasizes a postmodern approach to Hemingway's tale, it is impossible to include any such recurring symbolic clues that might help the audience track the characters' moral demise. By its very nature, postmodernism is a non-symbolic approach to storytelling. Its open form leads to a more deconstructionist, Dadaistic use of visual metonymy, in which the traditional metaphorical value of recurring, romantic symbols has no place. As a result, Farr's romance with North seems much more detached and aloof than the intimacy shared by Collins and Andreson. One sign of this increased detachment is the difference in lyrics and delivery of the two signature songs in each film. In the 1946 film, Andreson falls in love with Collins after hearing her sing "The More I Know of Love," whereas in the 1964 remake, an anonymous vocalist sings "Too Little Time," while North and Farr dance. The lyrics of Collins's song suggest an awareness of the paradoxical pleasure and pain of growing closer to someone, which foreshadows her tumultuous relationship with Andreson. However, the words of the song sung by a third party in the later film imply a more emotionally distant relationship, which will have insufficient time to develop given the circumstances. Perhaps this is why Shelia Farr leaves behind no mementos for Johnny North. Compared with her earlier femme fatale analog Kitty Collins, Shelia Farr lives in the more fast-paced, violent, postmodern world of the 1960s that leaves no time for the development of a sentimental love story.

It is exactly Collins and Andreson's sort of quick-boiling, slow-simmering, romantic undercurrents that many of the most memorable love stories in the Hemingway canon are based upon. In the original texts and film adaptations of *The Sun Also Rises*, *A Farewell to Arms*, and *For Whom the Bell Tolls*, each love affair begins with a moment in which the code hero's male gaze is acknowledged and reciprocated by the female object of his affection. The remainder of each work is spent in unveiling the iceberg of unspoken feeling underneath the still waters of their unwavering glances that initially bind them together, even though waves of adversity seek to tear them apart. Yet, rather than trusting the audience to read the actor's facial expressions and gestures to intuit the presence of something below the surface level of interaction, for some reason Siegel's film seems to feel the need to spell out with absolute clarity the reasons why Farr and North would continue to be attracted to one another. Instead of learning that Kitty Collins is a high-maintenance woman who cannot be controlled by any man merely from Ava Gardner's dress and body language, viewers of the 1964 *Killers* hear Sheila Farr say directly to Johnny North, "Nobody drives me," and "I like fancy things" (Siegel). This need to state the obvious plagues Siegel's adaptation, and removes much of the mysterious, unspoken allure of the 1946 film, not to mention defeating the whole purpose of Hemingway's iceberg theory, which is that emotions felt most deeply are often the ones best left unspoken.

The emphasis on action and plot movement in the 1964 *Killers* also leaves one other important Hemingway theme on the cutting room floor. That theme is best described by a favorite quote that Hemingway had of Turgenev's, "The heart of another is a dark forest" (*Short Stories* xii). Throughout his life and work, Hemingway had a fear of darkness, both actual and metaphorical. In the case of his story "The Killers," Hemingway expressed this fear through Ole Andreson's inability to sleep at night in a dark room, due to his restless conscience. In other works, such as *The Sun Also Rises*, Hemingway heroes like Jake Barnes also wrestle with their doubts in sleepless nights of paranoid self-analysis. Due to this persistent use of contrast between the clear and clouded sides of a man's soul, almost every film adaptation of a Hemingway work has used dim lighting and night scenes to correlate with times in which the hero's strength and confidence is at its lowest ebb.

However, in Siegel's *Killers*, every scene is as brightly lit as a sunny California day. Although Gene Phillips has argued that this is simply another of Siegel's ironies, that "evil is just as likely to strike in broad daylight as under the cover of darkness," this choice simply doesn't work, when one considers again the differences between Hemingway's modernist story versus Siegel's postmodern adaptation (77). Hemingway's use of darkness, as echoed in the 1946 film version, underscores places in the story during which Ole Andreson and the world have turned their backs on each other. In one particularly well done scene from the 1946 adaptation, Burt Lancaster, playing the Swede, lays facing the wall in almost perfect darkness while his assassins sneak up to kill him. This scene, which is lifted directly from the story, demonstrates the complete internal darkness that the Swede feels in the moments just before his death. Ole Andreson is a man who has betrayed not only his own moral code, but who has also sacrificed the ethics of his sport, boxing, in an effort to win the love of a woman who double-crosses him. In Hemingway's world, an athlete who rigs a sporting event is considered to be of the lowest possible moral character, a violator of the purity that only comes from fair competition. As such, he deserves to wallow in the dark night of his soul until he is executed, which is exactly what Lancaster's Swede does.

However, in Siegel and Coon's film, Johnny North is a poor substitute to display Hemingway's essential sporting man's struggle. Rather than making a definite choice to turn his back on the ethics of his sport, North is rendered unable to drive competitively by a random crash at the track, brought on by a few too many nights of partying late with Sheila Farr. North suffers very little, if any, of the existential crisis that the Swede does as a result of not being able to compete any longer in his chosen sport, due to his own moral failing. Only a brief mention of his regret is displayed in a scene with his mechanic, and this comes in a well-lit hospital room, where North is recuperating from his injuries surrounded by people to attend to him. This situation, of an athlete who, through little fault of his own, ruins his career but nevertheless still has at least one friend and a host of medical staff waiting to help him transition into another life stands in stark contrast to Lancaster's Swede, who must face his world after boxing mostly in lonely darkness. In short, if Siegel was attempting to use postmodern irony to show that evil could occur in broad daylight, the result failed to achieve the emotional depth that only modernist darkness could convey.

Finally, it is important to note that although director Don Siegel is the production team member most responsible for the meaning lost through odd staging and casting choices, screenwriter Gene Coon is the ultimate source of a script which purports to adapt a Hemingway story, when in reality it creates an entirely different work. Siegel, who went on to direct such films as the original *Dirty Harry* (1971) and John Wayne's final film, *The Shootist* (1976), certainly seems capable of creating a cinematic world in which a man who lives by a Hemingway-esque moral code slowly has his conscience eroded away through adverse life experience. However, Gene Coon, who is best known for his work on the original *Star Trek* series for television, spent the majority of his career in the far more restricted world of 1960s sci-fi television, in which budgetary concerns and ratings dictated production far more than creative collaboration. Considering that he was working within the confines of having to fill exactly ninety-three minutes of screen time, to allow room for commercials, it is a wonder that Coon's screenplay managed to come as close as it did to the themes of Hemingway's original story, even though it was ultimately banned from television because of excessive violence.

What remains of the 1964 *Killers* is best described by two then-contemporary film critics at the time of release. Writing for the *Christian Science Monitor*, Louis Chapin claimed, "It seems that everybody's supposed to know who Hemingway is, but nobody's really expected to read him" (qtd. in Laurence 178). Chapin's observation is accurate, considering that by 1964, Hemingway has been deceased for three years, but his highly-publicized reputation as a literary tough guy had pervaded American culture so thoroughly that the mere mention of his name evoked a specific sort of manly-man image, regardless of the fact that the author's actual work was far more complex. Further, the *New York Times*'s Eugene Archer said, "Hemingway is the victim in all of this. All that remains of his original story is the author's name, big and enticing in the advertisements, giving discredit where it is far from due" (qtd. in Laurence 178). Archer's comment is right on target. In the five decades since his death, Ernest Hemingway, the master stylist and emotionally sensitive writer, to quote Hank Williams, Jr., has been "standing in the shadows of a very famous man": Ernest Hemingway the literary celebrity. Unfortunately, Siegel and Coon's adaptation of *The Killers* is one of many instances in which the much bigger ouroboros of Hollywood has negatively eclipsed and overshadowed Hemingway's actual work.

Islands in the Stream (1977)

Franklin J. Schaffner's adaptation of Hemingway's *Islands in the Stream* was the first film to be made from the author's posthumously published works. The novel itself was issued from the author's estate under the guidance of his widow, Mary Hemingway, who pieced it together from notes on what would have been his four-part epic of the sea. For the first time with the print edition of *Islands in the Stream*, a story about an aging artist, his blended family, and his attempts to cope with a lifetime of regrets, Hemingway seemed to be writing directly with an eye toward his legacy in a straightforward, yet sympathetic fashion. Given Hemingway's choice to present his life through fiction this way, the choice of Schaffner and his production team to replicate this sentiment throughout their adaptation makes for a great deal of thematic consistency among collaborators, even if it does not produce a completely cohesive piece of cinema in the arc of its storytelling.

The genesis of this consistent vision begins with the friendship between Hemingway and Denne Petitclerc, the screenwriter who adapted *Islands in the Stream*. Petitclerc was the ideal man to play real-life apprentice hero to Hemingway's Papa persona. Petitclerc's father had abandoned him in a department store in his native Washington when the writer was only five. Later, Petitclerc claimed that this sense of abandonment greatly influenced his writing work, and caused him to write "stories with a strong father-son bond, because he had no idea what that was like" (Petitclerc). While still a young reporter for the *Miami Herald*, Petitclerc wrote Hemingway a fan letter defending the author's use of short, declarative sentences against a recent negative newspaper review. Petitclerc was shocked when Hemingway called him up in the newsroom a week later, with an invitation to go fishing in Cuba. The two would remain friends for life.

According to the *New York Times*' obituary of Petitclerc, on one of these fishing trips Hemingway mentioned an unfinished book that he thought would make a good movie. Nine years after Hemingway's death, that book would eventually become the novel *Islands in the Stream*. Hemingway, usually a diligent writer, stalled out on completing revisions for the novel "perhaps because Hemingway found the work so intimately biographical that the task proved increasingly too difficult and delicate" (Phillips 148). What resulted in Petitclerc's film adaptation is the persistent feeling that the work primarily represents Hemingway, through his fictional alter ego Thomas Hudson, in his favorite role as code hero, with his sons as apprentice heroes. What makes *Islands in the Stream* so interesting from a critical viewpoint is that the real-life inspirations for these apprentice heroes were not only Hemingway's biological sons, but his artistic descendants, including Petitclerc and many others, as well.

One of these other intellectual descendants of Hemingway was the star of *Islands in the Stream*, George C. Scott. Growing up in Michigan, Scott wanted to become a writer like his idol, F. Scott Fitzgerald. However, after high school Scott joined the Marines, where his duties included several years as a gravedigger at Arlington Cemetery, where Scott claimed that he "picked up a solid drinking habit that stayed with me from then on" (Scott). After his Marine service ended, Scott attended the University of Missouri School of Journalism, where he also became interested in acting for the first time. During this subsequent career, Scott developed an on-screen reputation for playing gruff, tough characters, and an off-screen persona to match, which included a string of failed marriages and outbursts of temperament. In short, Scott's entire life leading up to his portrayal of Hemingway hero Thomas Hudson prepared him for the role, and made the actor a real-life apprentice hero who continued the Hemingway ouroboros on film.

Wisely, director Schaffner built upon these similarities between author and actor by having Scott costumed to look as much like Hemingway as possible. Throughout the film adaptation of *Islands*, Scott sports a large white beard, various guayabera shirts, and the sort of dark tan seen in photos taken of Hemingway during his Cuban years. Combined with Scott's natural gruff vocal delivery and mannerisms, the overall effect of this portrayal is circular. George C. Scott, inspired to become the artist he was by men like Hemingway, effectively becomes Hemingway onscreen by playing Thomas Hudson, a Hemingway character, who is merely an autobiographical avatar of the writer himself.

Despite the close personal and biographical parallels among author, screenwriter, and lead actor that helped create a moving portrayal of Thomas Hudson, many meaningful details in Hemingway's original novel were left out of the adaptation. Considering that Schaffner's adaptation is otherwise a fairly faithful, conversionist narrative, these deletions and recharacterizations must be carefully examined. First, the majority of what has been called Hemingway's barroom dialog has been minimized or deleted. Mostly gone are the portions involving Thomas Hudson's reliance on drink and picking up random women in order to cope with the intense feelings of loneliness that he experiences while living by himself with his memories on the island. Only one redheaded woman, whose character goes unnamed in the film, is left in the early scenes to represent the type of life Hudson lives alone. In all likelihood, these omissions are made to maintain the focus of the central plot of the film, as adapted by Petitclerc, which is centered squarely on the relationship of Hudson to his three sons and the regret he feels at his inability to be more of a constant presence in their lives. Also, the preservation of Hemingway's posthumous image as a stoic, code hero himself might have been tarnished if Petitclerc had chosen to convert the text more closely. Considering the close, father-son dynamic between the two friends, Petitclerc would not have wanted to present that image.

However, the absence of Hudson's attempts at self-medication in the novel contribute greatly to the reader's sense of the character's intense sense of regret and despair, which so closely mirrored these same feelings in Hemingway's own life. Another noticeable omission, which could have provided more insight into the psychological state of both writer and character, is the absence of the conversations that Hudson has with his black-and-white cat, Boise. According to Carlos Baker's biography of the author, Hemingway actually owned a tuxedo-marked cat named Boise, who lived with him as part of his innumerable collection of felines in Cuba. In the novel, Hudson referred to Boise's parallel as "Boy," partly as a shortening of the cat's name, and partly in honor of the fact that Hudson had acquired the cat when one of his two younger sons requested to be allowed to keep him after finding Boise as a kitten eating leftover shrimp in a bar. Of course, by the time that readers meet

Boise, Hudson's sons have been killed, and the cat is one of the only things that Hudson has to remember them by. As a result, the first sixteen pages of the Cuban section of Hemingway's novel are spent in monologue, both internal and external, of Hudson talking to the cat about his regrets regarding the loss of his sons and wife. The despair that Hudson feels when he is unable to talk to any living being other than his cat, about the loss of his sons and his ex-wife in a car crash, is echoed in the ironic tone of these pages, as Hemingway records his alter ego's thoughts:

> Now the boy was gone and the kitten had grown into an old cat and had outlived the boy. The way he and Boise felt now, he thought, neither wanted to outlive the other. I don't know how many people and animals have been in love before, he thought. It probably is a very comic situation. But I don't find it comic at all [*Islands* 208].

Hemingway's portrayal of the bond between man and animal here is typical of his later writing. In *The Old Man and the Sea*, a short novel which was pulled out of material originally intended from the same sea-epic series that spawned *Islands in the Stream*, the old fisherman Santiago shares a similar bond with the massive marlin that he wrestles in an epic battle. As the fish grows weary in the fight of its life against the fisherman, Santiago begins to project his own emotions onto the animal. The fishing line that binds the two together becomes an odd sort of paternal umbilical cord, as the psychological struggles of man versus animal meld into a single whole, demonstrating Hemingway's ever-increasing awareness of the individual man's interconnectedness not only with the whole of humanity, but also with the entire natural world.

This same sentiment is echoed in *Islands in the Stream*, when Hudson's middle son, David, hooks a huge swordfish. The battle of wills that ensues between boy and fish reaches epic scale, with his father, Hudson, urging him on as code hero to the boy's apprentice. After a day's struggle, the fish breaks the line and gets away, leaving the exhausted boy to sob, "It sounds crazy, but in the worst parts, when I was the tiredest, I began to love him. I'm sorry we lost him, but I'm glad he got away" (Schaffner). In this scene, the boy David learns one of his first important lessons on the journey from boyhood to manhood in the Hemingway world: that nature and man are inextricably intertwined, and as one being dies, or suffers, so do we all. Young or old, all men's destinies are as ever-changing, yet just as eternal, as the sea.

This type of occurrence is also what Hemingway attempts to depict in the interaction between Thomas Hudson and his cat, Boise. Boy, as he is repeatedly called, becomes the mirror of Hudson's repressed grief not only for the loss of his sons, but also for the loss of his role as a father figure, or Papa, once those sons have exited his life. However, as the cat becomes almost a surrogate son and co-mourner in the passage, Boy may also be taken to represent the lost boyhood of both Hudson and his author, Hemingway. When he is with his sons in the novel, Hudson seems to be reliving his own boyhood through fishing, boating, and other father-son activities, which also parallel Hemingway's relationships with his own sons in most accounts of their lives together. Although much has been written about Hemingway's highly publicized Papa persona, very little consideration has been given of the man who actually spent a great deal of his adulthood living out every adventure-loving boy's wildest dreams of going on safari, becoming a soldier, and seeing the world. Through Hemingway's depiction of the relationship between Hudson and his favorite cat, readers can sense the boyish Tom Sawyer-and-Huck Finn side of the author who often touted *The Adventures of Huckleberry Finn* as America's greatest book.

However, Hudson's dialogue with Boise the cat also reflects the grown-up feelings of romantic regret that the more adult side of Hemingway's personality had to come to terms with, as a direct result of his choices to live a man's life based upon reacting to immature impulses. Later in the scenes with Boise, Hudson expresses regret about how he has been unable to hold on to either of his wives, mostly because of his own selfishness and independence. Near the end of this sequence, Hemingway again records Hudson's desperate sense of loneliness as he struggles with the truth that the failure of his marriages has largely been his own fault:

> "I never had a girl that waked when I did," the man said. "And now I haven't even got a cat that does. Go on and sleep, Boy. It's a damned lie, anyway. I had a girl that woke when I did and even woke before I did. You never knew her, you've never known a woman that was any damn good. You had bad luck, Boise. The hell with it.
> "You know what? We ought to have a good woman, Boy. We could both be in love with her. If you could support her you could have her. I've never seen one that could live on fruit rats very long though" [*Islands* 216].

Notice that Hemingway's word choice to describe the females in his life changes over the course of this passage from "girl" to "woman." This change is significant, because it reflects the sense of maturity that the older Hudson has in retrospect when reflecting upon his past romantic relationships versus the way he felt as a younger man when he was actually involved in them. Hudson's boyishness is reflected in the petty, immature resentment of never feeling as if a girl really understood him, recalled in the little action of waking up simultaneously. However, when Hudson tells Boy to go on back to sleep and confesses that it is a lie, because he knows that at least one girl did have this deep sense of connection with him, Hudson is effectively trying to put away his childish need to have a girl who could read his mind. The girl Hudson is referring to is his first wife, whose real-life parallel is obviously Hadley, Hemingway's first wife. Read with that fact in mind, the discussion between man and cat becomes yet another in Hemingway's long list of fictional apologies to the woman whom he most often regretted letting get away.

By the end of the passage, Hudson acknowledges that this sort of boy-and-girl love is irretrievably in the past, and that he and the cat, a representative of his young adulthood need to be understood, should compromise and find a more mature love. This change is reflected by Hudson's statement that both he, as a grown man, and Boy, or his boyish side, could be in love with a good, mature woman. Still, Hudson realizes that even in his adulthood, he still may lack the emotional maturity to support a real relationship with a grown woman, who needs more than basic affection, or fruit rats, to sustain her. By the end of Hudson's discussion with the cat, Hemingway has basically confessed through the character that he regrets that his own immaturity caused an end to what he believed to have been the love of his life, if he had only recognized it.

The omission of this passage with Boise the cat, and other scenes like it, causes the film adaptation of *Islands in the Stream* to lose some of its most powerful self-reflectiveness. This loss is significant for viewers familiar with Hemingway's biography, because it denies fans an ideal situation to catch a glimpse of the author whose life inspired his characters. To be fair, however, the film does attempt to retain some sense of this internal struggle through the emphasis placed on Audrey's portrait. Audrey, Hudson's first wife, is clearly intended to be the Hadley equivalent in the adaptation. In the film, Hudson paints an actual portrait of Audrey, which he shows her when she arrives at his island home with the news that the only one of his three sons from their marriage has perished in the war. Although he collected and displayed a great deal of art at his home in Cuba, the only portrait Hemingway painted for Hadley was a self-pitying one of himself. In hopes of winning back both Martha, his then-current wife, and the sympathy of Hadley, his first wife, Hemingway often wrote both women long letters about his lonely existence at his farm in Cuba while he was writing *Islands*. According to biographer Carlos Baker, "With Martha and his sons away, Ernest complained that the large and empty Finca was lonelier than limbo.... He drank a great deal, listened to records on the Capeheart player, and then fell asleep on the floor while the cats hunted mice in his luxuriant beard. Such, at any rate, was the self-portrait he painted to engage Hadley's sympathy" (384–85). By including scenes of interaction between Audrey and Thomas Hudson, Petitclerc's script retains a great deal of the vulnerable intimacy of Hemingway's original work that shows audiences a very different side of the author than the popular press often portrayed.

Besides these psychological explorations into the characters of Thomas Hudson and his author, Schaffner's film uses a high level of incorporation to pull out many other relevant historical details from Hemingway's life that point to his construction of the original text. Gene Phillips states that Hemingway's choice to use his own sons and inspiration for Hudson's boys "make up a kind of collective apprentice hero" (149). This interpretation makes sense when Hudson's three sons are considered as representing the three chief parts of a typical Hemingway apprentice hero, such as Nick Adams. The oldest son, Tom, represents Nick's sense of duty, both to his family and his country. David, Hudson's middle son, demonstrates Nick's grit and determination. The youngest, Andrew, most personifies Nick's paradoxical struggle between innocence and darkness within himself, which he must eventually outgrow on his way from apprentice to Hemingway code hero.

Most likely, Hemingway drew these characterizations from his own three boys, Jack, Patrick, and Gregory. Jack, Hemingway's only son from his first marriage to Hadley Richardson, was the family war hero, serving in military intelligence during World War Two. However, unlike his fictional counterpart, Jack survived the war. Middle son Patrick followed closely in his father's footsteps as an outdoorsman, becoming a professional safari guide and big game hunter as an adult. In the film, his fictional counterpart, David, foreshadows Patrick's actual life in his epic struggle against a huge swordfish, an he screens like a much younger version of Santiago in *The Old Man and the Sea*. Ironically, youngest son, Gregory, Hemingway's second and final child by second wife, Pauline Pfeiffer, never seemed to transition out of his father's paradoxical boyhood characterization, and he died in jail after a tumultuous life that included multiple marriages, brushes with the law, problems with drugs, and a sex-change operation.

Still, even though they became estranged late in life, Gregory Hemingway always considered his father to be a very loving man and agreed with his portrayal as youngest boy, Andrew, in *Islands in the Stream*. In her memoir of life with onetime husband Gregory, Valerie Hemingway repeated Ernest's description of his youngest son's character, which Gregory used for his own epitaph: "He was a devil too, and deviled both his older brothers, and he had a dark side to him that nobody except Thomas Hudson could ever understand. Neither of them thought about this except that they recognized it in each other and knew it was bad and the man respected it and understood the boy's having it" (214). What makes Hemingway's choice to replicate his own sons so closely in *Islands in the Stream* so interesting is that not only do the boys represent the three parts of Hemingway's typical apprentice hero, but also the three sides of the author himself. If one had to sum up the personality of Ernest Hemingway in a few words, it would be difficult to say more than he was a man with a high sense of duty to his country and family, who loved the thrill of adventure and the outdoors, but who also struggled his entire life to reconcile the darker and more innocent sides of his character. Of course, this description could be used to explain the character of most middle-class American men. Perhaps this blended characterization is the key to Hemingway's enduring appeal: he is an American Everyman to the exponential power.

The problem for a filmmaker, though, with casting Hemingway as Thomas Hudson and in turn Hudson as Everyman, is that it is virtually impossible to portray the demise of such a larger-than-life representative personage. One death cannot stand for every death, and yet some sort of ending must be made. This problem is the most likely reason that in both the novel and its film adaptation, the ending seems disjointed and abrupt. However, it could be argued that the only way to end such a life is through circumstances that are almost too random to be believable. Certainly, this is the way that *Islands'* director, Franklin Schaffner, chose to end his most notable film, *Patton*. In his collaboration with actor George C. Scott in the title role, Schaffner's version of the seemingly invincible general's life ends when Patton is killed in a freak automobile accident. After making it through numerous harrowing experiences on the battlefield, it seems a cruel, yet fitting, irony that the general's life would end when his duties were complete, and when he least expected it. The inference seems to be that if General George Patton had to face death head on, he would have been able to defeat it. Instead, death had to sneak up on him, when he least expected it, similarly to the way the hyena, a representative of death, sneaks up on Harry in Hemingway's short story, "The Snows of Kilimanjaro."

Hemingway seemed to agree with this sort of ending for a code hero that "death was just a dirty trick," which happened just as duties were completed and a time of well-deserved rest drew near (*Farewell*). Otherwise, the code hero, always prepared in battle-ready mode, would remain invincible. The death that Hemingway devised for Thomas Hudson, aboard his own boat and under enemy fire while completing a dangerous mission, seems more in keeping with the author's public persona than the one he created for himself through his suicide in 1961. Yet, given reports of Hemingway's daring exploits during his patrols of the Caribbean aboard the *Pilar* and also his time in self-directed military service in Europe when he was supposed to merely have been covering World War Two for the press, one has to wonder whether the author would have preferred a more Thomas Hudson-esque ending for his actual life. Regardless, viewers of the film adaptation of *Islands* who are well educated enough in Hemingway history to know about Hemingway's World War II service are invited to remember their hero's death as similar to Patton's: a quick, simple coda after his duties were done, not by his own hand, leaving a sea of unanswered questions behind. Petitclerc's choice to preserve Hemingway's disjointed final chapter in the life of Thomas Hudson, even though it comes across upon first viewing as abrupt, works when considered as a parallel intended to incorporate George C. Scott's portrayal of the demise of General Patton inside the circle of the Hemingway celebrity ouroboros.

Last, the film adaptation of *Islands* can be read not only as Hemingway's final attempt to explain to his readers through fiction what he had learned over a lifetime of experience, but also a summation of how Hollywood and the general public chose to receive this explanation. In the final lines of the film, Joseph, Thomas Hudson's friend and house servant, tells the dying Hudson, "I love you, you son of a bitch, you never understood about anybody that loves you" (*Islands*). After viewing the film, audiences can see that this utterance is true. The double tragedy in the film ending of *Islands* is that it confirms that both Hudson and Hemingway lived their lives so intently bent on trying to do things that would win the admiration of the world at large that neither ever stopped long enough to notice that they had already won the love of those closest to them. The inconsistencies in the film's storyline mirror their internal struggles. Sadly, both kept fighting battles for self-acceptance long after the war for public esteem had been won.

The Old Man and the Sea (1999)

From time to time in Hemingway criticism, attention is paid to the author's inspirations from the visual arts. Very often, this attention is directed at how the work of painter Paul Cezanne influenced Hemingway's writing style. According to Meyly Chin Hagemann, the genesis of this association stems from Hemingway's own admission in *A Moveable Feast*:

> I was learning something from the painting of Cezanne that made writing simple true sentences far from enough to make the stories have the dimensions that I was trying to put in them. I was learning very much from him but I was not articulate enough to explain it to anyone. Besides, it was a secret [87].

Considering Hemingway's claimed interest in the visual arts, it is surprising that only one animated film adaptation of his work has ever been made. That film, Alexander Petrov's forty-minute adaptation of *The Old Man and the Sea* (1999), is truly extraordinary. An Oscar-winner for Best Animated Short, Petrov's film is intriguing not only for its unique, hand-painted, oil-on-glass technique, but also for how it seems to reconnect Hemingway with his inspirations from Cezanne and with the common people and landscapes that the author strove so earnestly to portray with absolute realism. What results is a work of cinema so cohesive that it incorporates the collaborative creative visions of Hemingway, Petrov, and Cezanne, enclosing all three men in a sort of universal artistic ouroboros.

As a young man in Paris, Hemingway was a steady museum-goer, particularly to displays of Paul Cezanne's works. Lillian Ross noted in her *Portrait of Hemingway*, "I can make a landscape like Mr. Paul Cezanne. I learned how to make a landscape ... by walking through the Luxembourg Museum a thousand times with an empty gut" (60). Always proud of his lean years and how they connected him with the common man, Hemingway sought in many of his works to depict the men whom he felt were the salt of the earth as close to the earth itself. The ultimate articulation of this artistic mindset was in the final novel published during Hemingway's lifetime, *The Old Man and the Sea*. In the novel, the hero, Santiago, is not simply a common fisherman, but a symbol for the constant struggle between human determination and the uncontrollable natural world. Yet the question remains as to exactly what types of stylistic secrets that Hemingway learned from Cezanne were incorporated into his works. In his article on Hemingway and Cezanne, Ronald Berman has claimed that evidence of this influence can be categorized into three basic ideas: "First, that the painter's intellectualism was an important part of his total effect. Second, that he provided a new kind of technical language for art. Third, that the artist was himself a model for independent thought" (25). The remainder of this discussion will show how Petrov's film adaptation of *The Old Man and the Sea* proves Berman's three theories correct, by tracing common themes and origins in the men's works.

Beginning at the end of the chain of creative intellectualism, it is important to examine the background of Petrov's production first. Before the production of *Old Man*, Petrov was widely known in Russia for his unique style of hand-painted animation, which was in effect a new technical language. When Petrov became interested in producing an adaptation of Hemingway's novel, Martine Chartrand, a producer at the National Film Board of Canada, convinced the animator to produce a proposal and storyboard for her to market to gain production money. Pascal Blais Productions, a Canadian animation company that normally specialized in commercial work, became interested in the project and agreed to produce it. Immediately afterward, Bernard Lajoie, co-founder of the company, approached some Japanese investors to secure additional funding, and found IMAGICA Corporation willing to participate on one condition: that the film be produced in an IMAX-friendly format.

Lajoie designed a special camera and studio so that Petrov could complete the project using his unusual techniques. The first of its kind, the new studio at Pascal Blais became the model for Petrov's innovative, independent art form. In a study of the film, Alyson Carty and Chris Robinson describe Petrov's method:

> Petrov works on different levels of glass, animating a character on one level, while simultaneously animating a background on another and so on. Light is shone through the levels of glass and a photograph is taken. Petrov then manipulates the slow drying oil paint and another photograph is taken. This process was repeated 29,000 times to complete *The Old Man and The Sea* and the utmost accuracy was essential.

Petrov's painstaking techniques were the result of years of classical training at the Vonorezh Art School and film classes at the Moscow Institute. Feeling that his work had a more truthful, connectively visceral quality the closer he became physically to his media, "Mr. Petrov long ago forsook brushes for his own hands: with a few deft movements of his fingers, thumbs, or even the heel of his palm, he creates faces, hands, legs, trees, sky, and the shifting moods of a Russian lake during the spring thaw or a Caribbean sea at sunset" (Bohlen). According to Bernard Lajoie, Petrov's unconventional style created the sensation of "sitting in a museum looking at a painting, and suddenly the painting tells a story" (qtd. in Bohlen). This sensation of painting such a realistic animated film seems to be at last the ultimate articulation of what both Cezanne and Hemingway were trying to achieve: art that was so true it no longer imitated life, but actually came to life.

In order to understand the connection between Cezanne and Hemingway, it is first necessary to compare the biographical parallels between the two artists that provide the underpinnings for their work. According to Mary Cassatt and other contemporaries in the art world, Cezanne, in real life, had a contradictory personality that was similar to Hemingway's:

> As Cassatt observed, there was something surprising, even contradictory, about Cézanne. He spouted profanities yet could recite long passages of Virgil and Ovid in Latin. He scorned priests but went faithfully to Mass. He hated the official Paris Salon but kept submitting his work to its judges. He haunted the Louvre, copying sculptures and paintings into his sketchbooks, yet critics said he couldn't draw. He was obsessed with tradition and obsessed with overturning it. He felt himself a failure … and the best painter of his time [Trachtma 1].

A wayward Catholic, Hemingway was a writer whose editors often had to remove profanity from his works, yet he revered the classics. Hemingway kept company with the Lost Generation writers of Paris, and then made fun of them in his works and memoirs. Last, Hemingway claimed to draw inspiration for his writing from the Impressionist painters, even though contemporaries like William Faulkner often chastised his spare style. Perhaps most similar of all, Hemingway strove constantly to be the voice of his generation, while struggling with ever-increasing paranoia and self-doubt as he aged. If he were looking for artists with similar backgrounds to serve as models for his own work, Hemingway would have found much to relate to with Cezanne.

Also like Hemingway, Cezanne was committed to capturing the natural world and its common people, or in his words, "to make paint bleed" (qtd. in Trachtma 1). Particularly, Cezanne was a rebel in his early days, who wanted to shock the Paris art world with "a style that he called *couillarde*, or ballsy, suited to his early subjects—murders, rapes, and orgies. The young Cezanne wanted to make people scream.... He attacked on all fronts, drawing, color, technique, proportion, subjects ... he savagely demolished everything one loves" (Trachtma 1). For those familiar with Hemingway's early writings, this approach sounds very familiar. Hemingway lambasted literary mentor Sherwood Andreson with a mock-romantic parody novel, *The Torrents of Spring* (1926), which took its title and subject matter from a Russian writer whom Hemingway admired and often imitated, Ivan Turgenev. Further, Hemingway's other early novels, such as *The Sun Also Rises* (1926), featured plotlines centered on illicit love affairs and other subject matter that was deemed by Hollywood film producers to be too explicit to represent visually for almost three decades after publication. In short, Hemingway was in many ways his generation's equivalent to Cezanne, albeit in the verbal arts instead of the visual.

These parallel worldviews led both Hemingway and Cezanne to create work that was stylistically alike in its Impressionistic simplicity. Known for his depictions of the outdoor landscape and its ability to convey in literature the characters' emotions, Hemingway is often supposed to have drawn some of his artistic interest in depicting an emotive natural world from Cezanne. According to fellow writer D. H. Lawrence, Cezanne, like Hemingway, "built up a landscape essentially out of omissions" in a way that scholar Max Nanny claimed "has much in common with Hemingway's iceberg technique of leaving out whole contexts of meaning" (80). Also Nanny goes on to state that "Cezanne recommended that in painting nature ought to be recomposed 'by means of the cylinder, the sphere, the cone,' that is, by means of basic geometrical shapes" (80). Taken together, what this means is that Cezanne and Hemingway shared the belief that distilling their respective art forms to the simplest building blocks, such as rudimentary shapes or simple words, was often the best way to convey truth about the world in its purest form.

Cezanne and Hemingway's shared reliance on simplicity of form to convey realism and naturalism can be seen clearly throughout Alexander Petrov's animated adaptation of *The Old Man and the Sea*. Petrov's adaptation, despite its unconventional method, is clearly an example of the conversionist style of film adaptation. Although much is omitted for the sake of fitting the story into under an hour of running time, not a single line of dialogue in Petrov's film is different from that in Hemingway's original novel. Further, Petrov's painting style is Impressionistic, using short strokes and finger-blending of colors to capture the lightness and darkness that create emotion in his scenes, much in the same ways as Cezanne did. Also, Petrov was not afraid to employ Cezanne's shocking use of color contrast to accurately portray less-than-savory subject matter. The scene in which Santiago discovers the extent of damage that the sharks have wreaked on the marlin's bloody corpse is made even more poignant by Petrov's use of stark red color for the marlin's spilled blood against a background of calm green and blue seas. This same red hue was used on Santiago's ragged hands, enhancing audiences' emotional connection between the wounds of the fisherman and the destroyed brother he loved, but nevertheless killed.

Perhaps the most interesting visual metaphor in Petrov's film, in terms of connecting his adaptation to Cezanne's painting style through Hemingway's novel, is the continued employment of circles to suggest the narrative thread connecting Santiago's memories of the past to his present struggle with the marlin. As stated above, Cezanne frequently employed basic geometric shapes to suggest interconnection among natural objects. Hemingway repeats Cezanne's stylistic choice by staging Santiago's struggle with the marlin, and later the sharks, as a continual series of circles. Hemingway begins with a metaphorical circle. Santiago eats a bait fish for strength so that he can hold on to the great marlin until the fish tires and he can draw it close enough to the boat to stick in the harpoon. By replacing the marlin's link in the food chain with its fisherman, Hemingway further suggests that Santiago and the marlin are brothers in nature, even though the old man must eventually kill the fish. The marlin's death circles comprise the bulk of Santiago's battle with the fish. Hemingway's last literal employment of circles in the text comes when Santiago sees the sharks "swimming in circles" as they close in to tear apart the dead marlin (*Old Man* 114). All that remains in the center of the circle when the sharks are finished is a half-fish and a half-ruined fisherman with him. Returning to a metaphorical use of circles to complete the sequence, Santiago apologizes to the fish, saying:

> Half fish ... fish that you were. I am sorry that I went too far out. I ruined us both. But we have killed many sharks, you and I, and ruined many others. How many did you ever kill, old fish? You do not have that spear in your head for nothing [*Old Man* 115].

Hemingway's choice to have Santiago state explicitly that he and the fish are alike in their combat methods and natural struggle against life's adversities, represented by the sharks, completes the metaphorical circle of connection begun when the fisherman ate the bait fish intended for the marlin. To paraphrase Christopher Marlowe, that which creates both man and fish, namely the courage to face any opponent regardless of the odds, is what destroys them.

Petrov's film goes even further with Hemingway's circle metaphor, by depicting through an actual series of brilliantly colored circles the patterns of the old man's memory as he dozes while the dying fish completes his revolutions around the boat. Petrov's camera circles through the rotations of a sea bird that Santiago watches in the sky and then dives down under the water to capture the circling marlin. Next, Petrov's circles widen to enclose the old man's memories of lions playing on the beach and his triumphant arm-wrestling contest before pulling back to Santiago in his skiff, who thinks, just before the marlin jumps to signal their final battle, "I had rather be that beast down there, in the darkness of the sea" (Petrov). These scenes demonstrate Petrov's awareness of Hemingway's theme in *The Old Man and the Sea* that the struggles of men and nature are all interconnected in the grand scheme of life.

In their review of the film, Carty and Robinson draw further parallels between the works of Hemingway and Petrov on the story of Santiago the fisherman, using the concept of hands to indicate the two creative tasks, saying:

> It's all in the hands. In 1952, 53-year-old Ernest Miller Hemingway of Oak Park, Illinois shrugged off the decay of his own weary, abused body, an increasingly scarred mind, and the pulsating aches of his five tools of anguished expression to compose his tale of an old Cuban who battles his own decay, a crippled left hand, and a giant marlin. In 1997, 40 year old Alexander Petrov of Prechistoe, Russia struggled against a strange environment (Canada), a new and intimidating technology (IMAX), and with the use of his finger tips, transformed Hemingway's ode to masculinity from splashes of oil paint into a vibrant, coherent, fresco in motion.

This metaphorical approach to criticism of the adaptation is appropriate because both men used a hands-on approach to make their works as realistic as possible. Whereas Hemingway's knowledge of the daily struggles of the working class in Cuba was based on his interaction with blue-collar people while living at the Finca Vigia, Petrov's understanding of individual human struggle came from a lifetime of working in Russia, another Communist society with a history of oppressing its working class. The fact that Petrov was able so easily to comprehend and translate Hemingway's work, based merely from reading the novel, comparing it to his own experience, and then applying that understanding to create his own adaptation demonstrates the universality of Hemingway's themes and cements the international importance of the novel.

This is not to suggest, however, that Petrov was alone in his artistic interest in Hemingway. For decades, Russian literary scholars have wrestled with how best to interpret America's premier writer about the importance of stoic individualism within the context of communist ideology. Not surprising for those from a highly agrarian country, many Russian critics have praised Hemingway's treatment of Santiago's feelings of connectedness to the natural world of the sea and its creatures. However, others, such as Ivan Kashkin, the foremost Russian Hemingway critic, have spoken harshly about *The Old Man and the Sea* for Hemingway's choice to ignore "important post-war problems," and the author's "excessive preoccupation with technique, reliance on inner dialogue, and even impressionism" (qtd. in Prizel 445). According to Yuri Prizel, Russian critics during the Soviet years almost unanimously spoke out against Hemingway's works for failing to address political concerns of the proletariat more directly. Yet, the proletariat itself seemed to view Hemingway's treatment of Santiago's struggle as a common man against an inhospitable world more favorably. As an example of favorable public opinion of Hemingway's treatment of Santiago as the symbol of Everyman, Prizel cites an open letter of three students from Moscow University to the Soviet Press, published in 1956, saying:

> *The Old Man and the Sea* made a very favorable impression on them. Their interpretation was somewhat naïve and standard. Santiago, for instance, signified for them the struggling workers, while the sharks were evil forces (one thinks immediately of the "sharks of capitalism" a famous slogan of Stalin's days). Their only complaint was that the author did not express his own opinion of Santiago and instead let the reader decide for himself whether to like him or not [446].

Apparently, from this letter, it seems that Hemingway's themes were able to be interpreted as favorable to Soviet ideology, even if the author's iceberg theory approach to politics was not as overt as the average Soviet citizen was used to hearing.

Since 1970, Russian literary critics have sought to emphasize the lyrical and humanist qualities in Hemingway's novel more than they have attempted to pigeonhole the work as a testament to a lonely man facing an inhospitable, capitalist world. As Kashkin stated in his later career, "Hemingway was not a bard of death and violence, as Western critics claim, but a sad, tragic humanist" (qtd. in Prizel 450). This ability to appreciate the individual tragedy of human life has since surpassed uncovering hidden political ideology as the primary way of interpreting Hemingway in Russia today.

What makes this critical approach relevant to the study of Petrov's adaptation of *The Old Man and the Sea* is that it is highly ironic, considering

Petrov's reception in Russia both before and after he received an Academy Award for the film. Before receiving an Oscar, arguably the world's most capitalistic symbol of artistic achievement in the film arts, Petrov's work was largely ignored in his home country, and the filmmaker found it virtually impossible to secure funding for his projects without leaving Russia. However, after receiving the validation of an American award, "he was almost crushed on the platform at the Yaroslavl train station by a crowd of friends, fans, television cameras, and flower-wielding officials" (Bohlen). Petrov's response to the overwhelming reception had to be voiced by his wife, Natasha, because the filmmaker was too shy to address the crowd. She reportedly began with an obvious question: "Now you are falling all over us, but where were you before when we needed you?" (Bohlen). After recovering from the initial shock of his hometown's changed opinion about the value of his work, Petrov has since been more able to reflect on the changes in his public reception in Russia:

> In the eyes of a simple people, it is all a victory for Russia, something like a prize for football, or a sports prize.... Russia has gone through a long period when its authority was weakened, and people feel bad about that. That's why any prize, any victory, revives them. For me, this was all unexpected. I accept the Oscars with irony—no, that's the wrong word, with understanding. It is an exceptional prize, but it is not something on a state level [qtd. in Bohlen].

Fittingly for someone well versed in the Hemingway oeuvre, Petrov chose a sportsman's metaphor to describe his victory in the field of artistic achievement. The real irony of Petrov's film is that the animator's choice to adapt Hemingway's work about how the individual efforts of a common man can make him seem heroic actually transformed the filmmaker himself into a national hero.

Yet, like Hemingway's hero Santiago, who landed the giant marlin only to lose his prize to sharks before returning home, Petrov's Oscar has proven to be an empty award in some respects. Neither before nor after receiving the Oscar has Petrov been able to secure any funding from Russian investors for his projects. At present, production on Petrov's latest proposed film, an adaptation of a Russian novel, has been halted due to lack of funding. Even so, like a typical Hemingway code hero, Petrov has accepted Russia's unwillingness to promote its foremost animator with quiet stoicism. Like Santiago, who mentored the young boy Manolin in the art of fishing, Petrov volunteers his time teaching children the craft of animation at the Sea Gull Film Club in Yaroslavl, while waiting for his next big financing fish to shoal in. When asked if he plans to work abroad again, perhaps in Canada or the United States, where he has been able to find financial and critical success in the past, Petrov has denied the possibility, saying, "I always wanted to come home. And I did. That seems to mean something to people, that I returned, because it means there is something to return to. I hope it was the right decision" (Bohlen). Given Petrov's choice to assume the role of Russia's spokesperson through his work, one cannot help but believe that he will, like Santiago, finally find luck again.

Regardless, audiences are lucky to have this excellent adaptation of Hemingway's novel. The best film adaptations are those which cause the readers to think even more deeply about the work than ever before, to consider new ways of thinking about an old text because of visual cues provided by the filmmaker that offer a new way of seeing the original. Petrov's version of *The Old Man and the Sea* is a cohesive piece of highly incorporative cinema that not only represents a consistent artistic vision between filmmaker and author, but also between the author and his previous visual inspirations. In Petrov's adaptation, a painted-on-glass animated film imitates Hemingway's novel, which was written in a style that imitated Cezanne's still paintings. This concentric circle of inspiration creates a constructive ouroboros, as the great fish of artistic endeavor and her generations of fishermen continue their perpetual struggle in pursuit of one common goal: a realistic, truthful portrayal of man's ability to control his place in the universe.

The Garden of Eden (2008)

Although Ernest Hemingway began what has become his final novel in 1946, *The Garden of Eden* was not published until 1986, forty years after his death. Within the context of the Hemingway canon, *Garden* is an anomaly. The novel gives very little consideration to some of Hemingway's most common themes, such as war or mainstream masculinity. Instead, the novel focuses on Hemingway's less-considered territory of defining gender roles and the maturation that results from such exploration. However, *Garden* subverts the author's traditionalist views on these topics and replaces them with a much more complicated ideology and plot that is centered on the female protagonist, Catherine, as she redefines her sexual identity through lesbian and bisexual relationships. This shift challenges long-accepted critical interpretations of Hemingway's works. As Robin Slibergleid explains, "If Hemingway has long been taken to task for alleged misogyny—for creating female characters that are weak, subservient, and downright uninteresting—Catherine's struggle provocatively opens up the novel to feminist analysis" (101). The fact that Hemingway's unfinished, long-unpublished novel seems sympathetic to Catherine's explorations forces critics today to reconsider preconceived notions about the author's views on sexuality as much more feminist than ever supposed.

It makes sense that the Hemingway estate would have suppressed publication of *The Garden of Eden* for several decades, considering that readers might reject such a novel from America's foremost literary authority on traditional masculinity. However, in today's more open-minded socio-cultural climate, not only has the novel found a considerable audience, but its themes seem very timely for adaptation into film. Unfortunately, director John Irvin's adaptation of *The Garden of Eden* (2008) failed to find an audience, grossing only $22,083 in a three-week, independent release and receiving mostly negative reviews (IMDB.com). The problem with the film is not its subject matter, which would have been too controversial for a mainstream film adaptation in earlier decades (but which should have found an audience among the millennial generation), but instead an over-reliance on Hemingway's dialogue, which results in stilted performances from all actors in the production. As such, the film stands as a testament to how a faithful, conversionist adaptation can create a non-cohesive piece of cinema that makes a novel seem dated, when in actuality it was ahead of its time.

In written form, *The Garden of Eden* was highly incorporated with many details from Hemingway's life. According to daughter-in-law Valerie Hemingway, the author created many of the details about the protagonist, troubled writer David Bourne, from his everyday life:

> Like David, every morning Ernest got out of bed, sharpened those pencils, took out his copybooks, and wrote, wrote happy, tired, hungover, ebullient, depressed, whatever his mood it was cast off, discarded, and as the creative juices began to flow, he entered another world and if we were lucky and it was good enough he left it to us to enjoy forever [108].

To its credit, Irvin's film adaptation goes a long way to uphold Hemingway's dedication to the cathartic values of persistent engagement in the writing craft. Through David Bourne's voiceovers and writing scenes in the film, audiences are allowed a glimpse into how Hemingway may have relied on his work to help him define a sense of masculine identity and purposefulness.

Yet, Hemingway's writing rituals are not the only parts of the author's biographical life reflected in both his novel and Irvin's film. One of the most traumatic events of Hemingway's early career occurred when his first wife, Hadley, lost all the manuscripts to his earliest collection of short stories in a Paris train station. To the young Hemingway, the loss of this briefcase full of manuscripts represented not only the loss of his life's work up to that point, but what the author apparently perceived as a breach of trust between himself and his wife, who had failed to protect the work that meant so much to him.

As Valerie Hemingway explains, "Hadley was devastated, but Ernest was even more so. It was a situation akin to when a couple loses a child. There is a pervasive unspoken rebuke that eventually undermines and erodes the marriage" (108). Hemingway's sense of devastation from this event was reflected many times in his later writing, but nowhere with as much acrimony as in *The Garden of Eden*.

In the novel, David Bourne's wife, Catherine, intentionally burns both the manuscripts for his upcoming novel and the press clippings from his previous one. Catherine's reason for this action seems to stem from jealousy and a loss of control over her husband. Although Catherine, like Hemingway's first two wives, supported her husband financially so that he could write, she became resentful at the notoriety he gained as a result of his writing. In what appears to be an effort to regain a sense of dominance over her husband, Catherine has an affair with another woman. At first, Catherine flaunts Marita in front of David. Later, Catherine offers her to him as a substitute wife, thereby freeing herself of what she perceives to be her wifely obligations so that she can engage in further sexual experimentation without remorse. When David and Marita come to prefer each other to her, Catherine punishes them by destroying what both of them love most: David's work and the public acclaim that he gained from it. Given her complex scheme of revenge, Catherine should not be read or screened as a simple translation of Hemingway's animosity toward his first wife for the loss of his early manuscripts. Instead, Catherine is better considered as a composite of the author's conflicted feelings toward three different women: Hadley Richardson, Pauline Pfeiffer, and Zelda Fitzgerald.

Like David Bourne, Hemingway began an extramarital affair with a fashionable, rich, androgynous woman while he was in the process of writing his second novel. The parallels between Pauline Pfeiffer, Hadley's wealthy best friend, and the fictional character, Catherine Bourne, were obvious to those close to Hemingway. As Valerie Hemingway states:

> Catherine had some of the element of Pauline in her, an heiress, whose money freed the writer to live a more extravagant and carefree life.... Pauline had experimented with dyeing her hair blonde in 1929 both as a declaration of sexual freedom and as a birthday surprise for Ernest. Catherine was also reminiscent of Hadley, the wife who loses her husband's precious stories. The loss of the writer's work through his wife's actions was an experience Hemingway would never forget and probably never forgive [109].

Both during and after his marriage to second wife, Pauline Pfeiffer, Hemingway expressed a great deal of regret over leaving Hadley for her best friend. This sense of remorse can be sensed even from the title of his novel, *The Garden of Eden*, which begs the inference that a state of happiness between a couple will inevitably be destroyed when they succumb to temptation. What makes the novel critically interesting, in light of Hemingway's biography, is how the author displaces his real-life guilt through making the fictional wife, Catherine, the cause of David's moral decline. By making Catherine the "Devil," as she is so often called in the novel, Hemingway seems to argue that he was an innocent man who, like David Bourne, was lured into an extramarital affair through the sinister machinations of his wife and her lover.

Of course, this attempt is transparently false, and Hemingway must have known it would appear so, judging from the conversation between Bourne and his friend in the novel, Colonel John Boyle. When Bourne reveals his willingness to engage in an open marriage so that Catherine can explore her bisexuality, the Colonel says, "Remember everything is right until it's wrong. You'll know when it's wrong.... If you don't it doesn't matter. Nothing will matter then" (*Garden* 65). A few pages later, after Bourne and Catherine have bobbed and bleached their hair to match, Bourne looks at himself in the mirror and thinks, "You like it. Remember that. Keep that straight. You know exactly how you look and how you are," after which Hemingway adds the editorial comment, "Of course, he did not know exactly how he was. But he made an effort aided by what he had seen in the mirror" (*Garden* 85). From this exchange, readers can draw the provoking conclusion that both character and author were lying to themselves about their respective marriages and their roles in the destruction of those relationships. Of course, the psychologically intriguing yet unanswerable question is exactly why such lies were maintained. Perhaps if Hemingway had finished *The Garden of Eden*, a more definite conclusion could be reached. As it stands, the behavior of the fictional character Bourne and his real-life inspiration reads simply as the efforts of both men to reaffirm their senses of identity as honorable men when the ways in which they chose to deceive themselves proved otherwise.

Returning to the idea of Catherine as a composite of women Hemingway knew, it is important to consider not only Hemingway's guilt concerning his relationships with Pauline and Hadley, but also his general disdain for the relationship between his friend Scott Fitzgerald and his wife, Zelda. Once again, Valerie Hemingway offers insight into Hemingway's process:

> Catherine was a composite of several people. Zelda Fitzgerald comes to mind foremost. Ernest frequently spoke with anger at her jealousy over Scott's writing, and all the ruses she performed to distract and obstruct him, and of how weak Scott was to allow it. David Bourne was definitely not Scott [108].

As a man who valued his own psychological independence in romantic relationships, Hemingway was deeply troubled by Fitzgerald's seeming codependence on a wife who consistently attempted to undermine his career. If one considers, as stated above, that Hemingway thought so much of his work as to consider it equal to having a child, a wife who tried to stop a writer from working would be the equivalent in Hemingway's mind to a wife who secretly took birth control when the husband thought the couple was trying to conceive. This subversive, abortive attitude would have represented the ultimate betrayal to Hemingway, who most likely considered it part of a wife's duty to offer emotional support for her husband's career. Further, any man who allowed such a thing to happen would have lost the important sense of occupational purpose that Hemingway often expresses through his fiction as an essential component of masculine identity. As a result, in *The Garden of Eden*, Hemingway continuously has David Bourne return to the diligent practice of the craft of writing as a way to restore his sense of self after Catherine calls it into question by means of encouraging his engagement in her bisexual affair.

In his film adaptation of the novel, John Irvin does an excellent job of visually representing David Bourne's struggle to create a sexual identity for himself through writing. Irvin draws a visual connection between the concerns of fictional character and author by casting Jack Huston, an actor who looks very much like Hemingway, in the role of David Bourne and then styling him to look exactly like a young version of author. For his part, Huston gives a satisfactory, if somewhat subdued, portrayal of Bourne as Hemingway. However, Mena Suvari seems overwhelmed with the role of Catherine, and plays the character as a purely evil, self-centered, and smugly manipulative individual. Suvari's choice to portray Catherine Bourne as one-dimensional goes counter to Hemingway's construction of the character as a composite of three living, multi-dimensional women, who also inspired the somewhat more vulnerable Catherine Barkley from Hemingway's second novel, *A Farewell to Arms*. Although she is far more assertive, Hemingway's Catherine Bourne inherits much of the earlier Catherine's emotional co-dependence. Each time the later Catherine takes another step toward androgyny, whether it is through cutting her hair or attempting more masculine techniques in the bedroom, she asks David for reassurance of his affection for her, saying, "And you love me just the way I am? You're sure" (*Garden* 12). This need for acceptance in her marriage, when contrasted with her confidence that she can perform both as male and female for the world outside her relationship, makes Catherine Bourne a character with whom readers can sympathize through her struggle to define sexual identity even at the risk of losing her seemingly ideal coupling. The fact that Suvari's performance, and screenwriter James Scott Linville's script, reflect none of Catherine's internal struggle is one of the greatest mistakes in Irvin's adaptation, because it creates a thematic inconsistency between Hemingway's novel and the film.

However, the static portrayal of Catherine Bourne is not the only problem with Irvin's adaptation. The most troublesome issue is inherited from Hemingway's original novel, which is structured as a parallel narrative. As Silbergleid explains:

> At the center of Ernest Hemingway's posthumous novel *The Garden of Eden* sits the story within the story, the manuscript that the protagonist, David Bourne, writes about his boyhood experiences elephant hunting with his father. It's a story about a boy coming to terms with his relationship with his father and about a man trying to define his masculinity; a story that taps into multiple discursive sites, including race, gender, and species. It's a story that, to me, anyway, holds the key to the novel; a story that works as meta-narrative, focusing the "theme" of the book on storytelling itself [97].

Even within the context of today's literary climate, which has been conditioned by several decades of postmodernism to accept meta-narrative as a thematic concept, Hemingway's *Garden* remains hard to unpack. The flashback sequences, which depict an African safari that David Bourne and his father went on when David was a boy, can be read many different ways, ranging from a simple trauma narrative that forces an early emotional maturation for David to a complex scheme of sexually charged references that relate to David's later marital troubles. In all likelihood, Hemingway was in the process of employing his iceberg technique by interjecting several layers of meaning at various levels of thematic depth for readers who chose to find them. However, because he never completed the novel, Hemingway's placement of the African flashbacks remains somewhat inconsistent in the novel. Although some of the African episodes, such as the killing of the bull elephant, appear at meaningful times within the context of the then-present-day story of David and Catherine, others seem dropped in at random intervals, suggesting that Hemingway's structuring of the novel was never fully completed.

This inconsistency is magnified in Irvin's adaptation. Making a story-within-a-story translate smoothly from page to screen is never easy; however, when the original work was not consistent within itself, the problem becomes infinitely worse. The result in Irvin's film is that every time an African episode is interjected, it seems completely disjointed, as if part of an entirely other film. This sense of disruption was observed by the *L.A. Times*'s Mark Olsen.

> Every time the film switches over to dramatize a story that the writer is working on, a hunting adventure of a boy and his father, the momentum stops dead in its tracks. The true heart of the film is the tempestuous relationship between the writer and his wife and the way the presence of their mutual lover brings it to a boil, so why Irvin and Linville would be so thoroughly distracted by elephant hunting in the desert is anyone's guess.

Olsen is correct to point out that the drama between David and Catherine is the focal point of Hemingway's narrative. However, his observation that Irvin's manipulation of the African narrative is disruptive forces reviewers of the film to reconsider how he might have made the transitions into and out of these sequences more smoothly. One possibility would have been to make the African scenes shorter, and the cuts between real-time and flashback more directive as to exactly what each one was supposed to add to the viewer's understanding of the central plot.

For example, although it is earlier in sequence than in Hemingway's novel, a stronger visual metaphor could have been made if Irvin had intercut the beginning of young David's struggles with his father in Africa into the scene in which an older David tries to explain to the Colonel that he married Catherine, but he "didn't marry her family" (Irvin). This claim comes on the heels of the Colonel's telling David that Catherine's father intentionally killed himself and Catherine's mother in a car crash. A rapid cut to a scene of the cause of David's animosity with his father, and how it shaped his present-day life, placed just after David's denial that a person's family history affects later relationships, might have helped to heighten the sense of irony at David's being a haunted man who disclaims such influences.

Additionally, a more explicit visual presentation of the actual automobile accident could have provided a clear visual tag that Irvin might have chosen to pick up later to end the narrative thread, considering the fact that in Hemingway's original, unfinished notes, the author intended for the novel to end with Catherine's death in a car crash. This type of ending would have been more creatively consistent with Hemingway's theme in the novel that a person is the sum total of his or her unalterable past experiences, which translate into a life narrative. Instead, the actual ending of Irvin's film, which concludes with an almost baptismal image of David Bourne diving into the ocean, has no thematic consistency or sense of resolution whatsoever with Hemingway's novel. In sum, Irvin's slavish devotion to the exact dialogue and chronology presented in Hemingway's incomplete novel causes the African episodes to detract from, rather than supplement, viewers' understanding of the central narrative.

Considering Irvin's choice to present Hemingway's narrative as a close conversion of the original text, it seems odd that he chose to eliminate one of the most obvious visual connective devices that the author put into the plot to link the African episodes to the main storyline. Catherine's obsession with acquiring as dark a tan as possible escalates at the same pace with which she continues to make changes to her hairstyle and sexual preference. Given the persistent literary association in such Hemingway stories as "The Short Happy Life of Francis Macomber" with Africa as a dark continent in which the passions of married women run as wildly uninhibited as the animals pursued on safari, it is curious that Irvin does not seek to build more upon the symbolic connection between the content of David's African stories and his wife's efforts to acquire an increasingly darker skin tone. Although it is possible that Irvin was attempting, out of a sense of political correctness, to censor Catherine's preference continually to darken her skin tone as an endeavor parallel to exploring her bisexuality, that choice seems inconsistent, given the already highly controversial content of the remainder of the storyline. When viewed with this in mind, Irvin's choice to eliminate Catherine's tanning ritual appears to be just another nonsensical thematic inconsistency between the film and Hemingway's novel.

In the end, John Irvin's adaptation of *The Garden of Eden* incorporates many important historical and biographical details from Hemingway's life and work. However, it neglects other psychologically important themes that could have been presented more clearly through better implementation of visual tags and a more updated script that is less afraid to stray from the author's hard-to-film language. Still, with its much more open discussion of the author's less mainstream sexual viewpoints, *The Garden of Eden* is an important film that represents a possible starting point for more liberal-minded Hemingway adaptations in the future.

* * *

Since 1957, film adaptations based on Ernest Hemingway's works have followed the general Hollywood trend away from strict genre pieces and toward more eclectic films that reflect a combined artistic vision of all collaborators. Although the author's actual influence on an adaptation of his work reached its highest level with *The Old Man and the Sea* (1958), cinematic versions of Hemingway's novels have actually incorporated more of the author's biographical information after his death. As a result of decreasing restrictions by the Hemingway estate on portrayals of the author and his works, combined with increasing levels of tolerance on socio-cultural issues, future adaptations of Hemingway's works promise to reveal even more insights into the author's life and work that will doubtlessly broaden the circle of his authorial celebrity ouroboros.

Bibliography

Abbott, Mark. "A Portrait of Marlowe?" Marlowe-Society.org. The Marlowe Society, n.d. Web. 15 Jun. 2010.

Atkins, Irene Kahn. "Hollywood Revisited: A Sad Homecoming." *Literature/Film Quarterly* 5 (1977): 105–111. *MLA Bibliography*. Web. 12 Mar. 2011.

Bachand, Marjorie. "Short Stories by F. Scott Fitzgerald." Rev. of *The Curious Case of Benjamin Button and Other Jazz Age Tales*. Ed. Patrick O'Donnell. New York: Penguin Classics, 2009. Amazon.com. 14 Feb. 2009. Web. 23 Feb. 2011.

Baker, Carlos. *Ernest Hemingway: A Life Story*. New York: Scribner's, 1969. Print.

The Beautiful and Damned. Screenplay by Richard Wolstencroft. Dir. Richard Wolstencroft. 2008. Ontological Pictures, 2008. DVD.

Beaver, Frank Eugene. *Dictionary of Film Terms*. New York: Peter Lang, 2007. Print.

Bergson, Henri. "The Intensity of Psychic States." *Time and Free Will: An Essay on the Immediate Data of Consciousness*. Trans. F. L. Pogson. London: George Allen and Unwin, 1910. 1–74. Print.

Berman, Ronald. "America in Fitzgerald." *Journal of Aesthetic Education* 36.2 (2002): 38–51. *JSTOR*. Web. 12 Mar. 2011.

_____. "Recurrence in Hemingway and Cezanne." *Hemingway Review* 23.2 (2004): 21–36. *MLA Bibliography*. Web. 18 Jan. 2012.

"Biography of Audie Murphy." Arlingtoncemetery.mil. The Official Website of Arlington National Cemetery. Web. 18 Jan. 2012.

Bluestone, George. *Novels into Film*. Baltimore: Johns Hopkins University Press, 1957. Print.

Bohlen, Celestine. "Pride Projected on the Big Screen: Filmmaker's Oscar Becomes a Victory for Russian Culture." NYTimes.com. New York Times Online. 10 May 2000. Web. 18 Jan. 2012.

The Breaking Point. Screenplay by Ranald McDougall. Dir. Michael Curtiz. 1950. Warner Bros., 2011. DVD.

Brooke, Michael. "The Hays Code." *BFI Screenonline*. British Film Institute, 2003. Web. 12 Mar. 2011.

Brown, Thomas. "The Origins and Character of Irish-American Nationalism." *Review of Politics* 18.3 (1956): 327–358. *JSTOR*. Web. 12 Mar. 2011.

Bruccoli, Matthew. *Some Sort of Epic Grandeur*. 2nd ed. Columbia: South Carolina University Press, 2002. Print.

Bruccoli, Matthew, Scottie Fitzgerald Smith, and Joan P. Kerr, eds. *The Romantic Egoists: A Pictorial Autobiography from the Scrapbooks and Albums of F. Scott and Zelda Fitzgerald*. Columbia: South Carolina University Press, 1974. Print.

Callahan, John F. "The Unfinished Business of *The Last Tycoon*." *Literature/Film Quarterly* 6 (1978): 204–213. *MLA Bibliography*. Web. 12 Mar. 2011.
Carty, Alison and Chris Robinson. "The Old Man and the Sea: Hands Above the Rest?" *Animation World Magazine* 4.12 (2000): 1–4. Web. 18 Jan. 2012.
Cawelti, John. *The Six-Gun Mystique*. Bowling Green: Kentucky University Press, 1980. Print.
Cline, Sally. *Zelda Fitzgerald: Her Voice in Paradise*. New York: Arcade, 2002. Print.
Conductor 1492. Screenplay by Johnny Hines. Dirs. Frank Griffin and Charles Hines. Columbia, 1924. Televista, 2008. DVD.
Cousins, R. F. "Presle, Michelline." *International Dictionary of Film and Filmmakers*. Encyclopedia.com. 2001. Web. 15 Sep. 2011.
Crosland, Andrew. "Sources for Fitzgerald's 'The Curious Case of Benjamin Button.'" *Fitzgerald/Hemingway Annual 1979*. Eds. Matthew Bruccoli and Richard Layman. Detroit: Gale Research, 1980. 135–139. Print.
Crowther, Bosley. "*The Breaking Point*: The Screen-In Review." *New York Times*, 7 Oct. 1950. Web. 22 Oct. 2011.
The Curious Case of Benjamin Button. Screenplay by Eric Roth and Robin Swicord. Dir. David Fincher. 2008. Paramount, 2009. DVD.
"Denne Petitclerc, 76, Hemingway Friend, Dies." NYTimes.com, 27 Feb. 2006. Web. 18 Jan 2012.
DiGaetani, John L. "Benjamin Button and Baltimore." Tenth International F. Scott Fitzgerald Conference. Lord Baltimore Hotel Conference Room, Baltimore. 1 Oct. 2009. Address.
Dittmar, Laura. "Larding the Text: Problems in Filming *The Old Man and the Sea*." *A Moving Picture Feast: The Filmgoer's Hemingway*. Ed. Charles Oliver. New York: Prager, 1989. 54–63. Print.
Earle, David M. *All Man! Hemingway, 1950s Men's Magazines, and The Masculine Persona*. Kent, OH: Kent State University Press, 2009. Print.
Erickson, Glenn. "The Gun Runners: Don Siegel and Audie Murphy in the Cuban Revolution?" TCM.com, Web. 18 Jan. 2012.
Erigero, Patricia, et al. "Le Sancy." TBHeritage.com, 2005. Web. 20 Oct. 2011.
Ernest Hemingway's A Farewell to Arms. Screenplay by Ben Hecht. Dir. Charles Vidor. 1957. Fox, 2007. DVD.
Ernest Hemingway's The Snows of Kilimanjaro. Screenplay by Casey Robinson. Dir. Henry King. 1952. Fox, 2007. DVD.
"Essay: Second Acts in American Lives." Time.com, 8 Mar. 1968. Web. 21 Oct. 2009.
Eyers, Jonathan. *Don't Shoot the Albatross!: Nautical Myths and Superstitions*. London: A&C Black, 2011. Print.
A Farewell to Arms. Screenplay by Benjamin Glazer and Oliver H.P. Garrett. Dir. Frank Borzage. Paramount, 1932. Delta, 2000. DVD.
F. Scott Fitzgerald's The Beautiful and Damned. Screenplay by Richard Wolstencroft. Dir. Richard Wolstencroft. 2008. Ontological Pictures, 2008. DVD.
Fitzgerald, F. Scott. "Babylon Revisited." *Taps at Reveille*. 1935. New York: Scribner's, 1960. 331–341. Print.
_____. *Babylon Revisited: The Screenplay*. Ed. Budd Schulberg. New York: Carroll & Graf, 1993. Print.
_____. *The Beautiful and Damned*. Rpt. in *F. Scott Fitzgerald: Novels and Stories 1920–1922*. New York: Library of Congress, 2000. 435–802. Print.
_____. "The Camel's Back." *Tales of the Jazz Age*. Rpt. in *F. Scott Fitzgerald: Novels and Stories 1920–1922*. New York: Library of Congress, 2000. 823–849. Print.
_____. *The Crack-Up*. Ed. Edmund Wilson. Scribner's, 1931. New York: New Directions, 2009. Print.

———. "The Curious Case of Benjamin Button." *Tales of the Jazz Age*. Rpt. in *Fitzgerald: Novels and Stories 1920–1922*. Ed. Jackson Bryer. New York: Library of America, 2000. 797–1054. Print.

———. *The Great Gatsby*. Scribner's, 1925. New York: Collier, 1992. Print.

———. "Head and Shoulders." *Flappers and Philosophers*. Rpt. in *F. Scott Fitzgerald: Novels and Stories 1920–1922*. New York: Library of Congress, 2000. 310–334. Print.

———. *The Love of the Last Tycoon: A Western*. 1941. Scribner's, 1993. Print.

———. *Tender Is the Night*. 1934. New York: Scribner's, 1982. Print.

———. *This Side of Paradise*. New York: Scribner's, 1920. Print.

"Flesh and Desire: The Films of Frank Borzage." www.slantmagazine.com. 10 Jul. 2006. Web. 15 Aug. 2011.

Forrey, Robert. "Negroes in the Fiction of F. Scott Fitzgerald." *Phylon* 28.3 (1967): 293–298. *JSTOR*. Web. 12 Mar. 2011.

For Whom the Bell Tolls. Screenplay by Dudley Nichols. Dir. Sam Wood. 1943. Universal, 1998. DVD.

"*The Garden of Eden*." IMDB.com. Internet Movie Database. Web. 18 Jan. 2008.

Garfield, John. Statement before the House Un-American Activities Committee. Washington, D.C.: HUAC, 1947. Print.

"George C. Scott: The Man Who Refused an Oscar." BBC.com, 23 Sep. 1999. Web. 18 Jan. 2012.

Glaser, Madeleine. "Fitzgerald's The Beautiful and Damned." *Explicator* 51.4 (1993): 238–239. *MLA Bibliography*. Web. 12 Mar. 2011.

The Godfather: The Coppola Restoration. Screenplay by Mario Puzo and Francis Ford Coppola. Dir. Francis Ford Coppola. 1972. Paramount, 2008. DVD.

Gone with the Wind. Screenplay by Ben Hecht. Dir. Victor Fleming. 1939. Warner. 2007. DVD.

Gottheil, Richard, et al. "Benjamin." www.jewishencyclopedia.com. Ed. Cyrus Adler, et al. The Kopelman Foundation. 2002. Web. 21 Oct. 2009.

Gould, Mark R. "John Garfield, Film Noir, and the Hollywood Blacklist." Rev. of *He Ran All the Way: The Life of John Garfield*, by Robert Nott. @yourlibrary.org. American Library Association. 2011. Web. 5 Oct. 2011.

"The Great Gatsby." IMDB.com. The Internet Movie Database, 1990. Web. 12 Mar. 2011.

The Great Gatsby. Screenplay by Richard Maibaum and Cyril Hume. Dir. Elliott Nugent. Paramount, 1949. DVD.

The Great Gatsby. Screenplay by Francis Ford Coppola. Dir. Jack Clayton. 1974. Paramount, 2003. DVD.

The Great Gatsby. Screenplay by Craig Pearce. Dir. Baz Luhrman. Warner Bros., 2013. Film.

"Green Acres Star Eddie Albert Dies at 99." USA Today.com, 27 May 2005. Web. 18 Jan. 2012.

Griffin, Michelle. "Bad Reputation." TheAge.com.au. Fairfax Media. 26 June 2004. Web. 12 Mar. 2011.

The Gun Runners. Screenplay by Daniel Manwaring, Paul Monash, and Ben Hecht. Dir. Don Siegel. Seven Arts, 1958. Film.

Guterl, Matthew Pratt. "The New Race Consciousness: Race, Nation, and Empire in American Culture." *Journal of World History* 10.2 (1999): 307–352. *JSTOR*. Web. 12 Mar. 2011.

Harmetz, Aljean. "Jennifer Jones, Postwar Actress, Dies at 90." *New York Times*, 17 Dec. 2009. Web. 21 Jan. 2010.

———. "Van Johnson, Film Actor, Is Dead at 92." *New York Times*, 12 Dec. 2008. Web. 4 Jan. 2010.

Haskell, Molly. "Female Stars of the 1940's." *From Reverence to Rape*. Rpt. in *Film Theory and Criticism*. Ed. Leo Braudy and Marshall Cohen. Oxford: Oxford University Press, 2009. 501–514. Print.

Hassan, Ihab. "Toward a Concept of Postmodernism." *The Postmodern Turn: Essays in Postmodern Theory and Culture*. Columbus: Ohio State University Press, 1987. Print.

Hemingway, Ernest. *A Farewell to Arms*. 1929. New York: Scribner, 1995. Print.

———. *For Whom the Bell Tolls*. 1940. New York: Scribner, 2003. Print.

———. *The Garden of Eden*. 1986. New York: Scribner, 2003. Print.

———. *To Have and Have Not*. 1937. New York: Scribner, 1970. Print.

———. *Islands in the Stream*. 1970. New York: Scribner, 1997. Print.

———. *A Moveable Feast: The Restored Edition*. 1964. New York: Scribner, 2010. Print.

———. "My Old Man." *The Complete Short Stories of Ernest Hemingway: The Finca Vigia Edition*. New York: Scribner, 2003. 149–160. Print.

———. *The Nick Adams Stories*. 1972. New York: Scribner, 1981. Print.

———. *The Old Man and the Sea*. 1952. New York: Scribner, 1995. Print.

———. "The Snows of Kilimanjaro." *The Complete Short Stories of Ernest Hemingway: The Finca Vigia Edition*. New York: Scribner, 2003. 39–56. Print.

———. *The Sun Also Rises*. 1926. New York: Scribner, 2006. Print.

Hemingway, Valerie. *Running with the Bulls: My Years with the Hemingways*. New York: Ballantine, 2004. Print.

———. "*The Garden of Eden* Revisited: With Hemingway in Provence in the Summer of '59." *Hemingway Review* 18.2 (1999): 102–113. *MLA Bibliography*. Web. 18 Jan. 2012.

Hemingway's Adventures of a Young Man. Screenplay by A. E. Hotchner. Dir. Martin Ritt. 1962. Fox, 2007. DVD.

Hemingway's Garden of Eden. Screenplay by James Scott Linville. Dir. John Irvin. 2008. Lion's Gate, 2011. DVD.

Hemmeter, Thomas and Kevin Sweeney. "Marriage as Moral Community: Cinematic Critiques of Hemingway's *To Have and Have Not*." *A Moving Picture Feast: The Filmgoer's Hemingway*. Ed. Charles M. Oliver. New York: Praeger, 1989. 64–75. Print.

Hotchner, A. E. *Papa Hemingway: A Personal Memoir*. New York: Random House, 1966. Print.

"Irving G. Thalberg." TCMBD.com, 2011. Web. 12 Mar. 2011.

Islands in the Stream. Screenplay by Denne Park Petitclerc. Dir. Franklin J. Schaffner. 1977. Paramount, 2005. DVD.

Jacobs, Joseph. "Wandering Jew." JewishEncyclopedia.com. Ed. Cyrus Adler, et al. The Kopelman Foundation. 2002. Web. 21 Oct. 2009.

Jacobsson, Eva-Marie. "A Female Gaze?" *CID* 51 (1999): 5–28. Print.

James, Nick. "Face to Face." *Sight & Sound* 19.3 (March 2009): 28 *Wilson Web*. Web. 21 Oct. 2009.

Jefferson, Margot. "She Knew How to Whistle." Rev. of *Slim: Memories of a Rich and Imperfect Life*, by Slim Keith. *New York Times*, 24 Jun. 1990. Web. 12 Aug. 2011.

Kaminsky, Stuart. "Literary Adaptation: *The Killers*—Hemingway, *Film Noir*, and the Terror of" *A Moving Picture Feast: The Filmgoer's Hemingway*. Ed. Charles M. Oliver. New York: Praeger, 1989. 125–134. Print.

Keats, John. "Ode on a Grecian Urn." *The Oxford Book of English Verse*. Ed. Arthur Quiller-Couch. Oxford: Clarendon, 1911. 625. Print.

The Killers. Screenplay by Anthony Veiller. Dir. Robert Siodmak. Universal, 1946. Criterion, 2002. DVD.

The Last Time I Saw Paris. Screenplay by Julius J. Epstein, Philip G. Epstein, and Richard Brooks. Dir. Richard Brooks. MGM, 1954. Alpha Video, 2002. DVD.

The Last Tycoon. Screenplay by Harold Pinter. Dir. Elia Kazan. 1977. Paramount, 2003. DVD.

Laurence, Frank M. *Hemingway and the Movies*. Jackson: Mississippi University Press, 1981. Print.

Leff, Leonard. *Hemingway and His Conspirators: Hollywood, Scribners, and the Making of American Celebrity Culture.* New York: Rowman & Littlefield, 1997. Print.
Leitch, Thomas. "Adaptation, the Genre." *Adapation* 1.2 (2008): 106–120. *JSTOR.* Web. 19 May 2010.
Lencioni, Patrick. "The Painful Reality of Adrenaline Addiction." *Leadership Review* 5 (2005): 3–6. Print.
Long Island Momma Abigail. "Great Story, Great Movie." Rev. of *The Curious Case of Benjamin Button and Other Jazz Age Tales.* Ed. Patrick O'Donnell. New York: Penguin Classics, 2009. Amazon.com. 28 Dec. 2008. Web. 23 Feb. 2011.
The Lord of the Rings: The Fellowship of the Ring. Directed by Peter Jackson. 2001. New Line, 2002. DVD.
Margolies, Alan. "The Maturing of F. Scott Fitzgerald." *Twentieth Century Literature* 43.1 (1997): 75–93. *JSTOR.* Web. 12 Mar. 2011.
Marsh, Joss Lutz. "Fitzgerald, Gatsby, and The Last Tycoon: The American Dream and the Hollywood Dream Factory—Part II." *Literature/Film Quarterly* 20.2 (1992): 102–108. *MLA Bibliography.* Web. 12 Mar. 2011.
Marx, Jack. "*The Beautiful and Damned* ... with coke." www.news.com.au. News Limited. 5 Mar. 2010. Web. 12 Mar. 2011.
Matterson, Stephen. "A Life in Pictures: Harold Pinter's *The Last Tycoon.*" *Literature/Film Quarterly* 27.1 (1999): 50–54. *MLA Bibliography.* Web. 12 Mar. 2011.
Michael, Lloyd. "Auteurism, Creativity, and Entropy in The Last Tycoon." *Literature Film Quarterly* 10.2 (1982): 110–118. *MLA Bibliography.* Web. 12 Mar. 2011.
Miller, Kerby. "Class, Culture, and Immigrant Group Identity in the United States: The Case of Irish-American Ethnicity." *Immigration Reconsidered: History, Sociology, and Politics.* Ed. Virginia Yans-McLaughlin. New York: Oxford University Press, 1990. 96–129. Print.
Mullins, Wesley. "Quick, enjoyable read that does not spoil the movie." Rev. of *The Curious Case of Benjamin Button and Other Jazz Age Tales.* Ed. Patrick O'Donnell. New York: Penguin Classics, 2009. Amazon.com. 13 Jan. 2009. Web. 23 Feb. 2011.
Nanny, Max. "Formal Allusions to Visual Ideas and Visual Art in Hemingway's Work." *European Journal of English Studies* 4.1 (2000): 66–82. MLA Bibliography. Web. 18 Jan. 2012.
New International Version Study Bible. Grand Rapids, MI: Zondervan, 1985. Print.
The Old Man and the Sea. Animation by Alexander Petrov. Dir. Alexander Petrov. Pascal Blais, 1999. Direct Source, 2004. DVD.
The Old Man and the Sea. Screenplay by Peter Viertel. Dir. John Sturges. 1958. Warner Bros., 2000. DVD.
Olsen, Mark. "Movie Review: *Hemingway's Garden of Eden.*" LATimes.com, 9 Dec. 2010. Web. 18 Jan. 2012.
Pace, Eric. "Helen Hayes, Flower of the Stage, Dies at 92." *New York Times*, 18 Mar. 1993. Web. 1 Aug. 2011.
Phillips, Gene D. *Fiction, Film, and F. Scott Fitzgerald.* New Orleans: Loyola University Press, 1986. Print.
_____. *Hemingway and Film.* New York: Ungar, 1980. Print.
"Post-Traumatic Stress Disorder." *National Institute of Mental Health.* National Institute of Health, n.d. Web. 22 Oct. 2011.
Prigozy, Ruth. "Fitzgerald's Flappers and Flapper Films of the Jazz Age: Behind the Morality." *A Historical Guide to F. Scott Fitzgerald.* Ed. Kirk Curnutt. Oxford: Oxford University Press, 2004. Print.
Prizel, Yuri. "The Critics and the Old Man and the Sea." *Research Studies* 41 (1973): 208–216. *MLA Bibliography.* Web. 18 Jan. 2012.
Rapf, Joanna E. "The Last Tycoon: A Nickel for the Movies." *Literature Film Quarterly* 16.2 (1988): 76–81. *MLA Bibliography.* Web. 12 Mar. 2011.

Ross, Lillian. *Portrait of Hemingway*. New York: Modern Library, 1999. Print.
Roth, Eric and Robin Swicord. *The Curious Case of Benjamin Button: Story to Screenplay*. New York: Scribner, 2008. Print.
Schrader, Paul. "Notes on Film Noir." *Film Theory and Criticism*. Eds. Leo Braudy and Marshall Cohen. Oxford: Oxford University Press, 2009. 581–591. Print.
Schwarzbaum, Lisa. "*The Curious Case of Benjamin Button*." Rev. of *The Curious Case of Benjamin Button*. Dir. David Fincher. EW.com, 23 Dec. 2008. Web. 21 Oct. 2009.
Semuels, Alana. "*Marley & Me* and a Big Christmas Box Office." LATimes.com, 29 Dec. 2008. Web.
Server, Lee. *Ava Gardner: Love Is Nothing*. New York: St. Martin's Griffin, 2006. Print.
Shakespeare, William. *Hamlet*. Eds. Neil Taylor and Ann Thompson. London: Arden, 2006. Print.
Simpkins, Peter, Geoffrey Jukes, and Michael Hickey. *The First World War*. Oxford: Osprey, 2003. Print.
Slibergleid, Robin. "Into Africa: Narrative and Authority in Hemingway's *Garden of Eden*." *Hemingway Review* 27.2 (2008): 5, 96–117. Web. *MLA Bibliography*. 18 Jan. 2012.
Sloan, Tod. *Tod Sloan By Himself*. 1915. Rpt. San Diego: San Diego State University Press, 1988. Print.
The Snows of Kilimanjaro. Screenplay by Casey Robinson. Dir. Henry King. 1952. Fox. 2007. DVD.
Stagecoach. Screenplay by Dudley Nichols and Ben Hecht. Dir. John Ford. 1939. Warner Bros., 2007. DVD.
Statement of Ideals. The Motion Picture Alliance for Preservation of American Ideals. Eds. Walt Disney, et al. Hollywood, CA: SIMPP, 1947. Web. 22 Oct. 2011.
The Sun Also Rises. Screenplay by Peter Viertel. Dir. Henry King. 1957. Fox, 2007. DVD.
"*Tales of the Jazz Age*." Rev. of *Tales of the Jazz Age*, by F. Scott Fitzgerald. *Portland Evening Express*. 10 Oct. 1922: 19. Rpt. in *F. Scott Fitzgerald: The Critical Reception*. Ed. M. Thomas Inge. New York: Burt Franklin, 1978. 145. Print.
Tender Is the Night. Screenplay by Ivan Moffatt. Dir. Henry King. Fox, 1962. Film.
To Have and Have Not. Screenplay by Jules Furthman and William Faulkner. Dir. Howard Hawks. 1944. Warner Bros., 2006. DVD.
Townley, Edward. *Mussolini and Italy*. Portsmouth, NH: Heinemann, 2002. Print.
Trachtma, Paul. "Cezanne: The Man Who Changed the Landscape of Art." *Smithsonian*, January (2006): 1–4. Web. 18 Jan. 2012.
"Tyrone Power." IMDB.com, Web. 18 Jan. 2012.
Under My Skin. Screenplay by Casey Robinson. Dir. Jean Negulesco. 1950. Fox. 2007. DVD.
Villard, Henry Serrano and James Nagel. *Hemingway in Love and War: The Lost Diary of Agnes von Kurowsky*. Boston: Northeastern, 1989. Print.
Warshow, Robert. "The Gangster as Tragic Hero." *Film Theory and Criticism*. Eds. Leo Braudy and Marshall Cohen. Oxford: Oxford University Press, 2009. 576–580. Print.
Weintraub, Bernard. "Recalling John Garfield: Rugged Star KO'd by Fate." *New York Times*, 29 Jan. 2003. Web. 22 Oct. 2011.
Williams, Hank Jr. "Standing in the Shadows." *Country Shadows*. MGM, 1966. Vinyl.
Wills, Dominic. "Tobey Maguire Biography." *TalkTalk.co.uk*. Web. June 27, 2013.
Wilson, Robert N. "Fitzgerald as Icarus." *The Antioch Review* 17.4 (1957): 481–492. *JSTOR*. Web. 17 Mar. 2011.
Wolstencroft, Richard. "The Manifesto for Ontological Cinema, 1st Erignis." IdeaFix.com. Ed. Richard Wolstencroft. Sept. 2008. Web. 12 Mar. 2011.

Index

Adventures of a Young Man (film) 194–202
Albert, Eddie 165–166, 179, 186

Bacall, Lauren 118–122, 126, 144, 153, 178
balanced collaboration 6–7, 9, 31–32, 43–44, 54, 61, 63, 67, 79, 80–81, 85, 90, 100, 134, 155, 163, 170, 178
The Beautiful and Damned (film) 43, 81–91
Bergman, Ingrid 110, 114, 115, 117
Bergson, Henri 43–45, 48, 52, 67, 70
Bildungsroman 195
Blanchett, Cate 69, 71
Bogart, Humphrey 118–120, 125–126, 140–141, 144–145, 153, 178–179
Borzage, Frank 102–109, 170–171, 174
The Breaking Point (film) 101, 126, 140, 144–153, 178–179, 180–181
Brooks, Richard 10, 25–28, 31, 34, 127

Caporetto retreat 108, 174–176
Casablanca (film) 32, 125, 144
Cassavetes, John 205
celebrity ouroboros 1, 3, 42, 62, 91, 98, 100, 104–105, 118–119, 122, 128, 133, 136, 139, 162, 166, 170, 173, 210–211, 218–219, 226, 233
Cézanne, Paul 218–222, 226
Circe (myth) 133, 164, 207
Clayton, Jack 43–54, 66
cohesive cinema 1–3, 7, 9, 62, 81, 85, 91, 110–111, 118, 126, 134, 153, 157, 159, 178–179, 186, 191, 193, 202, 205, 210, 219, 226–227
Conductor 1492 (film) 10–17
consistent artistic vision 2, 7, 9, 11, 18–19, 22, 25, 29, 34, 37, 41, 45, 46, 68, 93, 103, 106, 139, 143, 153–154, 157–158, 162, 182, 183–184, 199, 202, 210, 226, 230–233
conversion style 3, 10, 42–44, 54, 67, 91, 145, 170–171, 178, 193, 195, 202, 212, 222, 227, 232
Coon, Gene 203–207, 209–210
Cooper, Gary 106, 110, 117
Coppola, Francis Ford 50, 53
The Curious Case of Benjamin Button (film) 34, 43, 68–80
Curtiz, Michael 144–146, 148–150, 153

DeNiro, Robert 58–59, 61, 66, 140
DiCaprio, Leonardo 95–96, 98
Dickinson, Angie 206

Epstein, Julius 28, 31, 33–34
Epstein, Philip 28, 31, 33–34

A Farewell to Arms (1932 film) 102–109, 111
A Farewell to Arms (1957 film) 35–36, 170–178
Farrow, Mia 53–54
Faulkner, William 119, 125–126, 221
film noir 10, 18–19, 22–25, 58, 102, 110, 112–113, 127–128, 131, 134, 141, 144, 204
Fincher, David 43, 68–76, 78–80
Flynn, Errol 165–167
For Whom the Bell Tolls (film) 102, 109–118, 202, 207

gangster film 18, 20, 119–120, 123–125, 128, 131, 133, 140, 145, 147–152
The Garden of Eden (film) 226–233
Gardner, Ava 128, 132–136, 155, 159, 163–165, 206, 208

Index

Garfield, John 101, 136, 139–142, 144–145, 147, 178
Gone with the Wind (film) 35–36, 171–175
The Great Gatsby (1949 film) 10, 18–25
The Great Gatsby (1974 film) 43–54
The Great Gatsby (2013 film) 91–100
Greek mythology 37, 55, 62–66, 129, 133
green (color) 51–52, 91–92, 99–100, 131, 133–134, 155, 176, 222
The Gun Runners (film) 126, 178–186

Hawks, Howard 118–127, 144, 182
Hayes, Helen 104–105
Hays Code 18, 20–22, 24–25
Hecht, Ben 171, 176–178
Hellinger, Mark 127–128, 132, 134
Hemingerald phenomenon 10–11, 25–26, 34, 43, 80
Hernandez, Juano 147
Hines, Johnny 10–17
historical manner 4, 10, 18, 31–32, 39, 44, 46, 53–54, 67–68, 77, 94, 112, 118–119, 124, 128, 137–138, 143, 171, 175–176, 178, 181, 202, 216, 233, 239
Hotchner, A.E. 194–202
HUAC 136, 140–144, 146, 147
Hudson, Rock 171, 177–178
Huston, Jack 230
Huston, John 128, 134

iceberg theory 131, 174, 206–208, 221, 224, 231
incorporated film 2–4, 15, 26, 58, 70, 91, 110, 122, 126, 149, 153, 163, 172, 202, 219, 227, 233
interpretation style 3, 10, 11, 21, 38, 40, 64, 66, 69, 70–71, 96, 104, 117, 138, 167–168, 178, 181, 205, 216, 224
Irvin, John 227, 230–233
Islands in the Stream (film) 210–218

Johnson, Van 32, 36
Jones, Jennifer 35–37, 42, 155, 171, 177

Kazan, Elia 43, 55, 58–68
The Killers (1946 film) 102, 127–136, 155
The Killers (1964 film) 202–210
King, Henry 10, 34–42, 153, 155–158, 161–170
Kunstleroman 195

Ladd, Alan 22–23
Lancaster, Burt 127, 135, 180, 208–209

The Last Time I Saw Paris (film) 10–11, 25–34, 36
The Last Tycoon (film) 43, 54–68
lost generation 33, 78, 84, 155, 164, 168, 169, 220
Luhrman, Baz 91–100

MacDougall, Ranald 144–145, 150, 180
Maguire, Tobey 96–98
Mainwaring, Daniel 180–183
Marvin, Lee 204–206
Mulligan, Carey 98–99
Murphy, Audie 180–181, 185–186

Negulesco, Jean 136, 138–139, 142–143
New Woman 115, 119, 121–122, 135, 159–160
Nichols, Dudley 110, 112–117
Nugent, Elliot 10, 18–25

The Old Man and the Sea (1958 film) 186–194, 233
The Old Man and the Sea (1999 film) 218–226

Peck, Gregory 155–156, 158
Petitclerc, Denne 210–212, 215, 218
Petrov, Alexander 218–226
Pinter, Harold 56, 61–63, 66, 68
Pitt, Brad 69–74, 76, 80
political manner 4–5, 10, 43, 67, 85, 87, 106, 107, 108, 111, 112, 114, 119, 123, 125, 128, 137, 141, 143, 146, 148, 174, 180–182, 190, 206, 224, 233
Power, Tyrone 165–166
Prelle, Micheline 143
psychological manner 4–5, 10, 23, 32, 41, 47, 54, 60, 67, 68, 92–93, 95, 106, 108, 111–112, 118–119, 128, 146, 176, 178, 182, 196–197, 199, 202, 212–213, 216, 229, 233
PTSD 148–149

Reagan, Ronald 206
Redford, Robert 52–54
revision style 3, 10, 14, 17, 19, 43, 71, 81–83, 90–91, 102, 104, 109, 117, 119, 202, 207, 211
Roth, Eric 70–71, 74, 77–78, 80

Schaffner, Franklin 210–213, 216–217
Scott, George C. 211–212, 217–218
Selznick, David O. 35–37, 42, 170–176, 178

Siegel, Don 178–186, 203–210
Siodmak, Robert 128–132, 134–135, 203–204, 206–207
six-question approach 1–3, 85
Sloan, Tod 136–140, 142, 144
The Snows of Kilimanjaro (film) 102, 135, 153–162, 163
socio-cultural manner 4, 10, 32, 54, 67–68, 119, 143, 177–178, 227, 233
Socratic method 128–132
Stagecoach (film) 59, 61, 110, 116
Sturges, John 186–193
The Sun Also Rises (film) 135, 155, 163–170, 207
Suvari, Mena 230

Taylor, Elizabeth 27
Tender Is the Night (film) 10, 34–42, 155

Thalberg, Irving 55–57, 59
To Have and Have Not (film) 102, 118–127, 144–145, 178
Tracy, Spencer 188–189, 192–193

Under My Skin (film) 101, 136–144, 153

Vidor, Charles 173, 175–177
Viertel, Peter 163–165, 168, 193

Western film 55, 59–62, 110, 116–117, 145, 151–152
Wolstencroft, Richard 43, 81–91
Wood, Sam 110–118

Zanuck, Darryl 153, 163, 165, 167–168, 170